Sand In My Shoes

Four Decades of Sandhills Stories and History

Marianne Beel

ISBN: 978-1-57579-385-6

Library of Congress Control Number: 2008927998

Cover photo by Marianne Beel.

Printed in the United States of America

PINE HILL PRESS
4000 West 57th Street
Sioux Falls, SD 57106

This book is dedicated to
L.C. Beel (1879-1970)

Leonard Beel was 23 when he rode the train from Iowa to Valentine to deliver bulls. He walked the prairie near the Gordon Creek and vowed to return and claim some of that land as his own, which he did. His Duck Bar brand was registered in the 1907 Nebraska Brand Book. That was a century ago. The brand is still registered and branded on the cattle.

L.C. was specific of how he cared for the land and expanded as he could. He said no one owned the land, rather the land owned you and must be cared for as such. He made a certain commitment to the land and some of us believe that his spirit remains. We are eternally grateful to L.C. for providing the opportunity to spend our lives learning what a family ranch has to teach.

He used the ranch until he was done with it and then offered us the opportunity. We cherished our time on the ranch and now we offer that opportunity to others. This is why we dedicate this book to the man who had the strength and vision to endure the hardships of the early years.

About the Author

Marianne Beel lived a full life: rancher, teacher, photographer, free-lance writer, columnist, correspondent, book editor, organization leader, wife, mother, and more.

She began taking pictures after her son sent her a camera in 1968. In 1971, she thought the *North Platte Telegraph* should cover the high school rodeo finals at Harrison in the Nebraska panhandle. The newspaper wouldn't send anyone but would use pictures and stories if she provided them.

She became the Sandhills area correspondent for the *Telegraph* and in 1977, began writing a weekly column called, "Sand In My Shoes."

Telegraph Editor Keith Blackledge said she was a "born reporter" who could write a feel-good feature or a tough investigative hard news story. She figured in several Telegraph Service to Agriculture awards while winning numerous awards of her own in *Nebraska Press Woman* and National Federation of Press Women contest. She placed third in the national sweepstakes competition in 1976 and won the Nebraska Press Women sweepstake awards three times.

Marianne Beel also was president, board member and contest director at various times for *Nebraska Press Woman* and a regional director for the national organization. She was selected twice, for the state group's top honor, "Communicator of Achievement," in 1980 and 2002.

At the same time, she was researching and writing much of the information for a two volume history of Cherry County, which she also edited. "Sandhills Century" was published in 1986 and earned her a first place national award from Press Women for book editing. The two-volume history contained 1,500 photographs and graphics on 949 pages. She served as president of the Cherry County Historical Society for six years and secretary for four.

Marianne Beel died July 17, 2007. She had written her own obituary, which the *Telegraph* published July 22 as the final "Sand In My Shoes" column.

Table of Contents

Marianne Beel

Introduction

It wasn't a desire to be a writer and photographer that brought Marianne Beel to the North Platte Telegraph. It was a desire to see young people recognized for their successes.

She told us we needed coverage of the Nebraska High School Rodeo Finals at Harrison. It was way out of our territory, but there would be competitors from areas we did cover. Wayne Jacobsen was regional editor then, and he told her we couldn't send a reporter, but she would be welcome to send us some pictures and stories.

We knew we had stumbled on a "natural." I've known and worked with some first-rate professional reporters and photographers. This busy ranch wife with kids to raise, cowboys to feed, and more sideline activities than I can list, ranks with the best.

She brought Sandhills ranch and community life to print for thousands of city as well as rural readers. Sometimes you find part-time rural correspondents who can write "good news" features but are clueless when it comes to what is called "hard news" about government, disasters, local controversies. Marianne has an insatiable curiosity - a valuable thing in a reporter - and she could do it all in both words and photographs. Her "Sand in My Shoes" column in the Telegraph once a week was something you didn't want to miss.

Photography was her first love, other than her husband and family. In pictures as well as words she documented the natural beauty of this unique part of the country and of the cattle industry that puts steaks on the tables of people who have never seen a cow.

She won photography, news writing, feature writing and column writing awards too numerous to list. She helped our newspaper win recognition for outstanding agricultural coverage.

We can all be glad for the work of Marianne's many fans to put some of that into book form, where it is available to those who have thrown away the columns they clipped to save, and to those who missed them the first time around.

Visit the Nebraska Sandhills and life on a ranch with Marianne Beel. Nowhere else will you find as authentic, lively and loving account.

- Keith Blackledge,
the "Old Editor" (retired) from The *North Platte Telegraph*

THE 1970s

Kennedy, Nebraska, Post Office. Marianne Beel,
postmistress, and Gail Lighthill, mail carrier.

Brands & Ownership

Brand: Quarter Circle - Lazy J
Owner: John Beel

Brand: Flying T
Owner: L.C. "Buddy" Beel

Brand: T Ox-Yoke
Owner: G.R. Beel

Brand: 7 J H P L
Owner: W. Robert Stetter

Brand: Bar Reverse C
Owner: Gordon G. McLeod

CALF SALE SAME AS ANNUAL PAY

- October 4, 1977 -

The past week, was a very important time on the ranch and probably as filled with tension as any week of the year — we sold and delivered our yearling calves. It was important, because it is our annual pay day; the one time a year when we have a product for sale. As ranchers, husband G.R. and I have no conception of life on a monthly or weekly income.

Marketing creates the tension. Seems, in most every other venture that the price is set by the business — for instance, if there has been a loss, the price the consumer pays for the product is increased to make up for it. Not so in agriculture. The farmer and rancher are at the mercy of a frivolous market that is subject to daily and even hourly change. Folks in agriculture have two choices — take a chance on a steady market and sell, or take a chance of rising prices and hold.

Marketing is pretty much a specialized job, especially in the cattle business. About 95 percent of the cowman's time is spent in production. That leaves him precious little time to market his calves — the result of all his efforts and his investments — at the right time and place for the most favorable returns.

G.R. prefers to sell at the ranch. He says there is no point in trying to ask what cattle are worth. He just wants all the market will bear — enough to keep the banker off his back for a while.

G.R. is happiest when he is among his beloved cattle. But when fall and sale time approaches, he seldom smiles. A man hiring on in the fall would probably wonder if G.R. has teeth.

Well, G.R. sorted and watched the cattle and watched the grass, and one day he said, "I guess it's time to sell...I'd like to sell them one day and deliver the next, so I wouldn't have time to worry if I sold at the wrong time." He says that if he gets away with a good price, the neighbors will say he is lucky; if he prices too low, he's stupid.

G.R. called Vance Whitehill, who is with Producers of Omaha and has been a repeat buyer for over 10 years. Vance said that he'd be up in a couple of days. In the meantime, G.R. tried to make his pencil stretch the market price to equal production costs, but he gave up.

Whitehill looked at the cattle, and, after a certain amount of bargaining, a price was agreed on. Delivery was to be in five days. There was no down payment or contract, just a gentlemen's agreement between two men. Outsiders might say that that is bad business, but it is one of the few surviving customs of the "old days" that we are able to enjoy with this particular buyer. His word is a contract, and so is ours.

Long before dawn on delivery day, the men and some helping neighbors rode off for the roundup. They left strict-orders that I be at the scales on time. (It has been my job to mark down and average weights and figure the total. Sometimes I help run the scales, too.)

I arrived at our scales early enough to have a second cup of coffee from the thermos and watch the eastern sky turn rouge red. A full moon, still bright and yellow, hung in the west. The temperature was 37 degrees, and low fog created mirage lakes in the lowlands.

Just as the sun eased over the eastern hills, the cattle appeared along the western skyline. One rider stayed near the front to keep them from running.

G.R. is very fussy about how the cattle are handled on the drive and while they are corralled and weighed. They must be moved and weighed before they go to water in the morning as "filled" cattle seldom result in a return buyer. At the same time, if the cattle are handled quietly and quickly in the corrals, the seller suffers less cattle stress and "shrink" over the scales.

The steers were weighed in a short time, and the riders returned to another pasture for the heifers. The next day, the process was repeated for the fall calves. The weather was chilly and a wind was blowing, so the cattle were easy to handle and there were no problems.

Each year, Vance says that the calves weigh more than he thought they would, and G.R. says, "They are weighing light."

I asked Vance why he returns each year for our cattle. "People want Sandhills cattle," he said," and yours are high-quality, good-doing cattle."

I'm glad to hear that, because some day our cattle may again bring what they are worth. I don't have to strain my memory too hard to remember when that annual pay check cleared up all the notes and interest at the bank — at least for a few minutes before we started borrowing for the next year. This year, with cattle prices still below production costs and expenses continuing to rise, we will be lucky if we can cut our note in half.

NOVEMBER, COLD STRANGERS AND POETRY
- November 29, 1977 -

November weather has been quite typical this year. It is a month of many moods — it teases and tempts with balmy weather, becomes mysterious and veiled by fog, and turns vindictive and spiteful with storms. Perhaps it is frustrating to be a month sandwiched between the gold of October and the shimmering white of December.

November and duck hunting are synonymous to me. On days when it seems only reasonable to seek a fire, husband G.R. says, "It's a good day for duck hunting."

Early in November, G.R. watched some northern ducks fly over. He and a friend from Hastings, Dick Peyton, were anticipating good hunting along our Gordon Creek. Then it stormed.

"Now the creek is frozen," I heard G.R. grumble as he dug through storage for his winter coveralls. He went off to feed hay to the weaned calves, then spent the afternoon in the shop fixing a motor. After that, he never seemed to find time for hunting.

But it got me to reminiscing about Novembers past, the weather and duck hunters — who are some of the nicest people I know.

About 20 years ago, G.R. left for some hunting on a morning chilled by drizzling rain and a threat of snow. When he returned much later, he brought three wet and cold strangers, one of whom obviously was not feeling well.

It seems G.R. had stopped at Ballard's Marsh, where the three Pawnee City men had camped in a tent. When he found the older man was chilled, he insisted that they come to the ranch. His greeting to me was, "This man is sick and needs to go to bed."

Now G.R. is a man of few words, and I had been married to him long enough to know to save my questions for later...but three strangers? Somehow I sensed that they all were staying.

The sick man looked miserable, so I showed him to an upstairs bedroom, plugged in the heating pad and made him hot broth. He mumbled something about "since I left Plumtree down in Tennessee, it's the first time I've been warm." I wondered if he was delirious.

5

The man in the "sick ward" was Morris VanHorn, a Pawnee City banker. His companions were Bill Price, a farmer, and Pawnee City Postmaster, Al Porr.

At the time, I was postmaster of Kennedy and ran a little fourth-class office here at the ranch, so Al and I settled down to talk shop. Cattle-rancher, G.R., and hog-feeder, Bill, found friendly debate in each other's choice of livestock.

They were delightful guests, and after the evening meal, we exchanged hunting and other stories long into the night.

I think the frustration of listening to us laugh into the wee hours must have cured Morris. The next day, he declared that we had saved his life and then joined the lively discussions.

Morris played the mouth harp for our boys, and we found that he had a sharp memory for things other than money matters. He would recite poetry for hours...long and fascinating poems, many I'd never heard. Our two little boys hung over his knees, completely fascinated.

I asked him about what he had mumbled that first night, and he said, "Oh! That's from 'The Cremation of Sam McGee'." Morris' baritone voice was expressive as he recited the poem in its entirety — all 14 stanzas. He introduced me to and created a lasting appreciation for the talents of poet Robert Service.

The three hunters returned to the ranch for many years, often bringing other friends. Those wet, cold strangers became warm friends. After Morris could no longer hunt, he would come back for the visit. One year, I remembered to put "Sam McGee" on tape.

Each November, when the first unseasonable chill sends me to seek warmth, I get out that tape. Many fond memories and our friends from Pawnee City seem to return to our home with Morris VanHorn's voice resounding from the tape:

"Now Sam McGee was from Tennessee,
Where the cotton blooms and blows.
Why he left his home in the South
To roam 'round the Pole, God only knows..."

ANIMALS MOVE IN CLOSE FOR THE WINTER
- December 13, 1977 -

I 'll admit to being a pansy and much prefer spring and fall weather to the minus 55 degree wind chill index of Thursday, for example. "This cold wind is pure hell on cattle," G.R. growled as he stopped for a hot cup of coffee.

It would appear to me the cold was a bit hard on the men, too. Tanks were frozen and the ice must be chopped, one wind mill was frozen and they had a flat tire on the hay sled.

However, if I can ignore the cold, there is something about this time of year I really like. The animals that were scattered in distant pastures during nice weather and seldom seen are now close to the buildings.

In a sense, everything is battened down for the winter.

For the first time since the 30s, this ranch has no cattle spending the early winter months on the wildlife refuge. Our lease, or special use permit, covers a deferred rotation area for wildlife conservation this year. The only problem this creates is the shortage of winter range at the ranch. As the dry cows have used most of the corn stalks, we are now feeding them hay and a little corn ensilage.

Instead of making the daily 24 mile round trip to feed the cows on the refuge, we must haul the stacks from Dewey Lake to feed them here.

We are extremely grateful for the abundant moisture and a hay crop that is more than double that of 1976. The cold weather is taking more hay, but with luck, we won't be faced with the shortage and rigid rationing of the three drought years.

Last winter, as we drove through the feed grounds one late afternoon, G.R. pointed to some hay caught between a cow's toes and grumbled, "Look at that waste. She's packing half the day's ration." (The situation really was just about that bad.)

G.R. does about all the hay feeding, as the amount varies with the weather. If it's warm, he feeds less. When it's cold and blowing, he usually feeds in the morning and again in late afternoon, especially the young stock. The extra hay creates a little more body heat, as well as, bedding for the night.

"With this outfit (big tractor, hydra-fork and stack mover), feeding is no problem," G.R. is quick to explain. "I could feed everything on this ranch 'til

I'm 90." (He probably will too, but I was hoping he'd let us retire at least by 75.)

Now the boss-man might say he has no problem feeding, but he sure had one last week. He's alone in the tractor and heads it in a general direction, then turns around to operate the controls of the hydra-fork. The stack was nearly gone when a resounding thud told him he had run over one of the liquid protein feeders.

I could quote what he said but that might be reminiscent of the "expletive deleted" era of a few years ago...Watergate.

Anyway, from the warmth of the house, I can see Tuffy and the rest of the saddle horses in the east lot. With them is a handful of Brahmas that we keep for the fun of it; we think there's beauty in the velvety lop-ears.

Through the tree lane to the south, I see the cows with fall calves. The calves are fuzzy in their "Teddy Bear" winter coats and snuggle down in the mounds of hay. I drove through them today and noticed the brands, just three weeks old, are healed and smooth. Cattle on this ranch have carried that same Duck-Bar brand since G.R.'s father, L.C., had it registered in 1907.

The spring calves on the west meadow resemble kids with faces sticky from lollipops. Their muzzles are coated with Molasses from liquid protein.

With corn on the feed grounds, wildlife too, has moved in close to the buildings. This morning, I caught a glimpse of the bright plumage of a rooster pheasant parading two hens across the lawn and into the shrubs. G.R. had told me 10 roosters were staying near the cattle. They have outwitted my attempts to catch all 10 in a photo.

Our pheasant hatch was above normal, as G.R. said he saw several large broods last summer. He had started, then delayed until a later date, mowing the weeds of the back lots. He saw a brood of 15 and knew flushing them from the tall weeds would be impossible.

Grouse have moved onto the corn pile and into the cottonwood grove. I'm always amazed that the uppermost and smallest branches will support their weight.

The eerie howls of the coyotes seem closer in the cold, crisp air. They, too, seem drawn to the circle of animals that surround the hub of buildings. Last night I heard the familiar "WhOOO" of the great horned owl in the south grove.

A feeling of closeness warms the cold a bit this winter. During the day, no matter which direction I look, I see the animals that give this ranch its purpose. Then, during the nightime darkness, we are surrounded by the sounds of the wild ones.

AS A CARD GAME, '77 DEALT BIG LOSSES

- January 3, 1978 -

Another year is gone...another entry in the log book of Father Time, another page in history. In the local vernacular, "1977 done bit the dust."

I got to thinking that each year is rather like playing a game of cards...52 weeks, 52 cards — and very seldom do we get to deal. In agriculture, Mother Nature does most of the dealing. But, if you play your cards right, you don't lose consistently.

Mother Nature dealt cold cards last January. But a pile of sorghum ensilage added bulk to our drought-shrunken, meager supply of prairie hay, so rationing was not severe.

In February, we blanketed the horses and pulled into Grand Island in zero weather for a cow-cutting contest for daughter Myndi. Even a barn full of animals didn't generate any heat in that unheated arena.

March came in, roaring like a lion — and forgot to stop. It stormed on the second, and nine days later dumped 15 inches of snow on top of the heavy coating of ice. We had a storm each week that month.

The March 11 storm was reported by KBR Rural Public Power at Ainsworth to be the worst in its history. Hundreds of poles were broken, causing a five-day electrical outage in our area. In the six-mile stretch from the substation to our ranch, 52 poles were down. Officials estimated damages throughout Nebraska at $3.5 million.

The March lion dumped a total of 57 inches of snow on Cherry County, making a winter season total of 80 inches. Temperatures didn't drop below the 20s during March, so the stress on cattle wasn't severe. But our ensilage pile was buried, and we had to go back to rationing.

We were calving cows during March, too. But the men spent day and night with them, and our losses were minimal.

The snows were a blessing and melted between each storm. Our drought-dried hills soaked up the moisture like a sponge. Precipitation during March was 4.10 inches — nearly half of the 11.21-inch total we received for all of 1976.

Lack of a late frost and a May rainfall total of over six inches brought grass to the hills, and we turned the cattle out to pasture three weeks earlier than usual...a good thing, because our stacked hay was gone.

Nearly every weekend during May and June, we pulled to a high school rodeo with Myndi. Sometimes the game was played in blowing sand, sometimes in pounding rain, and, just sometimes, balmy weather. The last week of June, the entire ranch crew put their energies into the State Finals Rodeo. Afterwards, we were all victims of "energy crisis."

There was no breather, though, as we went right into the hay harvest. A good crew of "haywaddies" had the hay harvested in record time and with less machinery breakage than ever. Our hay crop was more than twice the amount of the harvests of the previous three years, which were reduced by drought.

We finished the 29th of July, 1976. Ranchers haying into August were stymied with unusual amounts of rain.

Under the watchful eye of Skeet (husband G.R.'s "man Friday"), the irrigated circle of corn was said to be one of the best in the country. A narrow band of large hail sliced through the field on the 11th of August, but harvest was better than we anticipated. The ear corn and corn ensilage was a nice addition to our prairie hay for winter feeding.

The killing frost held out until late October. Colorful foliage and lush grasses made last October the best in my memory.

The temperatures were driven down in November and December, so we are most thankful for the abundant feed supply. But it's going fast.

Mother Nature's game was most intriguing this year. Official figures at the National Weather Service office at Miller Field in Valentine reports total precipitation for the year at 32.55 inches — an all-time record. The most moisture received previously was 28.91 inches in 1929. Our moisture during 1977 was only four-tenths of an inch less than the combined totals of 1974, 1975 and 1976, the three drought years.

During the year, we were playing another card game with a dealer named Farm Economy. That dealer seemed to hold a stacked deck and all the jokers. We couldn't win for losing.

Inflation pushed the prices up on all our necessities, and the cattle market remained stale. We sold our steer calves for only two cents a pound more than we did in 1971, while I paid two dollars a pound more for coffee.

Also, the beef referendum, which we supported, failed. We seemed to lose on every hand dealt.

But who wants to rehash a losing card game?

It's 1978, and we get a new deck of cards. Deal them out, Mother Nature. We can handle the game you deal...if we play our cards right.

⫰ ⊤ ⊓ ⱶ ⊃

RANCHING A WAY OF LIFE, NOT JUST A JOB
- February 7, 1978 -

Recently, The Telegraph published a letter to the editor from someone who said he was sick and tired of hearing about the plight of farmers and ranchers. His advice was for them to quit and get a nine-to-five job.

That advice might be easy to give, but the result might be the same as that man quitting his nine-to-five job to take one on a ranch: he might hate it. I wonder if the writer knows what a man is like who chooses to work and live in the country, why he is there and why he stays?

Possibly, the first thing he'd notice is a deep love and appreciation for the land and animals. Out on the land, a man has a chance to express his own individuality — perhaps more so than in any other occupation. Everything he does is an extension of his philosophy...it is not "just a job," it is a way of life.

Should a rancher quit after spending most of his life in the country, it is most likely not by choice. I wonder if the author of that letter has any idea how painful the decision to quit is for a farmer or rancher under present-day conditions.

No one in the Sandhills felt any elation when Doug Wrage had to make the decision to quit ranching. His dispersion sale was Thursday. There is no joy in a man's heart as he watches a herd of cattle that took 30 years to build be sold at auction.

Those good cows were not merely animals nor possessions; they represented a philosophy...as Doug Wrage represented the family livestock operation. He's a rancher — a cattleman, and a good one.

Doug was born in a ranch house 24 miles south of Wood Lake during the hay harvest season of 1923. He spent all of his life on ranches in Cherry County. That is, with the exception of the 2 1/2 years he spent in the Air Force as a radio gunner on a B-24 bomber. He was awarded the Air Medal, three Oak Leaf clusters and the Purple Heart.

11

Then he and his wife, Betty, worked together on a ranch near Wood Lake for three years. They went into partnership with Kurt Wendler near Beaver Lake and gradually built the base of their cow herd.

Building a ranch operation does not happen overnight. It takes close management and frugal living to accumulate just the necessities. After eight years with Wendler, Doug went into a 10-year contract with Ralph Baker and moved to that ranch near Alkali Lake. At the end of the contract, Doug leased the ranch and bought Baker's cows.

Now, this was a family operation. Betty and the youngsters helped with all phases of the ranch work, including hay harvest and winter feeding. In return, Doug said they gave the kids what they could, including a college education. The children went on to more profitable professions.

Baker sold his ranch three years ago, and Doug leased the Stetter place on the Boardman Creek west of Merritt Reservoir. Cattle prices were depressed that year and became worse during the next year. That was also the second year of the recent three-year drought.

Doug had accumulated more than 700 head of cattle and all the equipment it takes to put up the hay and feed them. He continued to do most of the ranch work himself, sometimes with the help of a single man. "I worked by myself all my life," he said, "and with conditions the way they were, I couldn't afford to hire anyone to do the work the way I wanted it done."

Last summer, while working alone and running a haybuster stacker, Doug fell from the top of the cage while making some repairs. He lay unconscious for about six hours. After he came to, he managed to drive his pickup truck to a phone and call for help.

The fall damaged the balance of his inner ear, and Doug's doctors told him that he could no longer work alone.

"I sure don't want to quit," Doug said, "but I'm forced to. I just can't afford to hire the work done...I'll have to get a job of some kind. I hope I can find one that will keep me in the country...a field man or something like that."

Doug said that he doesn't have the college education that some employers might require...the kind of education that he gave his kids. But it is quite apparent to those who know him that his working knowledge of a ranch could be invaluable to an agriculture-related industry. It is not easy to start as a hired hand and eventually build up a herd of over 700 high-quality cattle — that is an education not offered in any school.

So, I say to the writer of that letter to the editor, here is a Cherry County rancher who is quitting the business and who may possibly take a nine-to-five job. But I hope you can now see how painful the decision to quit can be...that it's not just quitting a job but leaving behind a way of life.

COLD MAKES FOR LOUSY CATTLE
- February 14, 1978 -

Sometimes I tell the bossman of this outfit that his initials, G.R., stand for "Grump and Rumble"...the Sandhills' answer to Archie Bunker. Recently, it was because of a tirade stemming from his frustration with the cold weather, cattle lice and government bureaucracy. His language was colorful and descriptive...but unprintable here. This time, though, he had my sympathy.

During the frigid weather of December, lice were showing up on the cattle. But it stayed too cold to spray for them. "Never did see a louse I could afford to feed all winter," he said.

Then a warming trend was forecast in early January. G.R. was ready and had every head of stock on the place sprayed during two days when temperatures bumped the 40s.

Lice are strange critters. The cycle of a louse is 30 days from egg to nymph to adult. And, unlike other parasites, the entire life cycle is spent on an animal.

Lice thrive in the very coldest of weather. They need moisture, so the infestation can be easily seen and the population estimated by checking the moist muzzle of an animal.

Spraying has to be repeated in about 20 days to catch the hatch from eggs not killed by the first spray.

To make a long story short, January turned out to be the third coldest on record in Cherry County. There was no chance to spray a second time. "Now we've raised another healthy crop of the little blood suckers," G.R. rumbled.

He is always careful to keep the louse population down, because it is possible for cattle to become anemic from a heavy infestation. For weak cattle, a spring storm can be a killer.

G.R.'s tirade on bureaucracy concerns jovial "Big Jim" Flannigan down at Sutherland. He operated a one-man factory for more than 30 years that produced a chemical mixture to control lice, face flies and other animal parasites.

Jim became a vital part of this country and said he sold his product to two generations of Adamsons and four of the Lovejoys.

He traveled a triangle from Sutherland to Gordon and east to O'Neill for about 800 customers. Jim offered a personalized service. He'd say, "Give me a pasture." What he meant was, he'd take a certain pasture and spend hours testing about four different chemicals in different amounts until he obtained a mix that gave him a satisfactory fly kill.

He'd mix the amount a rancher ordered and then deliver it, too. "That was the best part, as I could visit," he said. "Those people are the best damn hillbillies in the world."

Jim said government figures estimate that uncontrolled parasites can knock about 60 pounds from a yearling's weight. "Control would cost them about $1 a head, so that would be a gain of at least $13, figuring prices at 20 cents a pound," he said.

Flies and lice become resistant to chemicals, and Jim was in business to kill them. So every two years he would change his formula, subtracting the amount of some chemicals while adding to the amounts of others. And it worked... ranchers in this country never had to worry about it, as Jim took care of them.

This is where government controls started to pinch the operation. He had to change his formula every two years, but regulations and the red tape for approval of the change often took two years and longer.

"The environmentalists are all right," the big man said, "but sometimes a good idea gets out of hand. I was put out of business because I couldn't get approval in time for the needed change."

Jim admits it was partly his fault...if he spilled some chemical on the floor he didn't always cut out that section of the floor like he was supposed to.

Big Jim Flannigan has retired, but he says he misses the business and Sandhills people. Likewise, this ranch and many others miss Big Jim. He relieved the rancher of the "hunt and pick" method of finding an effective parasite control. He took care of us...and that is the reason G.R. grumbles about that (unprintable) government bureaucracy.

FEEDING CATTLE IN COLD EXHAUSTING
- February 21, 1978 -

We weren't too thrilled about our national status last Friday, when the Weather Service reported that we were the second coldest place in the country. To have one degree above the nation's low of 25 below zero at Burwell is a distinction we could do without. We lost two more fall calves.

It has been so cold for so long, and with so little sunshine, everyone is worn out; cattle as well as people.

G.R., my weary husband, says he just can't seem to get the cattle filled with hay. They empty the feed grounds as fast as he strings hay, and the extended cold is rapidly depleting the supply of hay. G.R. had to stop feeding in late afternoon to bed the fall calves.

Then, too, we are still feeling the results of last March, when more than 50 inches of snow dragged down, covered or broke most of our fences. We couldn't keep the bulls in their lots and are now getting a few unscheduled calves during this bitter cold. The calves have to be put in as soon as they are born...or better yet, just before. I can't even imagine the shock leaving the warm womb of the mother for subzero temperatures.

G.R. has had a heavy load. He and both of the hired hands have been ill, with one going to the hospital. At one time, I thought G.R. needed to be, as he could hardly drag. But the work remained, so he's been working days and taking his turn checking the expectant mothers in the springer lot at night. And he's had to put up with some lousy help...me.

I've taken my turns on the night shift so he could get some rest. That is, after enough tracks were made through the snow and we could return to using the four-wheel drive pickup with spotlight. Myndi, our teenage daughter, takes a turn on weekends and is a top hand. If a stubborn cow has to be driven in, she is as handy on horseback as any man.

Of course, when there's a problem, the men are awakened.

When it stormed last week and we were short of help, I started helping G.R. as he fed hay. It gets a little hectic when he's alone — driving through the tight herds of cattle, avoiding the drifts and operating the hydrafork, too.

I bundled into the warmest clothing I could find, including a fur-lined cap no one else would wear...I thought I looked a bit like a refugee from the Korean Army.

My first day out made me appreciate my "housewife" status. From habit, I took my camera, but we were both too cold to function properly.

There is no heater in the tractor cab. There is also very little room in the cab — just enough for the passenger to wedge between the driver and the door. I was that wedge...and "the closest" to the gates between all the lots.

It seems like I opened a jillion gates...up and down the steep vertical steps to the cab, feet so numb I could hardly feel them...grab the icy gate stick... lunge through knee-deep snow to drag the wide gate far enough for the feed outfit to pass.

The wind-driven snow bit at my cheeks and snow packed in over the tops of my boots. The cold made my nose run, but my handkerchief had become a frozen wad. I wished for a pair of "long handles."

Now, I don't drive that big tractor very often, and G.R. is short on instructions. I was pretty nervous driving through the drifts with the power of 100 horses under the steering wheel as G.R. fed. I was nervous trying to figure out the six gears... trying to hear instructions above the throb of the engine...when to put the tractor in hydradrive...and which snow-packed pocket to avoid. One I should have avoided, but before I could ask, "Should I go this way?" We were stuck.

G.R. didn't even yell at me...guess he was afraid I'd quit. I guess I'm a good example of poor help and why ranchers have abandoned horses for a big tractor and do the work alone.

When we went to the house for lunch and to get warm, I realized how the cold saps a person's strength. And it wasn't long before I realized how the body gets out of condition. I started getting calls from muscles I hadn't heard from in years.

It's getting better now as the body complaints aren't as loud and the steps into the cab don't seem as steep. But I'll be glad when it's spring and the snow that packs in over my boot tops will be replaced by sand in my shoes.

LONG COLD CAUSING CATTLE LOSSES
- March 7, 1978 -

The winter 1977-1978 has been a cold encounter of the lasting kind. The average daily temperature from December through February has set an all-time record low of 12.7 degrees...ninety days in the Sandhills deep freeze.

Last Tuesday, rancher G.R. said, "Thank God it's the end of this month." The next morning, March arrived with a new record low of 14 degrees below zero. On Wednesday, strong winds drove the wind chill factor to 40 below.

Should anyone ask me, I would suggest we quit the cattle business and raise polar bears and penguins. I think everyone is depressed.

Saturday morning, daughter Myki called at 5:45 a.m. from Omaha. She asked if she had got me up, and I asked her if she could smell the bacon frying. It was minus 21 outside.

G.R. had been up since 2:30 a.m., when he took over the night shift to keep a running check on the springers, as ranchers call pregnant cows. "Pure hell on baby calves," he reported at breakfast.

We've hired two extra hands. Didn't need the extra expense, but what do you do? There is only so much each man can do, and the frigid weather has made calving a 24-hour job. When the wind is blowing, two men take the night shift.

The extreme cold makes it hard to predict when a cow will calve. All the usual signs of imminent birth are not apparent, so we maintain a constant vigil. The minute a calf is born, it is taken to the overflowing barn and ear-tagged. The tags are recorded with that of the mother; it takes some of the work out of pairing them again in the morning.

G.R. said he could use a barn a mile long and a quarter-mile wide. I told him we'd get him the Astrodome for Christmas.

The men brought a chilled calf to the house Thursday. It was 10 below, and I was surprised it survived birth. When in the womb, the calf's temperature is 101.5 degrees. At birth, the wet little thing had the shock of a temperature drop of 111 degrees. That is a traumatic welcome to the outside world.

We put the chilled calf in the shower, and I scrubbed it with a brush for more than an hour. Quite often warm water and rubbing to force circulation will save a calf. This time it didn't.

17

Friday, they brought in another, a male, and placed him in front of the heater in my little office. He was a day old and had moved across the lot with his mother before he went down. If the calf's pupils have turned white, there is usually no hope. On this one, the eyes were just cloudy. I worked and worked with him, and this time it paid off. The next morning he went back to the shed with his mother.

I was really relieved. The loss of one little calf might not seem like much, but each loss means one less yearling to sell and a cow that has been fed for a year with no return.

The ice build-up on the ground and frozen cow chips have made every animal on the ranch footsore. It is nearly impossible to work cattle from the lots with a horse unless it is sharp shod with pads. We've wanted to shoe extra horses, but the farrier has been unable to get here.

The tires on the pickups and tractors are also showing stress. The concentrated build-up of frozen cow chips resembles sharp rocks. That seems to cut the tread right off a tire. Besides that, the rough ground causes added repairs, such as radiators that have vibrated loose.

One of the outside duals on the tractor is flat, but it's been too cold to do anything about it.

Conditions could be much worse. I recently talked by phone with a man in Sturgis, SD, who said that conditions in the northwest part of his state are critical. "Cattle are succumbing to the stress of the prolonged cold," he said. "Some operators have had a 50 percent loss, and some have had even more."

The loss, I'm sure, is not from negligence. At this ranch, everything is being done that is humanly possible. There is just no escape from the lingering, penetrating cold.

Yesterday, G.R. came to the house so leg-weary he could barely walk.

"I can't keep feeding this much hay," he said. "I don't know how much more it is going to take to get us to grass."

WARM WEATHER WELCOMED BY RANCHERS
- March 14, 1978 -

I t is amazing what a couple of days of sunshine and warm weather will do for the spirit. I've actually seen a few smiles lately. The mercury that dropped to a minus-21 on March 4 climbed to 52 on March 8. A lot of our ice and snow drifts turned into lakes. The water will be with us for a while, as the frost was driven eight to 10 feet down during the previous three months of record-breaking cold weather and water can't soak into frozen ground.

Ranch activities, last week, were in high gear. The men sprayed the cattle for lice. They had sprayed the first part of January, but the severe cold prevented the repeat spraying and the lice eggs hatched.

Then, in addition to daily feeding of hay and checking the cows, fences were fixed, horses shod and tractor repairs were made. Warm weather has relieved the pressure of constantly checking for newborn calves that might chill.

It seems more natural to see the cows and fall calves scattered throughout the hills and picking at winter grazing. For three months, I've seen them huddled in bunches, seeking warmth from the others.

The baby calves now run and play, or lie soaking up the sun. There are more than 100 cows and their babies scattered through the hills of the east lot. Eleven of those cows don't have calves, because their little ones were lost to the cold, or born too weak or premature. Not even our 24-hour vigil could save them.

Husband G.R. quietly marked the figure on the calendar. That's about an 11 percent loss — the worst I remember this early in the calving season. And that is in addition to the fall calves lost to the bitter cold.

The intense cold created more problems with the cows, too, especially with sore udders, possibly from frost bite. This seems to plug the teats, and the calves aren't able to open them. If close observation revealed a calf is not doing well, the cow goes into a chute and the quarters opened.

The sunshine reflected up by the snow has caused some of the cows to have sunburned udders, so there still must be checks to make sure a cow with a sore udder is not starving her calf.

But, at least the warm weather has lessened the strain on the hay supply. It takes careful management and rationing to stretch the hay supply until grass growth begins later this spring, and the extra-cold winter took quite a bite.

There is a lot more to this business of agriculture than most people realize. And it becomes a little depressing when your best efforts just aren't good enough.

Ilene Ostergard of Gothenburg sent a letter saying that she could certainly relate to conditions on a ranch, since she and her husband spent nearly 50 years on one before turning it over to their sons.

"Dad says he can't remember a year as bad as this past one," she wrote.

She also included a newspaper clipping in which a reader had written to say that disgruntled people in agriculture weren't making money because they didn't know their business and that low prices weren't the problem.

Her answer to that, I thought, was most accurate: "You are not to judge a person until you have walked in his boots for two miles."

I thank God that this is a country where people are allowed to voice an opinion, but there is nothing I'd like better than to see a few of agriculture's critics walk two miles in a rancher's boots. Should they accept the challenge to try on those boots, my bet is they wouldn't make it a quarter of a mile. They would find out what it is like to have no monthly or weekly check...or that there was no wage coming for their very best efforts.

This past winter has been hard for ranchers, but spring is just around the corner and with it, hope. The winter's extra moisture has assured us a good hay crop...unless we lose it to hail. I guess our critics would say that if we knew our business, we wouldn't let it hail...

'ONE ROOM AND PATH' OF '49 REVISITED
- March 28, 1978 -

Recently, I made a sentimental journey back to the scene of my first winter on a ranch. That was during the winter of 1949, the year of a big blizzard. After I left that first "house" in the spring, I never returned. I guess I've been afraid I might have to stay there again.

My husband G.R. and I had been married a couple of months and were in the process of building a house. There wasn't even an empty bunk house at the ranch, so we were living with G.R.'s parents.

That winter began on January 2 with a blizzard that sneaked in on the country unpredicted. My new husband and I had blissfully gone off to a movie in Valentine.

When we emerged from the dark theater, we were shocked to see the balmy, warm day had turned into a full-fledged, roaring blizzard. We hurried towards the ranch, which was 40 miles away, but only got about 20 miles from town when blowing snow reduced visibility to zero.

We inched our way to Everett Brown's ranch to wait out the storm. Four days later, a ski-equipped plane flew us home, and we left our car at the Brown's for the duration. About three feet of wind-driven snow had immobilized the entire area.

When we arrived at the ranch, G.R.'s father said, "You've got to get to Sawyer Camp." It didn't occur to me to ask questions about where it was or what it was like. But that was the way it was here. If L.C., his father, said to do something, we never questioned his orders. Of course, G.R. knew where we were going.

We loaded meager provisions from ranch supplies onto a drag sled pulled by four horses and started on our journey with the first light of morning. After some 12 hours of floundering through snow and giving the horse's time to rest, we arrived at Sawyer Camp, some 15 miles from the ranch. Not only was it a long way, but people didn't live anywhere close. It sat on a wildlife refuge.

To me, a camp meant something like 4-H camp...cabins and trees and having sort of a resort look.

Well, this Duck Bar Ranch camp wasn't any of those. Most of it was snowed under, but an old school house that had never seen a paint brush stood out like a sore thumb. The pole-shed barns were drifted under.

A photographer friend, Vicki Miller, had heard me tell about Sawyer Camp and the winter of '49. She was just a little skeptical about my story and wanted to see this place for herself. I agreed but told her it really wasn't fair to go during nice weather and in a pickup. We should have gone after a storm and on horseback.

About eight of those 15 miles is now oil road. When we left the oil, we hadn't gone far before Vicki started to mention the "gawd-awful" rough ground we called a road. I suppose we traveled about 10 miles an hour.

Being the passenger, Vicki had to open all the gates. Occasionally, she'd ask, "Are you sure you know where we're going?" I'd answer, "I surely hope so."

Though I had never returned to the buildings, I had taken hot meals to the hay crew down on the Sawyer meadow for many years.

Finally, we rounded a hill, and there was Sawyer Camp in all its questionable glory. Only now horseweeds reached to the top of the barn instead of snow. Everything looked pretty much the same, except the barn was in even worse disrepair and a wind break had fallen over.

The windmill and tank that supplied water for the house and cattle was still there. Then I saw the outhouse had been moved farther from the house. Vicki laughed and shook her head. "You really lived here, didn't you?" She kept repeating, "So this is your infamous 'one room and a path'." We opened the door to the porch, where coat hooks of years long past and school days long forgotten still remained at a child's height. Just as the first time I'd entered that shack, the smell of mice was overpowering. Exiled to that porch was the old pot belly stove that had heated (or tried to heat) the "house" that winter. We had fed the stove until it turned cherry red, yet the warmth always rose to the 12-foot ceiling and the corners of the building remained cold.

We opened the next door. Vic laughed and I was dumbfounded. I couldn't believe that one room was so small — maybe 15 by 20 feet. I just couldn't believe it...my mind remembered more room than that.

The tiny cupboard still hung from the wall and it was filled with the coffee cans needed to protect food from the mice. A crude bench hung from the wall for a "kitchen counter." A small propane stove stood where the kerosene burner once stood. The only other furniture left was an old chair. The building hadn't been used for 20 years.

Windows had been broken and birds had entered to nest and find sanctuary. The "signs" of birds and mice were abundant.

I told Vic that town folks called the shack "honeymoon cottage" when they heard we were off in "the wilderness" that winter. Then I told Vic the reason it was so funny. When we had been there three weeks, G.R.'s father had brought us down an Army cot and a hired man, Carl Schleve, to help us. We strung a wire and an Army blanket as a "room divider."

Living there was like living in a commune. I remember listening to Carl strike match after match to light his Bull Durham roll-your-owns, as he awakened often to smoke. Then there were sounds of mice scampering across the ceiling, down the walls and across the beds. Those months at Sawyer Camp were a lesson in togetherness.

I'm certain that little shack on the prairie made quite an impression on Vic, who is of the same generation as my oldest daughter, Myki. They both love the ranch, but I'm not certain either would like to start ranch life there at Sawyer Camp as I did.

Years later, I was asked to tell my story to a young women's group. So I told them in detail about living three months at Sawyer Camp and then moving to a smaller shack at Duck Lake Camp for two months while calving the cows. Both were with hardship.

We were back at the ranch in June when LC told me I was to feed the hay crew. Me? Feed 12-15 men three meals a day, some on Sundays; clean the bunkhouse and do some of the men's laundry. Shouldn't I have experience to qualify?

By the end of September and the end of hay harvest, I'd gone through 100 pounds of potatoes a week. You do the math on the rest of their food. The menu included meat three times a day and pie once.

Then L.C. brought me five men on the county road crew to room and board.

A young woman raised her hand with a horrified look, "And you're still there?"

SPRING CALF SALE BRINGS SMILES
- April 4, 1978 -

There is a promise of a bright sunrise as I write this. Bird songs nearly drown the throb of the big tractor that is already on the feed grounds. The new cycle of life has begun on the ranch; more than 400 calves with shiny white faces play in the sunshine. They are a sure-fire sign of spring, a renewal of life that spurs a smile and the eternal optimism that keeps a rancher in the cattle business.

But as surely as calves are born, there will be scours — a bacterial infection that can be a calf-killer. We haven't lost any to scours, but each day the men ride the herd and doctor calves with signs of it.

Calf scours is just one of the problems a cattleman faces during the year-round battle to get his stock from birth to market. And then it's the decision of whether to market your product at the ranch or a sale barn...and when. Decisions, decisions.

Take, for instance, the calves born last spring. We often sell at the ranch when we wean them, but the market was sour last fall. We weaned and waited, and the winter turned bitter cold. Selling was then out of the question, as the calves shrink in weight and that fall "bloom" of condition fades with the cold. I seldom saw a smile the rest of the winter.

By February, we were concerned about the hay supply. Leland Johnson of Thedford Livestock Auction came to the ranch to see if we'd bring calves there. The calves were "green" — no creep feed, just enough hay to keep them growing. Husband G.R. said that when they hit grass, they'd grow like weeds.

It didn't take Leland and G.R. long to agree on how to handle the calves; they both had a reputation at stake. Both wanted to present quality and condition for sale and no "fill," or extra water for extra weight. And, the calves had to be handled quiet and easy.

Because we were selling the entire herd, steers and heifers alike, the men decided it would be best if the cattle were trucked to Thedford on Saturday for the Tuesday sale. Sorting the animals into classes of sex and weight would be time-consuming. Then, G.R. wanted them weighed before the sale to see if they regained any of the shrink resulting from trucking and handling before sale day.

Selling cattle at any time is a little nerve-racking. The price depends on the buyers and the whim of the market that day. As the trucks left the ranch, the furrow deepened on G.R.'s brow. Johnson had wanted him to be there when they sorted, but problems at the ranch prevented it.

"I'm not worried, because those guys know what they're doing," he said. "They'll do a good job. They've proved that already."

Johnson will observe his 10th anniversary at the barn April 22. He envisioned year-round sales when he took over the barn and has accomplished just that. During those 10 years, the number of cattle handled in a year went from 16,000 to 44,000.

"There is more responsibility than most people realize when you sell a man's cattle," Johnson said. "When you are a commission man, you're often dealing with a rancher's income for an entire year."

He noted that country contact, advertising, care, and the right presentation of the cattle are all of vital importance to the producer, buyer and sale barn man alike. "Buyers and customers return only because they want to and have been treated fairly," Johnson said.

On sale day, March 21, 1978 everything went backwards, and we were late starting for Thedford. G.R. was nervous, and his frown only deepened as he wondered how the sale would go. If there was demand and buyers, fine; if not...

Just as we walked into the barn, the auctioneer said, "We're starting on the Beel cattle." I held my breath as G.R. looked at the black baldies in the ring, and then he said, "They look just right."

Those few words meant a lot of things: the cattle didn't show stress or fill, looking rather fresh off the range. It also meant that Johnson and his crew had handled the calves "just right."

The cattle sold above our expectations — in fact, they topped the market that day. It was the best price we had received for our calves in over four years. G.R. tried in vain to suppress a smile. He is a businessman, but he also has an ego. A buyer doesn't push the price out of sympathy but because he likes the cattle. A rancher takes pride in offering a good product, and the sale barn personnel does too.

G.R. was pleased to find the calves had regained three pounds of the weight lost to trucking shrink. Johnson was quick to spread the credit of success among his partners, Mark Nutter, Loren Sutton and Bill Stevens — "a great crew."

Friends teased G.R. for a loan, but he told them his banker was waiting in the pickup. However, he relaxed enough for a good steak and an evening at Thedford's Cow Poke Inn, visiting and "swopping lies."

SOUNDS HERALD THE ARRIVAL OF SPRING
- April 4, 1978 -

For more than a month, it has been spring...or so said the calendar. As I remember, March 20 did very little to tell me it was spring. There was no blossom fragrance on the breeze nor roll of drums to herald the season.

We mortals proclaim spring by a date on the calendar, but the Lord in His infinite wisdom slowly and gently stirs the earth from its slumber. It's a hushed and fragile season.

For me, spring arrives by sound before the Sandhills turn 10,000 shades of green. There was a heady feeling as birds clustered in our trees, performed their first concert of the season. I threw open windows so the sweet air and song could fill the house with spring.

For the past week, those sounds have gathered in volume until the Sandhills vibrate with song.

Meadow larks, with a daffodil at their throat, sing from a fencepost and robins are dusted with rose-blush from the dogwood. Kildeer zig-zag down the road repeating its name as its call. From the meadow, I heard the curlew's plaintive call rising above the busy chatter of ducks on the creek. High overhead, Sandhill cranes trail their low, loud, musical rattle while geese honk their way into the northern sky.

All of these are merely the harbingers of spring and the arrival of the night hawk says it is so. Long-time residents claim the night hawk seldom arrives before the final spring snow.

Very soon, it will be the season to stop and smell the flowers but now it's time to pause and hear the season of spring. So I have.

Each spring, I've yearned for the treat of visiting the courting dance of prairie chickens on their booming grounds. In all the years spent in the Sandhills, I've never seen a prairie chicken. Last week, I did.

The chickens are scarce in our area, but Larry Vaughn of the refuge, has photo blinds on booming grounds near Pony Lake. I could enter a blind before sunrise or in late afternoon with the latter unpredictable. I missed my 4:30 a.m. alarm.

Twelve hours later, I left my car a half mile from the blind and Larry drove me over the wet ground to leave me at the blind. A dozen chickens flushed at our intrusion so I entered the small cubicle a bit skeptical that they'd return.

After 10 minutes in the restricted confinement of a four-foot cubicle, I opened the observation slot and froze at the sight. On silent wings, the chickens had returned to the grounds and not 10 feet away, one rigid with alertness was staring me right in the eye. I couldn't smother the cough that rose in my throat while I closed the slot to go back into hiding. I was certain my sounds had cleared the grounds.

Suddenly a throbbing, hollow boom filled the air, reverberated from the metal cubicle and I held my breath in wonder. I was surrounded by sound which seemed to bounce and echo from the hills, the likes of which I'd never heard as it was enriched and intensified by resonance.

Cautiously, I peered from the blind to be thrilled by sight and sound. Dozens of prairie chickens were dancing on a blur of legs to the beat of their own drummers. Tail feathers flared, feathered horns rose at the back of their heads and brilliant orange swelled at their throats and then deflated with an erry boom. I counted more than 30.

What could describe that unique sound? Was it like strains from a haunting flute mixed with rhythm from a finely tuned timpani drum? Ooooom, boom, boo. The hollow oooom began low in pitch and then rose.

It was the shortest three hours I've ever spent.

At sundown, the activity diminished and the booming ceased but continued to resound in my head. Slowly, I became aware of duck chatter from a nearby pond and the coyote's call from the distant hill.

I was loath to leave the blind, but darkness demanded my departure. The birds disappeared into the night without a sound.

Their haunting song of spring, however, continues in my mind and I intend to return and record it for times when spirits need lifting.

COW CUTTING GETS IN YOUR BLOOD
- April 11, 1978 -

Y ou would think, by the number of horse shows and rodeos I've attended in the past 15 years, that I would have qualified for the National Finals Rodeo by now. However, my status has remained the same — just chauffeur.

Maybe I've improved a bit though, as the first time I pulled a trailer full of horses I was scared to death.

I've had to take the ditch with the car on several occasions to keep from hitting a slow moving vehicle that pulled onto the highway immediately in front of me. With the added weight of the trailer and horses, it takes a much longer distance to stop — and makes taking the ditch a disaster. If you have to slam on your brakes, there is a danger of throwing the horses down and possibly injuring them.

I'm sure people don't realize this, or they wouldn't pull out in front of horse trailers or semi trucks — especially when both lanes of traffic are busy.

I had to do a lot of defensive driving during the four days last week when I drove nearly 1,000 miles to pull daughter Myndi and her horse to various cow cutting contests. I'm surprised we don't read of more instances of trailer wrecks and killed horses. It's that season when a lot of horses are on the road.

Speaking of cutting contests, it was a thrill to see so many really good cutting horses at the coliseum in Lincoln. It takes a special horse and usually years of training so the horse works the cattle at high speed with slack reins and the rider giving cues only with leg pressure. To me, a good cutting horse is like a ballet dancer — grace and control in each move.

Carol Rose of Texas was at Lincoln, riding a four-year-old Doc Bar horse. Not only was the horse beautiful, it was a tremendous athlete and performed like a much older horse. I understand the Roses have priced the horse at $150,000.

I would hate to have the responsibility of pulling an animal that valuable. There were some very good horses at a cutting contest Saturday at Ainsworth. The all-day contest had 71 entries with "cutters" pulled in from all over the country.

I was disappointed in one thing, though. I was hoping Bill McKenstrom of Oklahoma would bring his turn-back horse, Chink the Chinaman. I had heard of the horse and wanted some pictures.

Bill said the horse is 30 years old — extremely old for a horse and the equivalent of 80 years for a human. Bill says he doesn't look that old, however, and is "one heck of a good turn-back horse." At one time, I guess, Chink racked up a lot of points in cow cutting contests.

Probably one of the oldest cutting horses used at Ainsworth was Niki Nak, owned by Pat Jacobs of Gate, Oklahoma. The mare is 18, and just four years ago collected enough wins to place her 7th in the nation. Last year, 11-year-old Rose rode her to 4th place in the youth cow cutting division of the nation.

The Jacobs are a cow cutting family. Pat and Nellie and their three children — Rose, Wade and Andy — all entered in the various classes. Nellie said they never compete against each other in the same class.

Myndi was tickled pink to place second to Pat in the $1,000 novice class. Then she picked up two 3rds and two 4ths in other classes.

Cow cutting can really get in your blood. Besides the people who make a living at training and showing cutting horses, many have taken it up as a hobby. For instance, Buss Olson, who rode horses for the Army at Ft. Robinson, now has a couple of cutting horses. And Rex Hagemeister had his 19-year-old Spotted Tail at Ainsworth, but used him as a turn-back horse and used a younger horse in the cutting contest. Mr. and Mrs. Sam Toole, who run Taylor's Supper Club at Denver, each ride and pull to a lot of shows just for the fun of it.

I'm kind of envious of cutters. I think it would be a thrill to be able to sit in the saddle during those neck-wrenching turns and make it look easy. You notice I said, "look easy," as I know it isn't. I've never tried it, as I'm afraid I'd land in the dirt on the first hard turn.

But you never can tell. Maybe someday I'll try it, but I assure you it will be in the privacy of our back corral where the sand is deep and soft.

SANDHILLS FIRES FRIGHTENING
- June 20, 1978 -

There are few things in the Sandhills more frightening than the smell of a prairie fire — other than the fire itself, that is. Often, the odor of the fire drifts for miles through the choppy hills of this sparsely-populated country, making it difficult to pinpoint the exact location of a fire. Sometimes, you'll discover a nearby fire that has gone undetected because the smoke wasn't seen or smelled.

Such was the case last Thursday, a day when the thermometer soared into the 90s. Conservation Officer Mick Gray had stopped by the ranch during a tour of the area. He asked husband G.R. who we depended upon in case of a prairie fire.

G.R. explained that there was a fire truck at a ranch to the west and another at the wildlife refuge to the east, each about six miles away. There are also two rural fire trucks at Valentine, the nearest town, about 40 miles away.

"Mostly we rely on ourselves, using wet gunny sacks, shovels and cattle sprayers," G.R. told him. "Because of the rough hills and the distance, it takes a while for the trucks to get here, and we hate to call them out unless we think we really need them."

Ironically, Gray hadn't been gone a half-hour when I saw G.R. zoom through the yard in his pickup and stop at the shop. Daughter Myndi ran to the house, changed her sandals for shoes, gasped, "Fire on 22!" and was gone.

I knew it wasn't prime fire time, and I decided the fire must not be a bad one or G.R. would have told me to call for help. I also knew that "22" meant Section 22 — a big pasture in rough hills, hard to reach even with a four-wheel-drive vehicle.

29

I had two of our little grandsons in my care, so I took them with me on a drive down the highway. I thought maybe I could see the smoke and locate the fire, but we saw nothing at first. Then, about a mile to the northeast, I thought I saw smoke — but that was the wrong direction for Section 22. I was confused.

I returned to the house and called neighbor Judy Reece, because the smoke appeared to be in their pasture. She said that they were not aware of any fire but would check.

About that time, the radio reported a fire about a mile west of us. The dispatcher said the report had been turned in from a location about six miles east of us — adding that the fire site given was only a guess. He said fire trucks had been sent out.

Knowing I'd have to direct the trucks when they arrived, I went back down the road to pinpoint the location of the fire. I met some neighbors and the refuge fire truck, which had been directed by Citizens Band radio dispatches to the smoke I'd seen to the northeast.

I rushed back to the house to call the dispatcher with an accurate location. I was told that an airplane had been sent out and found a fire directly north of our buildings — in short, there were two fires!

About this time, G.R. and his crew drove down out of the steep hills. They were smoke-blackened and appeared worn out. They had fought the fire for two hours in the deep pockets of the hills. The wind had changed several times, whipping the fire in different directions.

A short time later, the trucks arrived from town and soaked down the smouldering cow chips that would occasionally burst into flames. This eliminated an all-night vigil for us. The burned area covered about 60 acres.

G.R. later told me that the smoke had hung close to the ground, preventing detection. He thought that he and the crew would have little trouble putting the fire out, so he hadn't called for help. Besides, truck tracks in the soft sandy hills can help start severe soil erosion and lead to destructive blow-outs.

We decided that the next time, however, he should tell me the exact location of a fire so I could at least check to see if help was needed. That would also lessen the chances for confusion.

Apparently, bolts of dry lightening from a cloudless sky had set the fires about lunch time. Had the fires occurred in August, the situation might have been truly serious.

It's frightening to realize these hills can hide a fire for such a long length of time. It makes us most grateful to both the town and country residents of the Sandhills, who are willing to drop anything they're doing to rush to help fight a prairie fire.

IT ISN'T LIKE MOWING A LAWN
- *July 11, 1978* -

The Sandhills hay season is probably the most expensive time of the year...and inflation has pushed the costs much higher.

Take today's daily wages for five extra hands, each receiving three meals a day, multiplied by six (sometimes seven) days a week — and it's no small sum these days.

Then the machinery. A mower sickle that cost $7 in 1950 is now about $60. Rake teeth are $5 each, and it takes 80 to fill a big rake — and they break like tooth picks, especially with "green" hired hands and rough ground.

Husband G.R. defines a perfect hay season as an entire month of very little dew, rain only on Saturday nights, a "thinking" crew — and no machinery breakdowns.

It happened once. About two years ago — G.R. stayed in a mellow mood the whole summer.

We often manipulate G.R.'s initials to fit his mood, so his name varies. When he outwitted an ornery bull, we dubbed G.R. "Genius Rancher." When he struggled to sell cattle on a depressed market, it was "Grump & Rumble."

This hay season, he has become "GRrrr Bear." Then, of course, he has always been a bit of a perfectionist who has little patience with carelessness.

I could see the mood change as the crew drove in from the field about 9 o'clock one evening. A grease-covered G.R. stalked towards the house, bearing a definite similarity to a wounded grizzly bear.

I knew that haying conditions were bad on the wildlife refuge at Watt's Lake. The meadows hadn't been mowed for two years and were extremely wet and rough with bogs.

"Did you work late to finish at Watt's?" I ventured to ask.

"We finished all right," he growled, "but we broke up every damned piece of equipment we had."

A shower cooled him down, and he later told me the inch of rain had made haying nearly impossible because water now covered much of the mown

31

grass. "We stacked everything but about four stacks in the swath. We had to leave that because the rakes couldn't swim," he said.

The next morning, it rained again. "It's a good thing," G.R. said, "because we have machinery to fix. But it's going to be hard to keep the entire crew busy."

Our crew consists of some young men and a couple of teenagers, which I'll describe as apprentices.

G.R. left them at the shop while he went to Watts to bring the machinery home. When he returned, they were extinguishing a fire on his hay sweep.

A rumble started deep in this throat that was to build to a full-fledged roar before the day was over.

What happened? One of the men was welding the frame of the hay sweep, his vision restricted by the welding mask. One of the boys remembered that G.R. wanted the gas tank drained and — right — chose that time to do it.

A spark from the welder set the gas and the sweep afire. A big battery charger was sitting on the sweep, and it burned, too. To make matters worse, the sweep is 30 years old and many parts for it are no longer available.

Two more discoveries: A mower head sent to town to have the bearings pressed out and replaced had been returned untouched. And the belts sent for the lawn mower were the wrong size.

To mow the lawn, G.R. put the youngest boy on a little cub tractor generally used for mowing weeds. A city boy, he had taken tractor training so he could qualify for a hay job — but G.R. told him to be careful anyway.

The inexperienced youth soon drove into a wooden fence by the bunk house. He froze, forgetting that pushing in the clutch would stop the wheels from spinning. The wheels dug down into the yard until the tractor was stuck. GRrrr Bear said that he was "plumb worn out from cussin'." He demoted the boy to a weed whip.

The next discovery: the gas in the tractor was diluted with rain water because "someone" had lost the tank cap. Would you believe that, compared to "GRrrr Bear," a grizzly with a thorn in its paw sounds like an angel's whisper?

The calendar says we are two weeks into the hay season. Somehow, though, I have the feeling it might be a very long, "hot" summer.

HAYING OPERATIONS CHANGED LITTLE
- *July 18, 1978* -

There have been relatively few changes in the hay operation on this ranch during the past 30 years. The biggest change is the number in our hay crew...and the method of stacking the hay.

In 1949, my first summer on the ranch, there were 15 men on the hay crew. This year, there are four men and a girl.

Until the mid 1940s, this ranch used a slide stacker that required a four-horse team to pull the hay up into the stack. A man with a pitchfork stacked the hay. Then, about 1946, a surplus army half-track replaced the horses. It remained in service for the next 20 years.

In 1971, for one season, we tried a swather and hay buster stacker, which picks up hay from the windrow. It was a sweet clover year, the same as this year, and the men were constantly stymied with the woody clover plugging up the swather head as well as the rollers on the stacker. Husband G.R. got rid of them both and returned to a slide stacker.

It became increasingly hard to find a man to stack, so for the past four years we've used a farm hand and a metal cage for the stacking. G.R. says it's the cheapest and easiest way to put up hay.

This year the sweet clover is five feet tall in places. It's tough to mow, impossible to rake and ornery to stack. There is a lot of green foliage, however, and it will make good feed next winter. We had a stacking crew one day last week that was a family affair, and I learned firsthand about clover. I filled in for the straight raker, who was busy mowing, and G.R. operated the truck-sweep. Son John, daughter Myndi, and our ranch hand manned the scatter rake.

I had to rake in patches, trying to avoid the sweet clover. Once the long, dried stems were picked up in the rake teeth, it wouldn't dump into the windrow, so I had to stop frequently and pull it from the teeth.

G.R. prefers to just sweep up the clover, which makes more work for the scatter raker, because he wants to leave a clean meadow. Myndi does a good job and only has trouble keeping up when they use two sweeps. In return, she gets a nice suntan.

In spite of the usual machinery break-downs and rain, the hay harvest is moving right along. By mid-afternoon Saturday, the stacks for the day added up to 27, making a total of about 180 stacks so far. The crew was able to quit a little earlier than usual and disappeared for an evening in town.

As an indicator of our hay crop, I always use a little meadow just west of the house. In 1976, the third year of drought, only two stacks were put up there. This year I count 14. The difference is that we've had 13 inches of moisture so far this year; the average precipitation total for the entire year in Cherry County is about 20 inches.

We use that lot February to April to hold the "springers," as we call cows to calve in the spring. The hay is fed in different areas of the meadow, and the cow chip build up is concentrated. A harrow is used to break up the chips in the spring, and the natural fertilizer is also a boost to hay production.

Yesterday, we had a new addition to the "mow gang." Our graduate nurse, Myki, has returned to the ranch for two weeks before starting a job at St. Joseph's Hospital in Omaha. Though she's spent the past few years in the city, I think she's stayed a little bit "country." She says she gets homesick for the Sandhills and the hay fields.

Speaking of the Sandhills — I've recently noticed something missing this year. We have an over-abundance of sweet clover, grasshoppers and toads. Really — toads are everywhere. But there are no sunflowers or burred American licorice.

Last year, the road ditches and every hill and pocket had a golden glaze from all the sunflowers. I've seen only small, anemic-looking plants this year and a few ragged, grasshopper-eaten blossoms.

Also, the tails and forelocks of our saddle horses were matted with burs last year, but this year their long hair blows freely in the wind.

I'm sure there must be some logical explanation as to why there is a profusion of one plant species one year and nearly a total lack of it the following year. But I don't worry about it too much. For me, it's just another intriguing mystery of the Sandhills.

RED INK TURNS BLACK SLOWLY
- August 1, 1978 -

Our haying is nearly completed. There have been a lot of good days and a few bad days, but that's all part of the ranching game. You deal with the bad days and immediately forget them, such as the one I told you about when everything went wrong and G.R. resembled a grizzly bear. I've had a lot of ranchers laugh and say "that sounds like home." A city dweller told me, however, that column sounded a little bit like fiction.

I can relate to that. I can also quote Joseph Conrad: "Nothing lays itself open to the charge of exaggeration more than the language of naked truth."

A couple of weeks ago, I was visiting with a prominent Arthur rancher who told me, "It's amazing how many people in our own state really don't have an accurate picture of what ranch life is all about. I still meet people who think all ranchers do is drive to town in a big car and wait for the cows to have calves. Then we sell them and put the money in a Swiss bank."

I think, just maybe, some folks resist abandoning the romantic fantasy of "country living." They see examples on television all the time. You know how it is. The ranch crew on the televised program Big Valley is so involved in exciting day-to-day drama that you seldom see them hard at work…and every problem has a happy ending.

There is an exciting drama going on for cattlemen right now but it's driving them a little crazy trying to figure out a solution. Last week's cattle market was really "hot." Fall steer calves topped the market at 79 cents a pound. This is about the same situation we saw in 1973 when the same class of calves went to 80 cents and then the bottom fell out of the market for four years.

We always hesitate to sell that class of cattle at this time of year. They are loose from the green grass and the weight shrink from handling and hauling can be a considerable amount. Later in the fall, when the grasses start to dry, the cattle harden up and shrink less.

Each rancher has to evaluate his own particular situation. If he is short of pasture, the shrink loss might be ignored. If range is plentiful and the cattle are gaining several pounds each day, a cattleman could take less dollars later in the season for more weight and his range would be utilized.

Weight shrink might seem of little consequence until you put a pencil to it. Let's take a hypothetical fall calf that weighs 550 pounds and shrinks 5 percent in weight in the first three hours on a truck. Those 27 pounds figured at 27 cents come to $21. If the cattleman was selling 200 head it would be possible for the shrink loss alone to total $4,200.

The producers of feeder cattle don't know what to do. No one knows exactly how to price their cattle if they anticipate selling at private treaty. There is a shortage of feeder cattle and an abundance of feed. Cattle feeders have finally made money this year and much of the profit has to be put back into the industry, but no one seems to have a concrete answer of what will happen next month or the next. (Who says Las Vegas has a corner of gambling?) Should we ignore the season and sell on an "up" market or gamble and wait for more finish?

We made a decision, some time ago, to sell our fall calving cows at the sale barn at Thedford next Tuesday. One reason is to conserve our range. We need to leave some idle because it was hard hit during the three drought years and the Sandhills do not recover rapidly. The other reason of course, is to keep our banker at arm's length. The four years of selling cattle below production costs has boosted the red ink to large figures.

They are good cows; their calves topped the market in February and they will produce a similar set starting the first of September. We hope they will bring a good price. If they do, we hope folks not in the cattle industry will refrain from thinking ranchers are getting "rich." It is going to take a lot more than one year of decent prices to make up for the four years of red ink that we've all been through.

STORM DAMAGE
- August 15, 1978 -

Records were set for the length of extremely cold weather. Now it appears that Mother Nature is still on a tear. August 1, 1978, was a horrible day for the ranch, but husband G.R., daughter Myndi and I were at Huron, SD at the National High School Rodeo Finals. We were lucky to have our daughter Myki, our son John and his wife, Kathy, "holding down the fort" while we were gone.

"Be glad you're not here," John told G.R. that Tuesday night. "It's a mess."

Pea-size hail, driven by winds reported at 80-100 miles an hour, had pounded rangeland grass into the ground, twisted limbs from the big cotton-wood trees and put one through the roof of our garage, leveled our garden and shortened dozens of tall haystacks to about the level of a pickup truck's hood.

John and the hay crew spent two days picking up limbs and debris from the storm. About 1.60 inches of rain had fallen in a brief period of time, turn-ing cow paths into gullies and future blowouts. The downed limbs were put in these areas to reduce the erosion potential.

John went back to the job of putting the stacks back together with a fork lift. Some stack tops had slid to the ground, while some had completely disap-peared with the wind.

I had to feel badly about the garden because Kathy had worked in it all summer, pulling weeds and fighting the grasshoppers, only to lose it to the hail.

When we returned to the ranch, G.R. and John flew over the hailed area. They said that for miles there was a wide strip of range that had turned brown and looked as though a prairie fire had gone through it.

The Powder Horn Ranch of J.B. and Pat Fischer, south of Nenzel, was hit hard. Pat said that all of their cedar trees were barked, all of the roofs would have to be reshingled and windows were broken in every building, causing extensive water damage to the interior of the houses.

Pat said that a roar similar to that of a jet airplane continued in the distance after the hail had passed their ranch. Hail still covered the ground the follow-ing day.

The Fischer's 170-acre irrigated circle of corn was a total loss. J.B. plowed it under to plant rye.

Pat said the storm, which came from the northwest, was the most frighten-ing she had ever experienced. Then, on August 10 as she was returning to the ranch with a pickup load of rye seed, the sky again took on an ominous appear-ance in the northeast. She said that she outran it to the ranch, thinking all the while: "Oh Lord, it's coming to finish us off and get the windows on the other side of the houses."

That storm proved to be less violent and hit here about 10:30 p.m. with another 1-1/2 inches of wind-driven rain and enough hail to cover the ground. I kept my own frightened vigil at the window, certain that the black, twisting clouds contained a tornado. A switch in wind direction brought the storm back for another visit about 1 a.m. with lightning slashing the black skies.

Barb Stichka at the Big Creek Ranch said that the August 1 and August 10 storms caught her at the same spot along the Merritt Reservoir. During the first storm, she pulled under a tree for protection from the hail but was still afraid the car windows were going to break. After the storm passed, Barb said that hail was piled in drifts and clouds of steam rolled up from the lake and hills. When caught by the second storm on her way to the ranch, she said at least she knew where to find a tree for protection.

The storm damage to buildings and the irrigated corn crops isn't too hard to figure, but the damage done to the rangeland is difficult to calculate. The hail struck hundreds of acres of grazing land and only time will determine the damage to the grasses. The hail pounded the crowns right into the ground, then covered and froze them. Often hail damaged rangeland must be left ungrazed for at least a year before the vigor of the grasses returns.

We had planned to conserve some of our range that we felt was stressed due to the recent drought years and sold our fall calving cows at Thedford. At the time we made those plans, little did we know that same range would be ravaged by the devastating damage of hail.

GRASS MORE UNIQUE THAN IT SEEMS
- August 22, 1978 -

Many of us who live in the country —our city cousins, too, for that matter —might take for granted the profusion of grasses that cover the land. It's easy to do with familiar things.

Grass holds the soil, feeds our livestock and wildlife, and to me, is interesting to study. Until 1960, however, I thought grass was something to fertilize, water and mow. Cows ate it, the ranch crew cut it in the summer and fed it in the winter. Then I became involved with 4-H.

There was no one to lead the 4-H range management project, so I was elected. I protested that I knew nothing about grass and was told to learn with the youngsters.

Soil conservationist, Bob Lowe, was at Valentine at the time and spent hours in the field helping us learn grass identification, range condition, use and management. I was totally amazed that each grass had its own unique features and that we could find some 40 different grasses and forbes in an area about 20 feet square.

We learned to recognize them early in the spring, when they were mature in the summer and after they had dried up in the fall. We found, for example, that each blade of smooth brome grass has an indented "W" and that there is a "V" of fine hairs at the base on the leaf of switch grass.

We also learned that there's a sharp, pointed star of hairs at each node on drop seed, and in the winter, the sheath that held the drop seed head drops to become a soft flag in the wind...Sandhills muhly grows in a donut-shaped ring, and the leaves are short, stiff and very sharp. Cattle seldom eat it...Sedge is the only plant with a triangular stem...Little bluestem flattens and curves near the root, and the blade of prairie cord grass will cut your fingers if you slide them down the edge.

The more we learned about grass, the more intriguing it became. I couldn't believe that once I had looked at grass as a collective mass and had taken it for granted.

Bob Lowe gave me an essay written by John J. Ingalls that completed my appreciation of that vital and important part of our environment. I want to share it with you. Its title is simply: Grass.

Next in importance to the divine profusion of water, light and air — those three physical facts which render existence possible — may be reckoned the universal beneficence of grass. Lying in the sunshine among the buttercups and dandelions of May, scarcely higher in intelligence than those minute tenants of that mimic wilderness, our earliest recollections are of grass. And when the fitful fever is ended, and the foolish wrangle of the market and the forum is closed, grass heals over the scar which our descent into the bosom of the earth has made, and the carpet of the infant becomes the blanket of the dead.

Grass is the forgiveness of nature, her constant benediction. Fields trampled with battle, saturated with blood, torn with the ruts of cannon, grow green again with grass, and the carnage is forgotten. Streets abandoned by traffic become grass-grown like rural lanes and are obliterated. Forests decay, harvests perish, flowers vanish...but grass is immortal. Beleaguered by the sullen hosts of winter, it withdraws into the impregnable fortress of its subterranean vitality and emerges upon solicitation of spring.

Sown by the winds, by wandering birds, propagated by the subtle horticulture of the elements which are its ministers and servants, it softens the rude outline of the world. Its tenacious fibers hold the earth in its place and prevent its soluble components from washing into the sea. It invades the solitude of the deserts, climbs the inaccessible slopes and forbidding pinnacles of mountains, modifies climates and determines the history, character and destiny of nations.

Unobtrusive and patient, it has immortal vigor and aggression. Banished from the thoroughfare and field, it bides its time to return, and when vigilance is relaxed or the dynasty has perished, it silently resumes the throne from which it has been expelled but which it never abdicates.

It bears no blazonry of bloom to charm the senses with fragrance or splendor, but its homely hue is more enchanting than the lily or the rose.

It yields no fruit in earth or air, and yet should its harvest fail a single year, famine would depopulate the world.

꒡ Ტ ᕬᲘᕫ ᲛᲞ ᒍ

GRASS: A TRUE WONDER OF THE WORLD
- August 29, 1978 -

I hope those of you who read John Ingall's essay on grass in this space last week enjoyed it as much as I do ... and will perhaps take grass a little less for granted. To me, the essay was similar to a priceless string of pearls, with those carefully selected words beautifully strung together like a work of art.

The essay ended with a sentence that should make all of us realize the vital importance of grass: "... should its harvest fail a single year, famine would depopulate the world." To those of us involved in a cattle ranch, grass is our total dependency, the base for any livelihood in ranching.

We've had ample moisture in Cherry County so far this year — 17.53 inches, which is 3.37 inches above normal. Our hay crop is above normal and the hills are lush with native grasses. The waving sea of grass brings to mind how the entire year of our operation revolves around grass.

During the growing season, we carefully manage grazing to maintain the vigor of the grasses. If an area has been heavily grazed or been weakened by hail or drought, grazing will be deferred until vigor returns. The amount of vigor of native grasses regulates our entire operation.

The 4-H range management project mentioned last week must be credited with my appreciation and understanding of grass. During the 1960s, the 4-H kids in our club and I learned to identify grass, determine range condition, use and management as well as how to identify range sites. There was a tremendous amount to learn, and we spent a lot of hours in the hills.

I had three 4-member teams of grade school youngsters who became so accomplished in range judging contests that they dominated the county, district and state contests for three years. I was extremely proud of them but lost them to the fast-paced schedules of high school.

Cherry County Extension Agent, Harry Stokely, reports that membership in the range project has diminished drastically statewide and the Extension Service has taken a close look to see why. Because of the vast amount of technical knowledge to be covered, it was decided to divide the project so that less would be required of first-year members so as not to discourage them. The revised project books will be used next spring, and we all hope to see a renewed interest in the range project, which in my opinion is one of the most important.

Recently, I was able to enjoy a little benefit from my years with the 4-H youngsters. Our graduate nurse Myki and I were enjoying an evening walk across the meadow when she became curious if she could still remember the names of the grasses. (It had been 10 years.) We were both delighted that she could name all — with the exception of Scribner's panicum. "All those long hours you spent with us weren't a total loss," she laughed.

Then she offered a challenge: "Why don't you enter the state range judging contest this year and see how you fare?"

She really knows how to hurt a guy. I will have to enter the professional division, because I've won the women's division twice. After the second time in '64, officials said I had to enter the next class, made up of county agents, teachers, etc. The state range judging contest is set for September 30 at the Fort Niobrara refuge, so I had better do some homework... and fast.

In the meantime, there is nothing to prevent my appreciation of the beauty that cloaks the Sandhills now. The sun was hanging low in the west as I drove toward the ranch the other day and the ungrazed area by the wildlife refuge was an awesome sight. The backlighting, provided by the sun, accented each grass and played upon the purple and lavender of the maturing seed heads.

The silky tops of Sandhills muhly hung close to the ground, while lavender plumes of sand lovegrass, switch grass and sand bluestem towered above, glistening in the sun and bending with the breeze. The blossoms of white-flowered gilia, curly cup gumweed and evening primrose added a compliment of color.

All too soon, the frost will turn the grasses to rusty orange and the last native flower of the season, the heath aster, will disappear. Another season will end for our grass, but as John Ingalls wrote. "Beleaguered by the sullen hosts of winter, it withdraws into the impregnable fortress of its subterranean vitality and emerges upon solicitation of spring."

I really think that grass should be listed as one of the "seven wonders of the world."

꒜ ㅜ ᆫ 규 ᄀ

FALL BEAUTY: A GOOD CATTLE CHECK
- October 24, 1978 -

A h, the golden glow of foliage and invigorating air means it's "Indian Summer." Under a Harvest Moon, the yellow, ripened corn is filling the bins and the long-haired, grass-fat cattle are moving to market and the feedlots.

I have watched our fall calves born in August and September of 1977 grow fat and solid on the lush Sandhills grass. For me, there is nothing prettier than to see good cattle grazing in knee-deep grass — unless, of course, it would be the check from a good cattle sale, especially when the banker is running out of patience.

We sold 100 head of those fall steers at Thedford last Tuesday. We were pleased with the weight and the price, as they weighed more than 600 pounds and brought a little over 71 cents a pound.

It's been a crazy year, though, a far cry from 1977 — and '76 and '75 and '74. During those years, prices were low and the reception of buyers went from lukewarm to downright cold.

This time around, we've been contacted by buyers since last spring. In fact, some wanted us to contract our baby calves practically as soon as they were born for fall delivery. If I remember correctly, the price was around 55 cents a pound.

The decision of what to do is nerve-wracking to a rancher: Should he take the contract or wait and gamble? Some did, and some didn't. There was no assurance of an improved market, and cattle people were hurting from four straight years of selling at prices below the cost of production.

Well, I sat in the sale barn last week and watched some good spring calves that weighed just over 300 pounds sell for 89 cents a pound! Who could have predicted that the price would move up that much since last spring?

The man who fed our cattle a year ago said he made money for the first time in three years.

This is just another example of how crazy the fluctuation in prices in this business of agriculture can be.

While at Thedford, I asked a farmer what corn was selling for now, and he answered, "Tears, just tears today." I knew it was less than $2 a bushel, which is below the cost of production for most farmers.

It doesn't seem fair that, when cattle prices are up, corn prices are down. It would seem to me that when one part of the industry of agriculture can break even, another part loses money.

Back in 1973, we sold our spring calves for 80 cents a pound. I have a picture I took when they were being driven for delivery, and I named it "The Last of the 80-Cent Calves." Shortly after we delivered them, cattle prices took a four-year-long nosedive, while inflation pushed prices of other commodities higher.

Now, prices have gone beyond 80 cents — perhaps a more realistic price, compared to the cost of new Levi's. We're not going on any spending sprees, though. The bankers who have stuck with us to lend more and more money for operating costs have first dibs.

The ranch crew has been working and sorting cattle, and we are now ready to show our spring calves for sale. Maybe the price will go up, and maybe it will drop, but we can't worry about that. They are ready for market.

One thing I'll never understand is, why heifers almost always pay 5-10 cents a pound less than steers. No female equality in the cattle business, I guess.

While visiting with people after the sale at Thedford, I also learned from a purebred breeder that it usually takes up to a year for a rise in the prices for most cattle to be reflected in the purebred cattle industry.

I would doubt that business executives sitting behind desks have a corner on ulcers caused by big decisions — I think ranchers have their share. I asked a Thedford rancher for his opinion of the current gamble in the cattle business. His four-word evaluation was: "It's a fast track."

THE SANDHILLS FROM THE BACK SIDE
- September 26, 1978 -

T he other day, I read in the newspaper where "homespun forecasters" are once again predicting the winter. Recently, I forecast bad weather from the 16th on through the next week and I was "right on."

I can't take much credit though...it was inevitable. Any time G.R., the ramrod of this outfit, decides to take a few days away from the ranch, the elements can't handle the shock. Unsettled weather was a certainty.

For some time, G.R. and his friend, Dick Peyton from Hastings, have wanted to take horses on a pack trip across the Sandhills to see the country from the back side and where people live in the heart of the Sandhills. They would start near the Wyoming border and parallel the Niobrara and Snake Rivers back to the ranch.

Planning the trip was half their fun. G.R. would take care of the horses and Dick would handle the camp and food. Dick built a canvas tent, bought sleeping bags and put together camp fare equal to none. He had hard bread, smoked beef, dried foods and you name it...he had it.

G.R. had the three best looking horses on the ranch shod; they were going first class. I thought he should find a mule because Bo, a beautiful buckskin he selected for the pack horse, was about 10 notches above that job, I thought.

I guess Bo thought so too, because when G.R. was breaking him to the pack, Bo didn't take too kindly to all that rattling gear.

The men decided to make a three-day trial run on the ranch to test out their horses and equipment. To load the panniers on the pack tree, the men put Bo in the high-planked round corral used to test out broncs. The horse let them load him, then he broke loose and made about 10 laps around the corral with panniers banging against the posts...but holding together.

Later, in the larger corral, Bo had another "wreck" and broke off four boards from the corner of the barn, but the pack equipment hung together.

They rode through our Snake River pasture and camped along the Gordon Creek during their three-day trial run. They reported that Bo only ran away about seven or eight times, but always came back. They were ready. Before dawn on the morning of the 16th, they loaded the three horses in the trailer and son John drove them to Agate near the Wyoming border. By the time they started east, the wind in their faces had grown into a full-fledged gale.

The first person the men met was Jason Mead who lives in the only house at Agate. "Straight, slim and dignified," is how Dick and G.R. described him. "He must have been 70, but he looked better than we did," they said.

Then they met the man in charge of the fossil beds who said he'd love to join them ... if only he could. And, the wind grew stronger ... and colder ... and slowly brought rain. The horses were slowed by the rocky ground.

At the Raymond Wohlers Ranch 19 miles south of Crawford, G.R. was surprised when he recognized their ranch hand, Pat Soester. He had worked for us at one time and Pat teased him about traveling that far to ride horseback.

A mile down the road was the home of a native Sandhiller, Mrs. John Hughes, whose daughter is Mrs. Wohlers. "Turn your horses loose and sleep in the barn out of the rain," she told them.

"A delightful lady" is how the men later described her to me. During their visit with Mrs. Hughes (the men said she is 77 and "sharp as a tack") told them how her husband's father, John, had run the Old Running Water Stage Station just a mile west. "It was the only change for horses on the run from Sidney to the Black Hills," she told them. "The station was 25 by 100 feet with five big rooms and had everything...saloon, store...anything you'd want."

The men spent the night in the barn and headed out early the next morning. It was Sunday, the temperature was 38 degrees and the rain became heavier as they rode into an easterly wind. The roosters were crowing as they passed through the little town of Marsland.

PACK HORSE TRIP ACROSS SANDHILLS
- Date Unknown -

Last week, I began the story about a long wished for pack-horse trip across the Sandhills by husband G.R. and his friend Dick Peyton, Hastings. On their second day out, Sunday the 17th, they rode into a cold, wind-driven rain.

They only made about 12 miles by noon and the horses were refusing to push on with the driving rain in their faces. The men rode up to a shop where they could see men working. G.R. said. "Well, hello Jack Hunter!" Hunter didn't recognize him until G.R. told him they had gone to high school at Curtis together. You can imagine Hunter's surprise to find he knew one of the cold wet strangers who had ridden into his Box Butte Dam Ranch through the "back door." The afternoon was spent "swapping lies."

Hunter is another native Sandhiller, whose grandfather spent four years on the Texas trail before settling in Nebraska. Hunter offered the men a bed in the house but they were determined to sleep out. This time "out" meant "out" in the quonset "out" of the rain.

Hunter "trailered" the riders and their horses for about 10 miles over rocky ground the next morning and rode with them for awhile.

The drizzling rain, fog and "look alike" Sandhills made reliance upon a compass necessary for directions. This offended the "native" in G.R., and Dick with the compass was always right. They told me later that if they hadn't been such good friends they'd probably "killed each other" that day, when tempers grew short.

Arriving at a beautiful ranch location, they knocked at the door to make sure they were on the right track. They said they were a wet sodden sight to the woman who answered their knock. She was Mrs. Orville Ostrander and chortled at the sight of them. "My dad's 80 years old and he would just love to see the likes of you. Drop down and see Old Jules."

G.R. said he thought somehow he'd dropped back in time until he found out Mrs. Ostrander's father was a son of the Old Jules in Marie Sandoz' book and was named after him.

By five o'clock, the men and horses were equally tired when they came upon a set of wooden corrals. G.R. saw a pickup across the meadow and rode to ask permission to camp when a young man drove up who said he was foreman and "ran the place." "It would take a long time to get permission," G.R. was told. "Follow that road for about 10 miles."

The riders pushed their horses until they were off the ranch now owned by "non-natives" and onto "friendly" ground to camp.

The next morning they stopped at the next ranch house to ask permission to pass through. Mrs. Mack (Jerri) Malmberg met them with a friendly, "Put your horses in the barn and have some coffee. Later she teased, "Don and Jack are moving cattle from Newcastle, Wyoming about 250 miles to Lander. If you guys like to ride, why not go help them."

The wind remained cold as the riders continued on and the hills along the Snake River became rougher. The trip was wearing on men and horses alike.

They stopped at Fred Slater's place and learned of his interesting hobby of raising birds. "All kinds of birds," they told me later, "cages everywhere.

46

He told us he once sold a pigeon for $900. He has been working for the Minor Ranch for 21 years."

The riders crossed the Snake River and said they rode for miles and miles seeing only lush Sandhill's grass. An occasional salt box and windmill. (They later found that Minor Ranch pasture contained 38 sections of land.) Their pack horse had developed a sore spot under the pack and the men realized their trip was nearing an end ... if they'd only find a ranch and a telephone to call home for a trailer. They pitched their tent along the sandy and scenic bank of the Snake River south of Merriman.

A pickup approached; would they have to move? It was young Joe Minor who laughed and said, "The last time I saw anything like this was a man leading a donkey across the Sandhills."

Later, Dick Minor, Joe's father joined the campers and "lie swapping" brightened the night. Minor's reputation for a sense of humor is unrivaled and he is a friendly extrovert.

The following morning, Minor brought a trailer and hauled the horses to Minor Camp where the Minor family and crew were dipping 1,300 head of cattle. Minor then took the riders to the main ranch to a telephone and a shower. He tried to initiate a trade of his canoe for the horses and let the "so and so's" paddle home down the Snake River.

At the camp, the ranch cook threatened "You've got five minutes to eat and 4 1/2 are gone," but fed them a delicious meal.

Back home at the ranch, the men were bone-weary from the cold but elated about their trip of more than 100 miles in four days. They plan to return to the Minor Camp and continue east to the ranch another time.

Dick and G.R. said only in the Nebraska Sandhills could you enter a man's place through the "back door" and usually receive a friendly welcome.

ↄ T ⊥ Ⴕ ⊃

CONCEPTION RATE OF HERD INCREASES
- November 15, 1978 -

I have good news. The three college rodeo horses that were stolen at Torrington, WY, have been recovered. One team roping horse belonged to Gordon Witte of Crookston and his brother Duane called me with the good news.

We too, had a bit of good news emerge during the hectic fall season on the ranch. Tests have shown the conception rate of our cow herd was much higher than a year ago.

As soon as the calves are weaned in late October or early November, preparation for the next calving season begins with testing the cows for pregnancy. While the cows were in the chute, each was treated for grubs and lice with a pour-on insecticide and received a series of inoculations to help insure a healthy calf that will be carried full-term.

Shots of Vibrio, scours and vitamin A have become a routine program here. Vitamin A provides integrity of the mucus membrane, scours serum builds immunity in the fetal calf and Vibrio is to control a venereal disease. The only symptoms of the later are abortion or a low conception rate, so prevention is critical.

Butch Labore, Mullen veterinarian, and our crew went through about 500 cows in a long, hard day. Butch found only one of the 169 angus cows without calf. "That is exceptional," he said. Our hereford cows tested only five percent open which we consider above normal.

Last year, Labore said cows that he tested throughout the area were all the way to 50 percent without calf. He blamed stress from the severe winter as part of the problem and lack of the shots as another.

A low conception is disastrous to the cattlemen because by the time a cow is tested five to six months has been lost in the gestation cycle. Open cows are usually sold; they aren't paying for their keep.

We have found that the pour-on insecticide is much more efficient than the chemicals currently available for spraying. The pour-on is absorbed into the system, as compared to the spray, which kills lice on contact.

Directions for the pour-on should be carefully read, however, and several veterinarians and a county agent told me many people neglect this. Some pour-ons can be harmful to stressed cattle or certain breeds and the use can result in organophosphate poisoning. Atropine is antidotal.

I checked a can of pour-on and a little clock sign cautioned to take time and read the directions.

It noted that Brahman crossbreeds are less tolerant and the chemical must not be used on Brahma bulls. The chemical is probably absorbed too fast because Brahmas have sweat glands while other breeds of cattle sweat only at the muzzle.

If cattle are under stress from a drought area, for example, then trucked a long distance and the chemical applied, it could be fatal. Other warnings are against use on calves less than three months of age or animals stressed from castration, excitement, dehorning or convalescence. The cut-off date for pour-on use is early November. Cattle grubs migrate through the system and if they are killed while in the respiratory system, swelling can occur or if grubs are killed while in the back area near the end of their migration, the animals system has a difficult time disposing of the dead material.

Another warning that might be overlooked is disposal. The empty can should be rinsed with one-half gallon of water, one-fourth cup detergent and one-fourth pound of lye and the rinse solution and punctured can buried at least 18 inches deep. The chemical is toxic to fish, birds and other wildlife and should it be poured down a sink-drain, contamination of the underground water supply is possible.

Most of the information was news to me.

RANCH WIFE'S POEM DUBS WINTER
- January 23, 1979 -

Last year, I dubbed our winter a "Sandhills Deep-freeze" and apparently some readers were in agreement; their letters said "right on!" This winter of '79 has been a disgusting replay of even more snow and colder temperatures ... but I hesitated calling it "Deep-freeze II".

Snow kept piling onto previous snow and the winds turned it to ice. It didn't seem to matter if the men left in pickup or tractor, their answer to my questions, "How did it go?" was "I got stuck."

I went with G.R. recently to cake the cows on Watts Lake when that day's temperature eased up to 30 degrees. His well-traveled trail was packed ice, slick from the warmer temperatures and we slid off into deep soft snow. Yes, we were stuck.

I've abandoned most trips to town as a preventative measure ... to keep from getting stuck. The six miles of highway between the ranch and the wildlife headquarters can drift shut in an hour's time which is the amount of time a trip from town would take.

Last Tuesday, I left for Alliance with the southerly wind drifting snow and driving the wind chill factor to a minus 31 degrees. G.R. had preceded me down the highway by only about five minutes in a four-wheel-drive pickup. His tracks, however, had disappeared in the drifts across the road. I plowed through one drift, skidded on the ice and stopped only inches from the snow clogged ditch ... inches from being stuck.

As I drove west along Highway 2, Ruth Donahue's snow stories about the Mullen area became reality. Winter feed areas were criss-crossed with bladed tracks drifted shut by blowing snow. The few cattle I saw along the highway looked in good shape though. They've had a hard winter, which says a lot for the ranchers there. It takes hard work and careful feeding, during adverse weather, to keep the condition of cattle from slipping.

I saw a large herd of horses, with long winter coats, pawing through the snow cover to winter forage. Horses can subsist in this way, but winter grazing for the cattle was lost under the ice-snow cover in November. Montana ranch country was covered much earlier. They'd had a hard winter

It was a Montana ranch wife, Lucile Canfield of Richey, who named the winter for me in a jingle she wrote putting words to thoughts of her husband that she dubbed "The Windy Winter of Stuck." I thought enough people could relate to what she wrote that I want to share a portion:

"The Windy Winter of Stuck"
The drifts are deep and the drifts are hard
this windy winter of stuck.
But still the cattle must be fed so
I've tried it with pickup and truck.
I've shoveled snow and I've cussed snow,
and longed for a southern clime!
Then I goose the old pickup with chains
on the front and try it another time.
The snow is deep and the wind bites
cold and drifts keep piling high.
But you have to feed cows when feeding time comes,
Or else just watch them die.

It goes on to talk about TV, useless because of day-long work, although parades and bowl games were on. The saga compared a ranch operation to a football game with cold cows as the only goal posts and the audience an occasional cow.

You don't have a team to charge the line;
You're alone out there in the snow.
You've only a shovel to back your play;
and no fans cheering your throw.

50

There is more about wind, drifting snow and the white world of winter on a ranch. There is no doubt in my mind that she is a ranch-wife who captured her husbands thoughts quite accurately. I can even imagine the last lines as coming from G.R.

They say that hamburger, come spring,
will be high. Here's hoping I have some to sell.
Just one more winter like this year and last,
and I'm consigning these cattle to Hell!

⅃ T ⅃ Ⅎ ⌐

SANDHILLS RANCHERS BATTLE SNOW, SHORTAGES

- February 2, 1979 -

A good share of national news has been claimed recently by ranchers fighting a losing battle in a snow disaster area. We are grateful the battle wasn't completely lost because of the tremendous emergency effort by state and county road crews, Civil Defense, National Guard and innumerable volunteers.

An Omaha reporter was surprised when the emergency was declared and asked, "What happened — why didn't we have previous warning?" Probably, Cherry County Sheriff Jim Ward had the answer: "The ranchers have battled a serious snow situation for two months and have simply run out of resources."

This winter has broken records for cold and prolonged temperatures set just last year of 8.5 for December through February. The December-January average temperature recorded at the Valentine Weather Bureau this year was 8.3 degrees. January temperatures averaged 4.1 degrees to upset the previous record low of 5.8 degrees in 1937. Two January days were above freezing and 22 days were zero or below. Night after night, the mercury dropped to the minus 20s and winds drove the wind chill factor down to a minus 40-60.

Most operators have seen their "bumper" hay crop disappear in doubled daily rations to the cattle for needed energy. Cattle are forced to sleep on the ice pack because lack of the usual winds in early December failed to blow areas free. All of Nebraska lies under a solid ice cover.

We battle a hay shortage on this ranch and must rely on special use permits of the Valentine Wildlife Refuge. Last year, officials didn't want cattle winter-fed on the refuge and we hauled the hay to the ranch. This year, the program was reversed; cattle were to be fed where the hay was stacked.

For the past two months, son John has battled his way to a group of cattle 14 miles from home on the Sawyer flat between Pelican and Dad's Lake. G.R. has gone six and nine miles to two herds along Watts Lake.

The situation deteriorated when G.R.'s tractor blew a head gasket and it was four days before we could get a new one. John began an alternating program of feeding a two-day supply on Sawyer and then pulling to Watts Lake.

On four consecutive days, the men tore G.R.'s tractor down, made repairs and replaced the head gasket only to have the tractor travel less than a mile each time.

The men tried to move our TD-14 Caterpillar to Watts Lake, but a track broke in the crusted snow. It has been too bitterly cold to work on it out in the middle of the meadow.

We bought a new feed tractor with a dozer blade three weeks ago. The equipment dealer is so swamped they haven't had time to weight the tires and mount the blade. We're still waiting.

We wanted to doze a trail to bring the cattle home from Sawyer because we've had a few unscheduled calves and lost three. They'll have to follow just the tractor track.

Some of our cows have been consigned to the Thedford sale for two months, but until Sunday, trucks weren't able to get into the ranch. They've taken a big chunk from our calving hay supply.

The present cattle market will take a little edge from the severe winter, but any proceeds have already been eaten up by added feed costs, machinery repairs and diesel fuel bills that have risen to an all time high.

Weather predictions for February of below normal temperatures and above normal precipitation, doesn't sound too rosy. Last week, I heard a rancher grumble, "We all have to be crazy to battle a winter like this for only 31 cents of the food dollar."

Most of the ranchers I know, however, are a bunch of independent "diehards" and somehow, they'll find a way to battle the winter of next year ... and the next ... and the next.

RANCHERS FIND HUMOR IN BITTER COLD
- February 13, 1979 -

G.R. and I watched 100 head of our cows sell last Tuesday at Thedford. That sale will mean a savings of about 2 1/2 tons of hay each day that was needed to keep them, besides cake and ear corn.

Apparently, there is a lot of hay for sale at various locations, but enough trucks aren't available to haul it. Gran Magnuson of Arthur has such a truck and his phone has been ringing night and day.

Leland Johnson at the sale barn told us that in the past two weeks, about 1,000 head of storm-stressed cattle have been sold there. We saw a package of big cows sell, and if I hadn't seen it, I wouldn't have believed it. Those cows weighed 485 pounds or about half what they should and were a pathetic sight —victims of the winter.

I guess we made one right move last fall when we sold our spring calves and fall calving cows. We didn't have to battle to get them through this second consecutive bitter winter.

We spent our first "evening out" of the winter to have one of the Cowpoke's famous steaks ... and some visiting. It's a good thing folks can maintain a sense of humor. It seems they can find some sense of humor in every "snow story," critic's remark or hay shortage.

We were told one tale concerning an elderly rancher who drove out to his place, saw some dead cows and asked the hired hand what was going on. The weary ranch hand reportedly drawled, "Oh, they just ate so much they choked. It's part of their self-culling program."

The main topic of humorless conversation was the inexcusable remark a Cherry County Commissioner made recently on local television. It seems he thought the snow disaster area didn't affect the old timer's too much and if the younger ones stayed home and minded the ranch instead of running around, they wouldn't be in trouble.

A couple of those young ranchers were quick to point out, that critic lived about one mile from a main highway and no longer owned any cattle...and had spent most of the winter in a warm climate.

Ironically, we were talking with a young rancher who had left the family station wagon at the garage for an oil change. He was called to the phone and returned with a sheepish grin on his face. "That was the garage," he said. "They said there were only 200 miles put on the car since the oil was changed instead of 2,000. I didn't look at the sticker...just remembered it had been two months." Of course that brought accusations of "running around too much and not taking care of ranch business."

It's unfortunate if long time residents forget their youth and think they were born "old timer's." I think the best investment any of us in this country can make is to support our young people.

There are two generations working this ranch, and I doubt if either G.R. or John will tell you the winter hasn't been harder than normal. One recent day went something like this: the hub on a rear dual broke while they were feeding the bulls. They removed the wheel in temperatures far below zero with the wind chill index at minus 25 degrees.

Then, they had to move 280 head of cows about six miles from Sawyer Flat to Watts Lake because our hay on Sawyer was gone. John led them with a feed tractor and stack of hay and G.R. followed with the pickup, horse trailer and saddle horse. Our tractor with a dozer blade is still broke down, so they trailed the cattle down an icy oil strip. The cattle were already foot sore from the continued ice pack of the hills.

Just as they reached their destination of the Watts Lake pasture where they were going to feed the cattle, a front tire was ruined. Some type of steel stake was covered from sight by the ice cover, punctured the tire and fluid spurted out in a geyser. The men removed the wheel in the cold wind and drove to town to have a new one filled with sodium cholide used for weight and traction. The expense caused by that hidden stake was $230 for a new tire. I wonder if that could be classified as a "hidden" expense of beef production?

cl ꞇ ꞁꞮꞁ JꞘ ꞁ

SOME SNOW MEMORIES PLEASANT
- February 27, 1979 -

Three items came in yesterday's mail that are related to the 24th Medical Company (Air Ambulance) of the Nebraska Army National Guard and the snow emergency of January 24 - February 7, 1979.

I would like to share them with you —and no — I'm not going to rehash the cold, snow and winds that literally paralyzed West Central Nebraska. What I offer is a little insight to members of the helicopter crews.

I was fortunate to accompany helicopter crews twice during flight missions over the Cherry County Sandhills. One mail item was photos of the choppier landing here at the ranch. Snow is swirling into a storm from the rotors and in the background, saddle horses can be seen running in fright from the noise.

The crew was friendly and very considerate. At first, I think they were worried I might become air-sick. When they found I loved to fly, they allowed me to move to the "hell hole," a seat near the rear of the craft facing the window and a perfect vantage point for photos.

The flights afforded me a "whirly-bird's" eye view of the snowbound country. Cloaked in a solid coat of shimmering ice, the Sandhills were magnificent — if one didn't think about the hardship below.

The pilots maneuvered so I was able to capture photos of deer and coyotes, as well as, snow-clogged ranches. One crew member reminded me he had a cup of coffee in my kitchen in 1976 when a storm downed hundreds of power poles in our area.

The second item in the mail was a clipping of Marcella Dvorak's "Country Mile" column from Schuyler. Marcella had used a letter from her daughter, Judy, while stationed at Valentine as a medic with the 24th.

I want to share some of Judy's observations of the Sandhills:

"The Sandhills of our state appeared all around us as far as the eye can see. Each Sandhill, large and small, was blanketed with snow, giving the illusion of great waves in Mother Nature's ocean of snow.

"The clear, blue sky without a cloud, and the sun shining brightly made the snowy earth below us look every bit as beautiful and impressive as the Rocky Mountains.

"Our missions included flying tractor parts to remote ranches, checking for drifted roads, stranded ranchers and cattle, transporting officials — and Med-Evac when necessary.

"To work for more grateful communities is impossible. The people of Valentine, Mullen, Ainsworth, Alliance and everywhere in between demonstrated hospitality that we won't soon forget.

"They say that an emergency is when everyone works together to help out. In this emergency the whole state pulled together, and it took Mother Nature and her powerful winter weather to show it to me."

I think I can speak for ranchers in West Central Nebraska when I say, "We are most grateful to all members of the National Guard who came to our aid."

Most Guard members hold a variety of jobs in private life and answer the call to an emergency on a moment's notice.

It now seems coincidental that I met Judy and her husband Greg Smith momentarily at the Valentine airport. Greg was a pilot and Judy a registered nurse on the second helicopter. Because of their love of flying, the couple had been married aboard a helicopter in Minnesota.

The last item in the mail was a letter from another medic, Marcia Altwine, with an enclosure I especially treasure. Guard flight crew members noticed the souvenir patches I sew on my canvas camera bag gathered from special places. They said I should have the unit patch from the 24th which "We wear with pride."

The letter said in part, "It was a pleasure to share our love for flying with someone who enjoys the same experience."

That patch will claim a special place on my bag. I accept it with a great deal of appreciation for and pride in the members of the Nebraska Army National Guard.

NEBRASKA WEATHER TAKING ITS TOLL
- March 13, 1979 -

Reminders of the 1978-79 winter remain, although the warm March days are rapidly melting the ice cover. Cherry County had the dubious distinction of another record-setting winter for low temperatures. The Valentine weather station reported our December through February average temperature was 10 degrees compared to the 12.7 degrees which set a new record last year.

The snowfall there was recorded at 37.7 inches. The fall was dry so the snow melt is soaking right into the ground. It will help a bit to recharge the Sandhill aquifers, but G.R. said he has never seen the Gordon Creek so low for this time of year.

March is much warmer than last year. Last night the temperature was 12 degrees compared to 21 below last year. But March is noted for fickle weather and I remember the devastating March 27-28 storm of 1975. That blizzard came near the end of calving season and caused more than a $3 million loss in this county alone.

We lost two calves to the frigid weather in January, and several at the beginning of the season were born weak and died. This morning G.R. said a nice big crossbred died for no apparent reason. Possibly, the cow lay too long and did not remove the sack from the calf's head soon enough. It wasn't from a prolonged birth because the men had checked the cows within the hour.

Predictions of calf loss were made during the long winter. The beef shortage continues to reflect in the market. We heard where 400 lb. calves sold at Winner for $1.24 a pound last week.

I have a newspaper clipping given to me by Norma Eatinger of Thedford. Although the cartoon was printed in 1967, it could well have portrayed this past winter.

The drawing is of a whimsical pony, "Redeye," that is blissfully walking through knee deep snow saying, "Look at the little snowflakes covering the trees...the bushes...the grass." Redeye stops with sudden realization. "GRASS!" he said and leans down to say, "Hey you! Get off my breakfast."

Snow this winter covered every meal of the day for all our animals, and wildlife losses have been severe. The antelope loss is reported to be high.

I have a daily reminder of the winter here in the house...a crop eared and bobtailed cat.

Myki rescued it from the cold at Christmas time, but not soon enough. The cats are wild and she couldn't get her hands on it until the weather had done its damage.

We named it Zero, and it recently lost about two inches from its tail from being frozen. The cat remains wild until I sit or lie down on the couch. Then it smothers me with purring appreciation.

We found the other cats, all wild as March hares, were spending the winter on top of the chimney, capturing any warmth that escaped there. Each morning they cautiously came to the back door for food.

One morning, one appeared with a collar that forced its head into a rigid position. Curiosity hadn't killed that cat, nor gain it precious jewels...merely a cheap cut-glass necklace.

Apparently, it had been rummaging in the trash barrel and found some tempting morsel in the bottom of a quart jar. It must have broken the jar, but the rim and a jagged piece remained around its neck.

I couldn't catch the wild thing to remove the glass so it could eat. Finally, on the second day, the cat was tempted by some raw hamburger and I hid a trusty hammer behind my back. I scored a bull's eye on the first try, the glass fell away, the cat shook its head and went to eating. One more winter crisis solved.

I told G.R. we had to prepare for next winter by putting a hail screen over the chimney. I'd hate to have one of the little wild things misstep and result in a cat-clogged chimney.

<!-- decorative symbols -->
ᘮ ᐪ ᓄᕮ ᒉ ᒣ

WE NEED TO APPRECIATE WILDLIFE
- March 20, 1979 -

Sunday marked the beginning of National Wildlife Week; Monday was Agriculture Day. It seems fitting the observance of both, fall at the same time. Both are designed to build awareness.

Left to its own devices, nature balances its own with an interdependence of one species upon another. The advance of man into nature's domain has necessitated control.

Man must become aware and understand the importance of wildlife and its habitat for harmonious co-existence. But first, man, the landowner, the hunter and the wildlife official must come to full understanding and cooperation.

Natural habitat once stretched across the width and breadth of this nation. As the sod curled behind the mighty plow and disappeared beneath concrete deserts, wildlife fled to the untillable mountains, the wooded streams and the vanishing prairie.

Greedy hunters pursued the game with reckless abandon. Drastic restrictions stopped the wanton killing before the buffalo became extinct...before the beaver, deer and antelope disappeared...and the ducks, geese and grouse.

The elimination of one species disrupts the delicate balance of nature. As the raptors, the eagle and owl diminish under the hunter's gun, their main diet of gopher and mice flourish.

The coyote hunts the gopher and man hunts the coyote. Greed for the coyote's pelt is straining that species. The sport of hunting has been lost in the illegal use of helicopters, spotlight night-time hunting and snowmobiles. The coyote is defenseless against these methods.

Illegal hunting usually results in even more restrictions and limited or closed seasons.

Hunters pay thousands of dollars annually in hunting licenses to support wildlife law enforcement and administration. Yet continual illegal practices keep law enforcement costs spiraling.

Some hunters erroneously think a hunting license entitles them to unlimited territory. The mere courtesy of asking permission to hunt on private property is abandoned; landowners resent this. Abuse of land and property has caused more land to be posted and denied to hunters; hunters resent this.

What stake does the landowner, who is usually involved in some phase of agriculture, have in wildlife? Possibly more than meets the eye.

Each landowner pays taxes for the privilege of ownership. He carefully manages that land to support the livestock and produce crops which is shared with wildlife. Life is the land...and land is life.

Snow this season covered the broadleaf forage of antelope and 50 percent of Cherry County's antelope perished. A closed season is possible. Survivors found nourishment in stacks of alfalfa while deer moved onto corn piles and stacks of prairie hay. Both species shared the feed grounds with cattle for hay, often in short supply for the cattlemen.

Flocks of hungry grouse moved in around rural buildings. Many people who had no grain bought it to feed the birds. Pheasants and grouse shared the livestock winter feed grounds.

To enhance wildlife habitat, rural people have planted shelterbelts, fruit bearing shrubs and left fence rows and run ways unmowed. Often these same people are non-hunters.

The delicate balance of nature is displayed when eagles rise effortlessly on invisible air currents then drop bullet-like at a careless rabbit or mouse. Or when a woodpecker fractures the stalk of a dried sunflower for insects hiding there. Or while vultures soar and search to keep the prairie free of carrion. And when a coyote patiently awaits the emergence of a gopher from its burrow.

National Wildlife Week is intended to build an awareness of wildlife and its habitat which is essential for survival and co-existence with man. Man's callous greed once threatened certain wildlife species with extinction. Man's understanding and concern has brought them back. The preservation of wildlife is the obligation of all mankind.

IN THEORY, A COW IS ONLY BLUFFING
- April 3, 1979 -

I told you last week how I spent some of my early years on this ranch at a cow camp during the calving season. G.R. would often ask me to join him while he assisted the birth of a calf. He might have me hold the lantern, open a gate or whatever.

I haven't gone near the cows for years because at camp I found the deep "compassion" G.R. has for anyone who might be intimidated by an old cow.

Late one cold night at Duck Lake Camp, I went to the little barn with G.R. while he pulled a calf. I noticed a board was missing from the pen at the rear of the chute but thought nothing of it.

G.R. had finished and asked me to get his shirt and jacket from the post along the chute. From the corner of my eye, I caught a glimpse of that cow coming through the hole...and she had blood in her eye.

I had heard G.R. say a cow won't hit you if you stand still but my body screamed, "Get out of here!"

I have absolutely no memory of the next few seconds because the next I knew, I was standing outside on noodle-limp legs. The heavy, sliding barn door was still closed except for about a three inch crack.

Believe it or not, I was skinny way back then, but not that thin. I think I willed myself through that door...just before the cow hit it.

I could hear my "worried" husband through the barn wall, "Funniest thing I ever saw," he laughed, "she was blowing right in your hip pocket."

"Where are you?" I asked him. He said he had climbed up on the chute and would I go to the opposite door and get the cow's attention so he could get out of the barn.

"Don't worry dear, she'll never hit you," I called as I marched grumbling back to the shack we called home. He came to the house later, no longer laughing. "It was cold out there, you took my shirt," he said. (The lantern hung in the barn all night.)

He has maintained his theory that a cow won't hit you and I've watched him doctor calves when the cow will charge and stop before she hits his hip pocket. But he stays close to his pickup. One time, he said a crossbred cow followed him right into the cab. Another time, I saw a Brahma cow put him over the fence. He's modified his theory to specify hereford cows.

We now have some Angus cows that we bought last fall. G.R. says they aren't one bit afraid of a man and are very good mothers, protective of their calves.

G.R. and John use a steel mesh calf cart on runners to move the pairs to another lot. They say it's easy and fast because the cow can see the calf and follows right along. The cart can be pulled by the pickup or a man on horseback. This day, G.R. was driving and John would catch and load the calf.

John picked up one little Angus calf but the cow objected. She took after John and around and around the cart they went. He said he didn't want to lose the calf and the old cow "wanted to eat me for breakfast."

G.R. said he stepped from the pickup to help John. "She won't hit you John," he called and then hurried back to the safety of the cab. "I laughed so hard, I thought I'd die," G.R. told me later.

John said he was about winded by the time he finally got the calf loaded. He failed to see the humor his dad found in the situation.

G.R. said if he had thought faster, he could have driven ahead and let the cow have a clean shot at John. "Thanks a lot Dad, your concern overwhelms me," John grinned, then laughed at the memory.

I've never read that a 'strange' sense of humor is essential to be a rancher... but it just might help.

"Sense of humor heck," G.R. grumbled, "You have to be downright crazy!"

SOME THINGS CHANGE, SOME DON'T
- Date Unknown -

Perhaps next year, we'll offer board and breakfast for winter skiing. Or maybe we should offer accommodations by the week and turn the bunkhouse into a dormitory. During the past four months, more than 60 inches of snow has fallen here, including 12 inches that fell Friday and 10 inches Monday night.

In addition to cross-country skiing during colder weather, downhill skiing is great fun in the Sandhills.

When the kiddos were younger they loved to ski. For lack of a chair lift, I pulled them at the end of a rope to the top of the hills with the Jeep.

They weren't into cross-country skiing, but we improvised. Sometimes, I'd saddle a fast horse and pull them with the lariat looped around the saddle horn. It was a bit like water skiing.

At other times, I'd pull them cross country with the Jeep...the boys preferred that because it was faster. But using the Jeep came to an end the time I was looking back at the kids instead of forward. When the Jeep smashed into a deep snowdrift, the impact zapped the radiator. For some reason, G.R. was crabby about the whole thing and thereafter took a dim view of the sport.

Repairs back then, however, didn't seem to be so expensive. G.R. and I were talking about that very subject just last night.

I believe he told me that new, in 1968, the Oliver tractor cost about $10,000. This winter he had to replace the clutch, pressure plate and a shaft. Bill for the parts alone was $1,300, which seemed to me an abnormal percentage of the purchase price.

Sometimes it's hard to place rising costs in perspective, but his analogy made it clearer.

"On the average," he said, "it took about 12 calves in 1968 to pay for a plain, four-wheel drive pickup. Today the same type of pickup would cost about 35 calves."

Shop foremen aren't spared from complaints caused by the high cost of repair. One that we'll call Bud, says he takes a lot of guff from customers who protest the amount of their bills.

Sometimes, however, there is a lighter side that emerges after a complaint has been rehearsed, but never delivered.

Such was the case after a customer we'll call Jake (for reasons that will become obvious) had Bud's crew do some work on his four-wheel drive pickup. The bill was sizable, as most bills are.

Before heading to the ranch, Jake parked in the big parking lot to pick up groceries. Still annoyed at the bill as he started for home, he was shocked when a howling metallic noise erupted under the front end of the pickup. Jake was furious, certain that the lock-out hubs, which he'd just had fixed, were trying to disintegrate.

Before they did, however, Jake hoped to drive to the garage and vent his wrath on the shop foreman. He was so furious his face turned beet-red as he rehearsed what he would say.

The noise grew louder...more threatening...so Jake stopped. He stepped to the front of the pickup, and there, twisted like a pretzel, was a metal grocery cart that was being dragged across the concrete, firmly lodged in the pickup's undercarriage.

Jake's face didn't even change color. Rage-red turned to embarrassed-red.

After considerable effort, the cart was dislodged and Jake drove on to tell Bud about the biting speech he'd prepared and abandoned.

Bud laughed and said that customers often get the cart before the "horse," but this was the very first time the practice had diverted an irate complaint.

∂ T ⌐Iⁿ JⱢ Ɔ

RODEO CONTESTANTS GIVE BEST SHOT
- Date Unknown -

As I write this, superb rodeo action continues simultaneously in three arenas at the National Finals Prepster Rodeo. I'm still at West Fargo, ND, where 1,153 top contestants from 31 states and two Canadian Provinces are giving rodeo their "best shot."

The Fargo rodeo committee has overcome a tremendous handicap to put on a fine rodeo. A week of rainy weather before the first performance had turned the arena and the surrounding camping area to an impassable quagmire of sticky gumbo. On Sunday, July 29, huge bulldozers moved into the arena to push aside the gunk to a depth of 19 inches before they reached dry dirt.

Some 100,000 yards of dry sand were hauled into the three arenas to make a rodeo even possible. The arena dirt is deep, has slowed some times and caused horses to be hurt. But ... better than mud.

Cars and campers had to park along roads and anyone who pulled off became stuck. G.R. said the gumbo was the stickiest he'd ever seen. "I'm going to take some home to glue a pickup fender back to the body," he quipped.

On the heels of the mud, the committee was faced with a rash of horse and saddle theft although they had thought security was adequate. "Everyone will remember it happened at Fargo," one said.

Bad luck has seemed to plague so many of our contestants. Merely hours before she was to compete in team roping, Jnell Kennedy caught her roping hand in a door tearing fingernails loose. During competition, she lost her grip on the dally.

Billy Gallino had to ride a saddle bronc shortly after having a front tooth broken off near the gum-line. I'm certain he was in great pain.

Then a sunfishing bareback twisted J.R. Clark out of balance and something was injured in his back. He hasn't been able to compete, of course, and has been in a lot of pain.

Skeeter Thurston had the good luck of getting a reride on a horse that wouldn't buck... three times. His bad luck was the horse never did.

There has been some good luck, too, however, and it has been exciting to watch Nebraska hands stand at the top among the best of them. And believe me, these kids are good.

And, meeting new people is always an extra bonus of rodeo. I had the pleasure of meeting Larry Jordan, publisher of World Rodeo and Western Heritage who is full of plans to expand his high school rodeo coverage. He puts out a very interesting product covering every phase of rodeo and is expanding heritage stories.

G.R. and I met a fun-loving group from the Cajun state of Louisiana who kept us laughing for hours. One man, who was at Fargo with his son participating in steer wrestling, turned out to be Jim Miller. He told us he won the bareback riding the year Harrison hosted the national finals.

His friend told us a little story. "Jim was in the saddle bronc riding, too, and drew Jesse James, a horse that was young at the time, but established a national reputation as a mean bucking horse. Someone warned Jim that the horse would pull the rope from his hand so he wound it around his fist like a bull riding rope.

"Old Jesse dumped Jim and dragged him around the arena until his arm was six inches longer," his friend said. "When the pick-up man got the horse stopped they asked Jim why he didn't let loose of the rope."

By this time, Miller's friend was laughing so hard he could hardly talk but he swears that Miller dusted himself off and said, "Back in Louisiana, when we put a halter on a horse we figure he's broke to lead and we have to bring him to the chute."

Being at Fargo has been a most enjoyable experience... I wouldn't have traded it for anything. The thing that makes rodeo so great, are the people who participate in it and those who are fans of the sport. I'm glad our two girls got us involved.

THE FREE LIFE...AND WILDLIFE
- May 9, 1979 -

I feel so lucky living in the country and free...especially when someone suggests a ride on a balmy May afternoon. I think of the jillion things I'd planned...then say, "Let's go!" Rancher G.R. — mechanic G.R. today — was going to the Gordon Creek pasture to fix a windmill. "Maybe we'll see some duck nests and the old badger that's digging along the road," he said, as we left.

The Sandhills have turned a soft green, which deepens to emerald on the wet meadows. Each pool, puddle and pond was speckled with wild waterfowl. They must know nothing of segregation, because plover, curlew and killdeer mingle with mallard, pintail and teal as they explore the waters.

We drove along in silence, because idle chatter would break the magic spell. We silently revere the goodness of this land that we call "God's country." The fresh green of the hills and bright blue of the sky and water surely are God's colors. And He has painted this space with a panorama of wildlife.

The badger wasn't home, but a nesting teal flew from her nest as we happened to drive close. Briefly, we studied the down-filled nest with three eggs, hidden on a little knoll close to the water.

It was an exhilarating afternoon —breathing fresh, pure air that has never known a factory chimney; dipping fingers into creek water so clear you can see the bottom, and enjoying the vast expanse to the horizon that is broken only by soap weeds and budding plum brush.

We had just returned to the house when we got a phone call from G.L. Piercy, a young neighbor about the age of our son John. G.L. and John were classmates during their years in country school. G.L. then left, but returned to his parents' ranch last fall. He has become another pair of eyes for me, as he enjoys photographing wildlife, too.

G.L. was excited. Beavers had moved into the creek that wanders through the center of their building site, and he had been able to watch them. The light was nearly gone, but I took my camera anyway.

I met the young man and we walked through the trees along the creek, trying to be quiet. Dry leaves crunched and twigs cracked under our boots, but I found I was holding my breath in hopes our advance wouldn't frighten a beaver, should one be out of the water.

He silently pointed. Not 50 feet ahead, a big beaver was clipping off a willow shoot next to the water. It was the first beaver I'd ever seen in the wild. The creature knew we were there yet seemed totally unconcerned. It was great!

I suppressed a giggle at the noisy chewing, which sounded like a set of bad dentures. The beaver sat on his haunches and, with rapid clattering chomps, stripped the bark from a tender twig as he rolled it in his front paws. Finally, he slipped into the water and disappeared.

We saw another one that also ignored us. A pair of mallards landed in the water by a big split willow tree not far from us. G.L. said their nest was in the fork of the tree, noting that she had just started to lay eggs, as there were only three at that time.

The sun disappeared, and we tramped through the underbrush along the creek. It was a sanctuary carpeted with moss, with willows and cottonwoods brightening with spring. G.L. welcomes the birds and even the dam-building beaver to share the creek in his front yard. He gave me a memory-gift of that peaceful spot.

We decided to try an experiment in the dark. Beavers work mostly at night, so we wondered if they'd allow us to watch them by the pickup spotlight...and they did!

But we couldn't figure out what they had in mind. One would swim down the stream to the shore, investigate the site, then slide back into the water and go to another spot. A second and a third one followed the actions of the first.

I guess we became a little giddy and let our imaginations run wild. We decided they must be government beaver, because they couldn't seem to decide what to do about a dam. We wondered if their environmental impact statement had been approved. Had inflation affected their budget? When would they become "busy as a beaver"?

Watching them was great fun. How lucky we are to be a free people, able to jest freely about our government...and to live in the Sandhills, where we can be entertained by wildlife in their natural habitat.

RAIN MAKES A WORLD OF DIFFERENCE
- June 19, 1979 -

What a difference a rain makes! Last Friday, the men were dust covered and grumpy. Three consecutive days of temperatures above 100 degrees seemed to fry everything but the clouds of grasshoppers that sprang from the grass.

During two of those days the men worked on the irrigation system in the intense heat. A freak wind had twisted and ruined a tower and dry conditions made it critical to get water to the corn; popcorn this year.

I told G.R. if it was just later in the season, we could forget the irrigation, let the heat do its job and harvest the popped corn. All we needed was the butter. His icy stare restrained any further comment from me.

Saturday he was all smiles. We had more than two inches of rain during the night. The Merritt Dam road was reported to be washed out by three inches of rain. Our Snake River pasture adjoins Merritt, so it was nice to know that pasture received badly needed moisture.

The grass in this area had been slow. Dry conditions combined with the late freeze May 10 had ranchers worried if their rangeland would carry their cattle.

I heard one rancher say, "It doesn't look like there will be enough grass for the grasshoppers...say nothing of the cattle."

The Sandhills are amazing. Anything can be grown here provided there is enough water. Overnight, grass seems to have grown two inches. We've gotten another reprieve in this business that is so dependent upon the weather...and the whim of the market...and a jillion other factors.

During an airplane flight from Kansas City to Indianapolis recently, I was reminded of how little city folks understand our country and the cattle business. My seatmate was a district judge en route to Washington, D.C. When he learned I lived on a ranch he said, "That must be a relaxed way of life compared to the 'rat race' of city living."

This man was very distinguished looking, so I decided I'd get his impression of ranch living before I offered any input. The only problem he could see was how did we get our cattle fed during the winter? During the rest of the year, his opinion of ranching was "a matter of nature taking its course."

I knew I'd found a 'live one' and proceeded to educate that man about ranching. First, I couldn't resist telling him that most ranchers had looked for a sideline to supplement their "part-time" 12-hour day, seven days a week job. Cattle had been sold at considerable loss from 1974 through 1977.

He said he'd never thought about the year it takes just to get a baby calf on the ground. Or, that bulls had to be tested for infertility caused by severe cold weather or injury. Or, that cows had to be tested for pregnancy because ranchers could no longer afford to keep a cow that didn't produce.

He was astonished to learn that venereal disease in cattle is an important factor of infertility or early abortions. I gave him the example of vibriosis which has no clinical symptoms but is an insidious bacterial disease. Because the bacteria must be at a laboratory within two hours for diagnosis and distance makes that impossible, a herd history must be relied upon to determine the disease. A lowered calving rate, prolonged calving season or a combination usually point to vibrio. Now vaccination is a common practice as prevention.

He was extremely interested and asked a lot of questions. I explained everything from foot rot through scours. He decided city life wasn't the only rat race.

Before we landed at Indianapolis, I told him a little story that made him laugh and he said he was going to tell it when anyone thought all there was to the cattle business was waiting for calves to be born.

Our three-year-old grandson, Terrill, was getting impatient while keeping a vigil during the birth of a calf. At the first sign of birth, he wanted to leave. His innocent and nonchalant evaluation that the future of the calf was assured when he said, "It's okay. I can see its shoes."

⊂⌋ 𝐓 ⌐⊥⌐ 𝐉⊢ ⊃

JAUNT TO THE HILLS A PLEASURE
- July 3, 1979 -

How nice it would be, if all of life could be as enjoyable as an afternoon spent among the Sandhills after the welcome rains. The moisture has revitalized the prairie much like a rain turns the desert to a riot of color.

And, it's a shame that we sometimes have to find an excuse to get away from the "rat race" to enjoy what nature has to offer.

Early in June, my excuse appeared at the door, a couple of strangers...but not for long. A biology professor, Dr. Ron Weedon and his pretty assistant, Mullenite Joyce Phillips were in this area looking for a plant that is native only to the Sandhills. Without a second thought, I joined them in the search.

I had been suffering from a case of doldrums. Although writing can be a great pleasure, sometimes what must be written drains every bit of enjoyment from the day and energy from the body. I was glad to escape from my typewriter.

We tramped through the hills, my newfound friends and I. We spoke the same "language" because we loved the solitude and serenity of the hills. And... we loved what we saw: the dainty blossoms of daisy fleabane, fluffy plumes of prairie junegrass, and a variety of yellow, pink, blue and lavender blossoms.

I stopped to study the swollen buds of a prickly pear cactus that pushed upward from sand which had blown deeper and deeper with a southern wind. The plant was nearly buried. I marveled at the persistence of that plant, fighting the odds against the sand and never quitting. As I photographed it, I found a comparison to our everyday life.

That cactus was occupying its rightful place in life, gathering its energy from deep in the sandy soil to nourish the blossoms that would mark the spot and say, "I am here." But winds moved from a sandy blowout in an attempt to eliminate the plant from its place in the world. Plants and humans often have to fight to retain their rights.

Yesterday, I retraced my path to the cactus and found that persistence had won. The blaze of delicate golden blossoms were totally incongruous to that harsh and barren spot.

A promise of the hills covered with the creamy-white soapweed blooms, however, was not fulfilled. Wind and hail twice during one day apparently damaged the blossoms and they are deformed and scarred.

The delicate flowers of early spring are fading. The prairie junegrass foliage has tightened and dried. I can relate to that because I, too, thrive in the cool season and wilt under the scorching heat.

But the sun "worshippers" are making their presence known. Blackeyed susans dot the meadows and prairie coneflowers which resemble a golden ice cream cone hide among the prairie grasses. Blue vervain mimics the sky color and the wild rose, the pinks of sunrise.

The prairie is especially precious to me during this season. Everything is bright with promise that all's right with the world. Only with the passage of time, do I know that blossoms can be stripped by insects, winds can cut, drought can drain and the sun can scorch. But I know, too, that plant life is meant to be. Although they are tromped and crushed, they'll survive and return in another season by a stubborn will to survive. As I sat on a sandy knoll overlooking "my country," I decided there is an unwritten law for the supreme enjoyment of nature: take from it only enjoyment and leave behind only your footprints.

At this point in my peaceful day the serenity was rudely broken. An old Angus bull spotted me on his way to the windmill for water. He was "king" of the area and I an interloper.

I had walked far from my vehicle and as the bull pawed the sand his deep beller changed to a threatening high pitched bleat. Chills ran down my spine. He was challenging my mission of peace but I stood my ground because I knew he was bluffing. Had I not known that, his bellers might have caused me to run. It did enter my mind.

GRASSHOPPERS LIVE 'THE GOOD LIFE'

- July 24, 1979 -

Recently, I stopped the pickup momentarily on the highway. Immediately, a grasshopper attached itself to the mudflap which touts, "Nebraska ... the good life." I thought about the relationship of size, symbolic of what the dreaded insect is doing to Nebraska.

There is no escape from the ravenous hoard. I found a plant in my living room which had large circles eaten from a leaf. A thorough search produced a well-fed hopper perched on a lamp shade. Apparently, it had hitched a ride into the house unobserved on a straw hat.

While some bushes in my yard go untouched, the foliage on a huge bittersweet bush had been stripped. Flower plants are gone, but we didn't plant a garden for the hoppers this year.

I drove down the asphalt towards Merritt Reservoir and the tires squished hundreds. Huge ones immediately started feeding on their fallen comrades. Yuck! Even worse is walking through the grass and having your flesh scraped by abrasive legs as they hike up under your jeans ... or fly in a cloud to hit you in the face.

My kiddos used to call them "hopgrassers." Whatever the name, a grasshopper is spelled repulsive.

I vaguely remember the dark clouds in the skies during the "dirty thirties." "All it takes is three days of westerly winds to bring more," my Dad would say.

Cherry County agent Harry Stokely tells me the only species of some 120 that is migratory is Sanguinipes. It can travel long distances on the air currents where other species are limited to a relatively short range.

Harry said six species are common in the Sandhills, especially the huge "homesteader." Harry says the homesteader, however, will cause less damage than other species one tenth of its size.

I found one I'd never seen before high in a blowout of a steep hill. The little hopper was about one half inch long and was black and white striped with orange spots. The bright little insect could only hop about three inches at a time.

Our neighbor, Gordon McLeod, has a meadow that is solid grasshoppers double deck; they're mating. His right hand man, Buck Wang, said they were going to hurry and bale the area to add extra protein to their winter feed.

It's no joke. I checked the feed-grounds behind the haysled last winter, and found the grouse and pheasants feeding on thousands of dried grasshoppers. I don't see many birds, however, chasing the live ones.

A fungus, deadly to the hopper and caused by cool damp weather, might be our salvation. Spraying the rangeland at $5 an acre is inconceivable when a small ranch would include 5,000 acres. I don't know how the USDA decided their "piece meal" spraying and eliminated huge areas. That spray control operation did, however, strengthen my conviction as to the effectiveness of bureaucratic intervention into agriculture.

The unforgivable part was stringing ranchers along until the hoppers were full grown and hard to eliminate.

Apparently, grasshoppers were devastating back in 1893. Gordon McLeod passed along a story told to him by Vincel Thomas who worked for his grandparents at one time. Thomas told of driving a herd of cattle from Perkins County north to the forks of the North Loup River when grasshoppers ate any forage that had survived the drought.

I shudder to think how much loss will be credited to grasshoppers by this fall of 1979. Here in Cherry County, wounds are still raw from a loss to agriculture of $9.5 million from cattle loss and added cost of feed and repairs. Ranchers are paying dearly for the increase in cattle prices.

Some time ago, we received a gift from our duck hunters of toasted grasshoppers encased in squares of chocolate. It was considered a delicacy, high in

71

protein. For the adventurous who are looking for substitute protein for beef, I might offer an unlimited supply. I will stick to beef.

꒜ ꒑ ꒐ ꒙ ꒒

RAINY DAYS BRING 'GRUMPY' SEASON
- August 23, 1979 -

I write this Wednesday afternoon. G.R. and Myndi ate an early lunch so they could get some hay stacked. That was an hour ago and it is now raining...again. That has seemed to be the story of our hay season this year. If the skies aren't threatening rain, they are dripping rain or pouring rain.

In the past couple of weeks we've seldom seen the sun. If sunny skies are reported at Valentine only 40 miles distant, quite often it is raining here.

The high humidity has made some gorgeous sunrise's splash in all their splendor across the eastern horizon. In early morning, light sparkles from native grasses which are beaded and heavy with dew. The mornings have been beautiful.

The men, however, don't seem to share any appreciation of Sandhills beauty right now. G.R. has become "grump and rumble."

I can't remember ever seeing the Sandhills so green at this date in August, but I also can't remember when so many meadows were yet unmowed at this late date.

At this time of year, during the hay harvest, there's only one thing worse ... no rain at all.

It is easy to remember the early morning hours during the 1974-76 drought. The grass was so dry it crackled and the men could have hayed all night if their energy would have allowed... or if hay was available. Our crop was cut to half and less those years.

At least this year the moisture has kept grass growth ahead of the grasshoppers. And yes, we have the bugs in dense population; walk through the grass and a cloud of grasshoppers lead the way.

The water level starts to rise in early fall and G.R. is worried that the meadow on Duck Lake will become so wet we won't be able to drive mow tractors on it. He and John flew over the area yesterday and G.R. said he saw hay meadows marred with deep tracks, equipment stuck and a lot of hay yet to be stacked.

It has been an expensive year for all, especially hay contractors. Besides the ridiculous price of fuel, we all battle the high wages whether rain keeps hired hands from the field or not.

I talked with a cousin who contracts hay. He said they battled for five days to put up a mere 40 acres. "We finally just quit," he said.

Not too many years ago we felt our teen-age crews were anxious to learn and most worked hard. We haven't had the best of luck lately.

Then we had a 15-year-old call for a hay job. He had never driven a tractor or worked in a field but asked for $25 a day. He said his brother was getting that but also wanted a job. G.R. told the youth his brother had better stay where he was.

That wage might seem appropriate in this day of double-digit inflation but speed seems to be the middle name of most young people ... when they get behind a wheel that is. Sometimes it would seem there is a game called "break the most rake teeth."

At the current price of $5.45 a rake tooth, it takes only five broken ones to double that day's wage expense. But rake teeth have gotten to be a minor item.

So ours has been a skeleton crew, G.R., John and Myndi right now. But Myndi leaves for college this weekend. I hope no one remembers me. Right now I wonder if we'll reach a point when we can plan a breather when "the work's all done."

PRAIRIE WOMEN PROVE THEIR WORTH

- September 6, 1979 -

I'm convinced that the "powers that be" of the Internal Revenue Service are all men. I'm also convinced that none had a rural background, and don't realize that country women were liberated long before anyone ever heard of Gloria Steinem.

My reasoning is simply that the IRS doesn't think that women contribute anything to a farm or ranch unless they have actual proof of dollars spent.

I'll have to admit that ranchers sometimes (on this place, at least) also forget a woman's worth. Just let a crisis happen, however, and for some reason there seems to be no limit to a woman's capabilities.

Take the other day, for example, when women made up 50 percent of an emergency hay crew. While G.R. was moving stacks on one meadow, Red Muirhead, ran a mechanical stacker, son, John, mowed hay with a swather and a young man from Omaha operated the side delivery rake.

The raker had to return to Omaha and the irrigation system broke down requiring John's attention. So where did he look for immediate skilled replacements? Women, of course.

A phone call brought Eldora, Red's wife, out from Valentine as replacement raker. John came to the house and asked "Mom, will you handle the swather for a couple of hours?"

A bit aghast, I said "But John, I haven't even been properly introduced!"

"That's OK, I'll draw you a picture." I want you to know his "lesson" took three minutes.

He sketched a steering wheel, which had to be in exact position before the motor would start. Then, he drew three levers: a throttle, a thing-a-ma-jig to activate the sickle, and one he said "to position halfway between the rabbit and the turtle." "It's simple," he said on his way out the door.

If you're confused at this point, you relate to my feelings at that time quite well. But then, how could I resist John's blind faith?

I'll say one thing for him: he's a good artist. But this is the young man who for 20 years failed to comprehend my instructions concerning the mechanics of a washing machine — turn a knob and push a button.

When I got to the field, I convinced Red to give me a five-minute mini-course at the controls. I was relieved to find the "rabbit and turtle" were fast and slow symbols for the gears.

Red told me not to get upset if I had a runaway because the swather is guided by rear "crazy wheels" and the controls are extremely sensitive.

After the 25th trip across the field, I quit wringing water out of the steering wheel from my death grip and started to enjoy my surroundings.

I realized my thoughts weren't practical, but what a shame to mow that beautiful waving sea of grass – denuding the meadow and exposing its nakedness to the outside world.

Indian grass was shoulder height and the seed heads caught the sun like burnished bronze before toppling to the sickle. From my high perch in the swather cab, I could see crushed grass where a deer had spent the night and worried that a fawn still might be hidden there.

Then I made a game of trying to determine how many species of grass were growing there and isolate the many shades of green.

The steering did indeed prove touchy. While daydreaming, I must have left a few long narrow strips of unmown grass. On one trip, I had left the swather head about six inches too high. Windrows began to acquire nice squiggly curves.

I thought the effect was rather nice. Like one of those nature sculptures that some artists create in the out-of-doors. At least the monotony of ruler-straight rows was broken.

It was nearly sundown when John came to the field, but did he mention the large area that I had mowed?...or that I hadn't "crunched" his machine?...had a runaway? Nope. He said "It looks like you made a few didoes."

I was speechless. "Now, what did you expect from a woman?"...that's what I should have said.

CALL OF THE WILD HEARD IN FALL AIR
- September 20, 1979 -

I love this time of year, especially the cool mornings. Next to spring, fall is my favorite. I find it difficult to remain indoors restricted by four walls. The fall weather is stirring the migratory instincts of the wildfowl. I awakened recently, just as there was light enough to see the horizon. The honk of geese had roused me and I got to the window just in time to see a flock skimming over the grove of cottonwoods in which our house sets.

The geese aren't ready to leave. I think they are just practicing...maybe trying out their leaders. The flock had been seeded in the Sandhills and return each year to nest.

The electrical lines and fence rows are living sculptures; blackbirds perch there like clothes pins on a crowded clothes line. Flocks of snow white pelicans huddle together on the blue waters of Sandhills lakes.

The other day, I stopped to watch Mallard ducks on a windmill pond. Their actions were almost regimented. They would swim around very nonchalant, then in unison it seemed, they turned bottoms up and the pond was spiked with ducktail pyramids.

G.R. is very helpful in getting me out of the house. He is short of help and has more jobs for me than I can handle. He cleverly prefixes his requests with, "You'll feel better if you get some fresh air," then adds... "while you ride the springers."

I had thought my day was planned to capacity so, with just a touch of sarcasm, I told him, "First I have to leave instructions with the cook, upstairs maid and the yard man."

I was careful in selection of a saddle horse from the riding string...and that in itself is frustrating. Eons ago when I was a teenager, I would always select the most spirited one...now I'm cautious. My concern really isn't a fear of getting bucked off. It's the ability to get back up that I question.

I'll have to admit, the ride through the steep choppy Sandhills was pure pleasure. We've had nearly 20 inches of moisture so far this year and I can't remember the hills ever being so green in September. The mature seed heads of prairie sandreed and sand bluestem were nearly the height of the horse, a prairie jungle in places.

I rode to the hilltop blowout where I took my kiddos to play in the loose white sand some 20 years ago. That spot was graphic evidence of change in the Sandhills because the blowout was now nearly healed. Sandhills muhly, silky prairie clover and the bluestems had invaded the loose sand and sent down roots to bind and lock the granules of sand together to resist movement by the shifting winds.

From the crest of that hill, unattainable by vehicle, I could see for a long distance in all directions the vast unbroken expanse of land. How fortunate we are to own this precious chunk of the planet earth, I said into the south wind.

The meadows have returned to a bright green after the hay harvest and the stacks are huddled together in the fenced yards similar to the pelicans on the pond. It seems everything is gathering together to face the onslaught of the inevitable winter. Cattle are butterball fat with layers of stored energy.

There is a special smell to fall...a spicy smell of cured hay and mature rangeland grasses. The crisp morning temperatures intensify that smell.

I did remember to check the fall calving cows and counted the seven baby calves that are fat and frisky from an abundance of mother's milk. What a miracle of solar conversion, I thought...grass to milk to beef.

I'm convinced that the Lord had ranchers in mind when He developed His master plan and created the Sandhills. Sitting on my horse atop that high sandy hill, I was assured that a plow would never venture there to violate the land.

FALL IS TRULY GOLDEN TIME OF YEAR
- October 4, 1979 -

The "gold fever" which is sweeping the country must be contagious because I seem to have caught it.

While the "panic buyers" are being smashed in the crowd vying to pay up to $415 an ounce for the metal, however, I've been collecting my gold at leisure. Some I will hoard and some I will share.

There is gold aplenty in these Sandhills and I've been collecting some on film and hoarding some as sheer enjoyment of a golden opportunity.

I've missed a lot of "gold harvest," because I'm a slow starter during the early-morning hours. This morning I wasn't.

G.R. and son John were ready to leave and check the cows and spring calves before sunup. One was going by land and the other by air, so I could take my choice and join one. Southerly winds were gusting to 30 mph, I knew the air would be rough. I was still sleepy so I chose to go by land with G.R.

We were out in open country when the first gold became apparent. In silhouette, the hills took on an appearance of the soft dark velvet of a jeweler's drape. Could a rare and precious 1907 $20 gold piece, balanced there, create more excitement than the early-morning sun, muted and softened by atmospheric haze? Not for me. I was glad I hadn't missed the sun turn from a blood-red to gold before clearing the ground-hugging haze.

No amount of gold could have purchased the enjoyment of those early-morning hours. A grouse watched us in calm curiosity from its perch on a windrow of hay. Mallard ducks on a windmill pond ignored us and continued on with their morning bath. Along the edge, a muskrat tidied the deck of its newly-built house. A swivel-necked hawk followed our passage from a perch on a fence post.

John was overhead in the little J-3 airplane by now, so for fun we paced him into the strong wind to determine his ground speed, knowing that his air speed was close to 60 mph. We kept parallel to him, only by slowing the pickup to what seemed a snail's pace of 20 mph.

The airplane overhead slowed even more, so we knew John was playing his "standstill game," which he often does in a strong wind. By cutting his power, the air speed dropped to about 30 mph, which was equal to the wind velocity and the plane had no forward movement. It hung suspended in space.

Unknown to John, we could see he was flying like a bird. About 100 feet below him, a hawk duplicated his maneuver. The hawk was headed into the wind and maintained a fixed position by occasionally flapping his wings.

G.R. and I headed on west and stopped at the crest of a hill to enjoy what we saw. Before us, the early-morning sun teased the hills until they became an undulating river of fluid gold. Bent and ruffled by the wind, the waves of that golden sea of grass rose and fell before expending its energy on the green meadow beaches. A spoken word would have shattered the golden tranquility of the morning artistry.

It was breakfast time on the meadow and crossbred calves, sleek and fat in their velvet coats, were coaxing that last drop of milk from their patient mothers. The meadows are as green as June, but behind the cattle, some of the cottonwood leaves have turned to orange and remind us it is truly fall and the "golden time of year."

I would like to fix that scene in time, suspend it and keep it forever for selfish enjoyment. So I did.

I caught the morning on film and I'll enjoy it when the snow piles deep this winter. And I've made myself a promise not to waste one more day of autumn and miss any chance I get to harvest a bit of Sandhills gold.

SNOWBOUND A SIGN OF COLD TIMES
- November 29, 1979 -

I'm trying to adjust for things to come with a hope that history does not always repeat itself. But Nebraska's late November weather has me nervous. For the past three years, it's been the pits.

For the past three years, someone in the family has been snowbound somewhere during November. Will this coming winter be the third consecutive winter of record cold temperatures?

Two years ago, Myndi and I were snowbound in Omaha for five days the week before Thanksgiving. The ensuing winter broke all records for cold temperatures. The December through February average daily temperature was a frigid 12.7 degrees.

Last year, G.R. and I battled wet snow to get to North Platte three days after Thanksgiving. Heavy snow delayed for 12 hours the initial flight of my trip to China. The three month average temperature dropped to a new record of 9.9 degrees.

This year, I made certain I was at home. But, the storm caught G.R. and John in Chadron on Tuesday and they returned home about noon on Thanksgiving Day.

I hate to throw in the towel, but if this November snow is an indication of an even colder winter in months to come, I'll be in New Mexico by next year.

Thanksgiving was a new experience for me this year; a quiet lonesome day. It was the first time that none of the children were at home on a holiday.

I can't complain, we had our family dinner on Sunday before Thanksgiving, because Myki, our nurse, had to be back at work on the holiday. Only one of the family was missing. But it didn't keep me from being lonesome on Thanksgiving Day. For the first time in 28 years, G.R. and I were alone.

The day wasn't entirely without event, however, because G.R.'s Doberman, Lupe, delivered two puppies.

While most women were carving turkey, I was mid-wife to pups.

And because it was so cold, G.R. moved Lupe into the porch bathroom where he also brings calves when they are chilled. "I'll move them out as soon as it's warm," he promised.

I'm not going to hold my breath until that happens, because we had three more inches of new snow Sunday. Some of you might remember when I had ten puppies born in my basement two years ago. I had to threaten murder before G.R. provided a heated dog house.

Speaking of families at Thanksgiving, I wonder how many had three state champions at their table. Gary and Mary Fran Storer of Arthur did, and I would think it might be some kind of a record.

The Arthur football team won the state Class D title recently, and the Storer's had three sons on that team. Lance is a freshman, Eric a junior, and Shane a senior. Gary said they are "mighty proud" of their sons and the three gold medals.

I'll bet the boys' grandmother, Helen Gies of York, is bursting with pride. She is reported to be a true fan and a great addition to the cheering section. On their way to the championship game, she and her husband had their car break down in Lexington, but they borrowed a car and were only a bit late.

Mrs. Gies now claims five grandchildren who are state champions. Her granddaughters, Becky and Bobbi Bernham, were members of the Class B champion basketball team at York last year.

I have that to look forward to when our three little grandsons grow and become involved in sports or other activities. I'll take my own cheering section.

It's lonesome when all the "chicks" leave the "nest," but the condition needn't be terminal when we have grandchildren to enjoy.

ᒡ ᛏ ᓚ ᒉ ᦔ

NEVER ALONE IN THE SANDHILLS
- December 6, 1979 -

S ome folks feel a strong reluctance to traveling through the sparse-ly-settled Sandhills, especially if they are alone at night. I'm sure that fear fosters negative thoughts about the vast area and they miss a communication with nature.

Personally, I find such a trip through the hills a treasured time of meditation ... a time to let my imagination soar and brush away the cobwebs. I'm grateful when the opportunity presents itself.

Monday night I had the privilege of attending the annual 4-H Extension banquet at Tryon and share a few Sandhills pictures with the "southern folks" of Logan and McPherson counties.

When I left the ranch on the 85-mile jaunt it was early evening and the western sky was lightly veiled with clouds. It seemed to take only seconds for the winter sun to slice through the haze and drop from sight.

As if in celebration of the sun's trip across the heavens, a pink blush of triumph spread from the horizon and pushed ever upward. Undulating color extended to touch the clouds in the southern sky before following the sun into sunrise for the other half of the world.

I wondered how anyone observing such a display of splendor could deny there is a Lord of the universe. Isn't each day another miracle?

Soon, an almost transparent disc appeared upon the eastern horizon emit-ting a halo of gold radiance. In my fantasized reflections I found it not unlike a Mass in church. The full moon was like the host as unseen hands of a priest raised it from a chalice. The stars became the flickering sacristy candles.

I felt no fear in that vast open-air chapel. I could feel His presence and was not alone.

Silently I offered thanks for the peaceful solitude of our big sky country. I was reminded that only a year ago I was traveling through the overcrowded, over-populated Middle East where now there is evidence of some of man's worst inhumanity to man.

80

My gratitude for our way of life intensified during a delicious meal shared with my kind of people far from the concrete jungle of the inner city. If I should be transplanted into the core of a frantic metropolis the daily stimulus of nature would be removed...it would seem an inhabitation of a spider's web world.

It was with inner peace that I began the long trip home. I knew it was possible to not see another vehicle. But somewhere I had read "Nature leaves no room for loneliness" and I find it true.

A leisurely pace allowed me to watch the Sandhills rise and fall to the horizon under a moon which had turned night into day.

During a previous trip on a star-bright and moonless night, I had found the stars symbolic of people. Each of the world's brilliant intellectuals ... the talented and the achievers were marked by a brilliant star.

Monday night, however, the brilliance of the moon dimmed the stars until they lost their significance. The moon became symbolic of the Almighty whose importance overshadows all others.

I was overcome by the giddy feeling of a natural "high." Contented cattle bedded down on the snow dotted the hillsides and horses slept on their feet. A jack rabbit won a game of "chicken" when he darted in front of the vehicle and the coyote changed course to lope away on his sideways gait. Near the river, I stopped to wait for a deer to cautiously step across the asphalt, and all was right with my world.

Although the hour was late, I felt I was welcomed home. Little cottontail rabbits darted out from the shelter belt like excited children. Before I entered the house, I called "It's just me" because from the cottonwood grove a great horned owl had roused to ask "Who?"

LIVING IN A LAND OF CHANGES
- December 31, 1979 -

We all knew we were going to pay for the 65 degree temperature Monday. For December in Nebraska, it was much too nice. When we awakened Tuesday to a 54 degree drop ... we knew darned well we were still in Nebraska.

G.R.'s like an old Indian when it comes to predicting a change in the weather. Sunday, the morning was gray but the sunset was bright and he said, "We're in for a change of weather."

Did you happen to see the sunset Monday night? It was a spectacular production in living color. I can't remember when the entire sky was quite so brilliant and the color remained for such a long time ... at least 30 minutes.

I happened to be out in the hills about 12 miles from home during the display and there were no obstructions to clutter the view ... but wouldn't you know? I didn't have my camera.

It would have been nice if Monday's weather could have lasted long enough to completely melt the snow drifts that have dragged barbed wire fences to the ground. All through the winter range area around Mullen, fences have sagged or snapped under pressure of the snow.

I don't know of any rancher who really looks forward to fixing fence in the winter time. Maybe someday, someone will invent a barbed wire that will store solar energy. When it snows, the wire could heat and cut through the drifts. Maybe someday...

Our crew had been swamped with fall work so we contracted for a mile of fence to be built through some rough hills of our calving lot. The hills are good winter protection but also made the mechanical post hole digger impossible to use. After a few days of digging by hand, the contractors failed to return, so our crew is finishing the job.

Son John said the sand is moist and loose so digging post holes is no big deal and he could dig one in about a minute's time. But it made us aware of how some people are unwilling to use unmechanized methods.

Moisture in the ground at this time of year is a Godsend to the Sandhills. It usually assures us of a good hay crop the following season ... and we seem to have a year-around fixation about the hay supply. We are largely controlled by 'if's.'

If snow covers the winter range ... will the stacked hay supply last? If range is overgrazed ... will there be sufficient moisture the coming season to bring back the vigor of the grasses? If we have another drought ... if ... if.

While driving through the hills Monday, G.R. and I saw a few pastures that seem to be carrying too many cattle. A boundary fence-line between two ranches tells the story. To one side of the fence there is very little forage left, while on the side, the dried bluestems waved in the wind.

"The Sandhills are pretty forgiving," G.R. said. "But if land is overgrazed for several years, you're asking for a world of trouble. That pasture wouldn't support a handful of cattle if we'd get another drought."

I noticed he was using 'if's' ... if the land is overgrazed ... if we get another drought. But perhaps foreseeing the 'if's' of cattle business in the Sandhills is what has preserved long-time ranches. When there is sufficient moisture, the Sandhills grass is some of the most nutritious in our land. It's great ranch country but only if it is managed wisely.

Healthy plants send down roots to a depth of their height. If those roots should lose their stabilizing strength, there is a huge underground desert waiting for release.

THE 1980s

Duck Lake Calf Camp
"Honeymoon Cottage"

Brands & Ownership

Brand: S Bar
Owner: J.D. Sears

Brand: Quarter Circle R
Owner: Alyce Wolfenden

Brand: Cross O
Owner: Ravenscroft Cattle Company

Brand: Y Reverse L
Owner: Swanson Ranch

Brand: Three Bar
Owner: John and Cheryl
        Ravenscroft and Sons

S R̃ ̇̇Ŏ Y ⊢/

'WHEN CALVES SOLD FOR A DOLLAR'
- *January 3, 1980* -

Ten years ago, we used to tease some folks to hear them holler.
And tell them all the things we'd buy when calves got to a dollar.
We'd buy a great big tractor with computers on the lever,
right after we'd marched into town and paid the bank forever.
We'd travel half-way 'round the world and probably never stop ...
spend winters in the southland where there's no ice to chop.
By '72, calves went up ten ... brought 53 that fall
and closer to that buck a pound than memory could recall.
In '73, we pulled the plug at 80 cents and sold;
just before the market broke and four long years stayed cold.
"Oversupply," the experts said when Nixon put the freeze on.
So calves dropped back to 32 while ranchers muttered "Treason."
The debt increased and bankers smiled while loaning ranchers money
to keep their heads above the pond and tightened belts weren't funny.
Then, Mother Nature joined the act in a fickle three-year pout.
She cut the rainfall into half and the Sandhills suffered drought.
After three, she felt remorse at the cowman's awful plight
and sent the rain ... threefold this time and feed was back in sight.
A good thing, too, because she left us snowstorm after blizzard
for record cold and cattle lost and mortgaged to the gizzard.
Bank interest rose, inflation soared but the price of calves was stale.
Some ranchers said they'd chuck it all ... just find time for a sale.
Last year "she" threw another fit and acted far from nice
when herds were culled the hardest way ... two years of snow and ice.
But last year was the magic one, when calves went to a dollar.
So, now we'd do those crazy things, with leisure sure to foller.
G.R. went to the tractor man who even shook his hand.
He said he had the perfect rig for only twenty grand.
"Now, I don't need a fancy one or the biggest that you've got"
But the man said, "Don't ya worry none, it's the smallest on the lot."
The pickup place was just as bad and a cost-of-living factor.
The price they asked ten years ago would buy a four-wheel tractor.
We've dollar calves and dollar gas and interest's out of sight.

So there's nothing different we can do. We've tried and it's a fright.
So don't you think a rancher's life is free from debt and grief?
When next you eat a good Big Mac, remember please ... it's beef.
But we're all well and eat real good, tho problems can get "weighty."
We're optimists ... we look ahead and say, "Thank God it's '80!"
Ten years from now, computers might make ranching all "white collar"
and looking back, we'll note the year, calves sold for just a dollar.

S ᚱ ☩ Y ⊢⟋

PLANE SNEAKS OVER THE SANDHILLS
- January 31, 1980 -

B ecause three generations of this family now live on the ranch, G.R. and I must resist frequent reminiscing of days gone by to avoid being accused of "terminal senility." Sometimes, however, something happens which relates vaguely to an instance of years ago to emphasize a dramatic change in the times.

A week ago last Sunday, G.R. and John were winding up an afternoon in the shop when they heard the pulsing drone of a large airplane. Being pilots, they are interested in anything which flies over, especially at low altitude.

"Why, it's an old four-banger of the 40s," G.R. said and the men wondered what a DC-7 was doing as it hop-scotched over the Sandhills at half-throttle about a mile east of the ranch.

Their answer came the following evening when Bob Brinda called. He lives south of Mission, SD and had also seen the airplane.

It seems the craft landed in a wheat stubble field where farms are few along the Missouri River south of Mobridge. It was after sundown and most of the nation was glued to the Super Bowl game on television...except three men fishing through the ice. Assuming an emergency, those men notified authorities.

The landing "strip" was apparently prearranged. The plane had Panamanian markings and was found to be loaded with 12 tons of marijuana said to be worth $18 million on the streets.

"It took a good pilot," authorities said, but escorted the man to jail. Another pilot was brought in to fly the craft from the field.

Speculation was the plane flew low to avoid radar at a time when everyone was watching the Super Bowl.

G.R. remembered another good pilot and related an instance back in the 40s when a B-51 bomber had engine trouble and the pilot landed it on a meadow north of Gordon McLeod's ranch just west of us. About the only damage was to the rear gun turret which was torn off.

"The faulty engine was replaced right out there on the prairie and another pilot was brought in to fly the plane out," G.R. said.

During the war years, he said, low flying aircraft became a way of life in the Sandhills. An airbase at Ainsworth was used to train fighter pilots and bomber jockeys.

The Valentine Wildlife Refuge, where we graze cattle, was used as a bombing range. Black powder was used to mark a "hit" instead of a real bomb.

"I suppose the pilots needed a little excitement occasionally so they buzzed our work horse teams," G.R. laughed. "We had some of the wildest runaways you ever saw!"

The training area for the fighter pilots was south of Nenzel on what is now the Samuel McKelvie Forest. "Sometimes, a pilot wandered past their gunnery range and scared hell out of a few people," he said.

"Frosty Melton told of the time he was in the middle of the Boardman Creek taking a beaver out of his trap when a fighter plane swept around the bend strafing the creek with machine guns. It probably scared the pilot as badly as it did Frosty."

As a whole, those low flying airplanes stirred more feelings of patriotism than wrath because the pilots were training for World War II, the war that was to end all wars. My own mother logged more than 2,500 hours for the Ground Observer Corp. while her son was off in the Air Force. Our present generation has no memory of those days.

Now, the world is again tense from threat of war. But, the aircraft of a week ago reminds us the battle against another war is continual ... a war against illegal drugs which leaves twisted minds instead of bodies and the battle ground is not confined to the city. As Bob Brinda said, "Someone was planning a 'trip' without leaving the farm."

To end on a more positive note, the daily mail reaffirms my belief that more people are interested in helping our young people. The quick response to my plea for Nestea labels to benefit the young people in high school rodeo has been great. Thank you, you are the greatest!

S R Ꝋ Y Ⱶ/

WILLING 'HANDS' BRIGHTEN THE WEEK
- March 13, 1980 -

For the past week, G.R. has been in the height of glory. He's had two willing "hands" at his beck and call. Myndi is home from Chadron on spring break and Myki correlated some vacation time from her Omaha job.

Way back when, at my first glimpse of a daughter after having two boys, I said, "This one is for me." Dr. Wilbur Johnson said. "Don't kid yourself. Fathers get the daughters."

How right he was. If we had 20 daughters, G.R. would have them all busy, because he needs the help. Of course, the girls would rather be riding horseback or working with the cattle than washing windows or scrubbing floors. I really don't blame them.

Sunday was a beautiful day with sunshine and balmy temperatures. I hardly saw any of them except when they came to the house with, "I'm hungry!"

Their biggest contribution to his day is driving the tractor through the calving lots and opening the dozens of gates. G.R. says his old legs get a little weary and I've been poor help this year.

Then the girls caught their horses and checked springers while G.R. checked the first calf heifers from those not claiming their calves. A constant companion in his pickup is his brave doberman pinscher, Lupe. G.R. is full of stories how Lupe puts cows back where they belong and saves him a lot of problems.

Myki came in laughing about a new experience for Lupe which wasn't handled with too much bravery.

Myki went with G.R. in the pickup to pick up a new calf and bring it to the calving shed. Myndi would bring the cow because she wasn't letting her calf nurse.

G.R. picked up the calf and pushed it onto the seat by Lupe and Myki. "Lupe threw a fit." Myki laughed. "She went right up the seat and out the pickup over Dad's shoulder to get away from that calf. The expression on her face was so funny."

Later in the day, I watched the three of them through my family room window in a calving season drama that has always frightened me. I was afraid to watch but more afraid not to.

For some reason, the crossbred first-calf heifers turn from gentle to downright mean after having their calf, and we're having problems with them wanting to claim another's calf. The girls were bringing a pair into the barn so the cow could be forced to let the calf suck. G.R. was on foot to open the gates.

All that heifer wanted was to get G.R. and "eat him for lunch." He used to say if one stood still a cow would never hit you, but these crossbreds have changed his mind. I mentally warned to be careful because those legs aren't as quick as they used to be.

After getting her into the first corral, he couldn't get the metal gate to the next corral open because the heifer would hit the gate trying to get at him. Finally, he was able to push it open and she took advantage of a clear shot at her target. .

Time and again G.R. jumped to the fence just ahead of the charge before they finally got the cow into the shed. As he opened the door a crack to push the calf in, I waited for that bundle of fury to hit the door and send him sprawling ... but nothing happened.

Having the three of them disappear into the barn where I couldn't see was worse than watching. Would someone be hurt?

They were only a couple of hours late for supper and came to the house laughing about their crazy day. I guess the girls liked the return to action and for G.R. it was pleasant to have the company.

We'll be thoroughly spoiled by the weekend when the girls leave in their separate directions. I have an idea that next week, yours truly will be opening gates and steering through the lots to avoid baby calves.

It will be just as well. The house will be too quiet for awhile as I adjust to the lack of the girls' laughter and "horseplay." I'll miss them terribly, but I'm glad they like to come home.

S ᚱ ☦ Y \-/

A STORMY LESSON IN PRODUCTIVITY
- April 3, 1980 -

I read in a newspaper where low productivity of American labor was contributing to inflation. I also read what Secretary of Agriculture, Bob Bergland, had to say at Petersburg, VA, about the family farm. It would appear he is in favor of letting them die, because, "they simply do not produce food economically enough," he said.

I would surely like to get that man snowbound on this family ranch. He would find out that his steak begins with a baby calf and we would allow him only five minutes to be a guest. We would teach him what long hours and productivity are all about.

It's possible that Mr. Bergland knows as much about a family ranch as the city reporter who called me Monday from the east coast. His opening statement was, "I understand you farm a lot of cows," and later, "what do you mean by pulling — and scours?"

At the time, I was flaky with fatigue from a morning of wading through deep snow which had the resistance of wet concrete. I was tempted to give a ludicrous answer such as, "We "farm" our calf crop similar to winter wheat and "pull" the calf from a stem and "scour" it with cleansers."

I didn't because he couldn't understand why we didn't put our herd in a barn. I mentioned we had nearly 400 calves on the ground and the Astrodome was in Texas. He lost interest when I told him our calf loss from the storm was minimal — so far.

I think it's hard for city folks with a 9-to-5 job and a 40-hour week to understand a round-the-clock, seven-day week. Each animal saved is vital for our debt payment and the price we receive for cattle simply does not keep up with inflation.

Each member of this family pitches in when needed. I would have been glad to have Mr. Bergland take my place on the tractor when G.R. and I took over the night watch Friday at 3 a.m. so son John could get 40 winks.

We had extra help because daughter Myki and another nurse, Rosie Kirlin, had arrived from Omaha amid snowflakes the size of silver dollars.

At daybreak Friday, Rosie asked for jeans and snowboots, saying, "It's a good time to get a ranch education."

While G.R. and I went blasting through snowdrifts to feed the cattle, the girls watched the herds and eartagged the new calves.

They rubbed circulation into two chilled calves in our utility bathroom and then with the deft touch of a nurse, tubed milk and protein into their stomachs for energy. The girls felt the frustration of moving their patients after two days, then coaxed a little premature calf to suck with an ear syringe and then from a bottle.

Rosie learned of "making do" when time is essential, the closest veterinary is 40 miles away and roads are snow-clogged.

While feeding, we came upon a cow having trouble, but she couldn't get up to be moved to the barn. G.R. tied the calf-pulling chain to a lariat snubbed to the tractor and told me to back it up slowly. Moments later, the big calf was struggling to its feet.

Another cow had a prolapse of the uterus and the men used the equipment at hand for the emergency. The hydra-fork on the hay sled elevated the cow's hind quarters, the uterus was replaced, and stitches taken.

Rosie saw other cows get into situations which would have been fatal if unobserved. One had laid down to calve against a fence with her back downhill which causes bloat and death if not rescued immediately. Again the tractor was used. Another went into a drift on the way to water and got stuck, but cows can't back up. The cow probably hadn't watered during the storm, but requires about 10 gallons a day and she won't eat snow. Rosie waded in to chase her out.

Five calves were pulled that day. Some were backwards and others had a foot turned back. An older calf wasn't getting enough milk, pump jacks for water broke down, and the list goes on...

Rosie said she hadn't realized a rancher had to be such a jack-of-all trades. She returned to Omaha Monday, saying that muscles were screaming that she didn't know she had and "I don't know how you stand the pace."

Now a second storm is in progress. I hate to be sadistic, but I would love to have Mr. Bergland and a few others share some of our weariness while we work to save our calves from a spring storm on a family ranch.

FARMERS 'PLACE THEIR BETS'
- April 30, 1980 -

April showers have only been teasers this year with an occasional sprinkle, but at least it settles the dust. We look forward to a three-day soaker in May. It's very dry.

But the chips are on the table and farmers have placed their bets. The corn is in the ground. Some adequate rainfall would certainly improve the odds for a profit by cutting fuel consumption.

If you would put a pencil to it, I'll bet the gambling in Las Vegas couldn't hold a candle to the gambling that goes on day after day in the world of agriculture. The odds are about the same.

We went to considerable effort to improve the odds of our calf crop, but you don't always win. We gave our cows expensive inoculations in November and January to prevent scours (diarrhea) in their calves. Because the cows were wintered in three separate locations, they were treated at different times.

Scours hit about two weeks ago, but it has become apparent the only calves seriously affected were from one herd of cattle that were treated while on the refuge. Many of those calves became terribly sick and died in spite of all our efforts. Calves from other cows were sick but recovered after treatment.

Now it would seem that the vaccine used on the one group of cows was not as effective. The last calf to die was sick only a day and, according to our records, nearly two months old.

So what does it mean to lose a calf? We can let the cow go and possibly spoil her udder if she's a good milk producer. All at once, there is nothing to take her milk. Or we can gamble and buy a two-day-old calf for about $150 to transplant. That calf, of course, might die too, God forbid.

We've been moving the cows and calves out to fresh ground and it's getting harder to check for scours. The cows move from the feed grounds into the hills and practically run themselves thin seeking green grass.

If anything on this ranch pays its own way, it has to be the two-seat J-3 Piper airplane that was built back in 1948. John can make a low-level aerial check of the cows in a half hour, but it would take a crew all day on horseback.

I went along the other day with the thought that another pair of eyes might improve the odds of missing something. Many of the pairs were scattered over a vast area. A calf lying flat out on its side is terribly sick and we could pinpoint its location from the air for a rider.

We found calves running across lowlands, sleeping in pockets of the highest hills and only one, thank God, stretched out in the last minutes before death. It had been treated several times to no avail.

One group of cows was gathered along the north fence. They know by intuition that their summer range is just beyond and they're anxious to go there. All we have to do is open a gate.

Very little escapes the eye from the air. It's easy to check the condition of pastures, and sometimes a fence line dividing ranch operations will note adequate range on one side and signs of overgrazing on the other.

I'm always intrigued by an aerial view of the Sandhills. Right now, the lowland meadows have turned to a fresh green color slashed by the clear blue water of the winding Gordon creek. A bright spot among the leafless brush on the creek banks was a huge clump of plum blossoms and eight white pelicans punctuated the blue waters.

So far, the green color is only teasing at the hilltops and tree groves, but it is there; the inevitable and welcome sign of spring.

I'm sure I'll sound disloyal, but the only sight which offended me on that morning flight was our corn field. Right now, the circle is a bare, brown scar which intrudes into the heart of rangeland. I'll feel better about it should alfalfa be planted someday that eliminates the exposed earth during this season of spring.

S R � Y ⊢/

SPRING NOT ALL ROSES ON RANCH
- May 14, 1980 -

We all knew that spring had arrived too early this year. Unseasonably hot days hurried the plum and apple blossoms and some gardeners had set out plants in their gardens.

Friday, I admired sweet peas and chokecherry blossoms. Sunday morning, they were all limp.

A new low temperature of 22 degrees just before dawn eliminated most of our wild fruit in the Sandhills. Eleven degrees was reported 52 miles north of Ainsworth at Wewela, SD.

Our mild, dry winter had everyone concerned, but thank God for the recent rains. The freeze would have been much more devastating to the prairie if conditions had remained as dry as in May.

I had hoped to photograph sweet peas on Mother's Day, but I wasn't interested in recording the results of a frost on film. Instead, I spent part of the day admiring potted plants in a greenhouse.

Time has seemed to pass incredibly fast this spring. Possibly, the warm weather has just allowed opportunity for added projects. The added ones have to be combined with traditional projects, such as fixing fence, so cattle can be turned out to pasture, and branding.

Every day, some ranch is branding and vaccinating calves to prevent disease. In most cases, the big roundup has been eliminated and cattlemen merely set up portable corrals right out in the pasture. It seems everything has been geared for efficiency.

Most ranchers use a vaccine which contains prevention of blackleg and malignant edema and a three-way vaccine adds pasteurella. Dr. James Butler, Valentine veterinarian, offers a warning for cattlemen considering the use of a three-way vaccine.

He said he had a report of 90 calves vaccinated with the three-way and five calves died almost immediately. The cause is anaphylaxis, or shock, which is a hypersensitivity produced by an injection of foreign protein material.

Butler said cattlemen using the three-way vaccine should keep a supply of Epinephrine to inject, preferably right into the blood, if symptoms of shock occur.

It's traumatic, to say the least, when a healthy calf is lost after going through nearly a year of problems to produce that calf. As I understand it, the University of Nebraska estimates it costs $325 to produce that baby calf.

Spring for the cattleman is certainly not all roses. Higher prices that were predicted just didn't happen. Then, our mild winter should have produced less calving problems, but other factors have taken toll.

Forty-seven ranchers, that I know of, have reported high losses by calf abortions or still-born calves after using a vaccine produced to prevent scours. The vaccine fell under suspicion after it was found that one batch was contaminated with another disease, BVD.

Cody rancher, Jerry Adamson, said he used other serial numbers of the vaccine and had no abortions but had calf scours return to his herd. When fecal samples of the calves were tested, the virus, reocorona, was found; the very same virus the vaccine was to prevent.

Adamson said he had cooperated with the University of Nebraska during the experimental development of the vaccine and had eliminated scours from his herd. "Now the vaccine is produced commercially and I'm back where I started," he said. "I think it's time the producers of biologicals take a long, hard look at their products."

We have progressed into a very technological world where biological products are essential to maintain a disease-free productive cattle industry. Biologicals have been described as a "panacea" to the industry.

What would happen if we had to return to the days before preventive medicine and cattle were subjected to survival of the fittest?

God forbid!

S ℞ ☿ Y ⊢/

WILDFLOWERS COLOR ROLLING PRAIRIE
- June 12, 1980 -

Have you stopped recently to smell the flowers? If not, please do. Our Sandhills, and the vanishing prairie, are laced with varieties of wildflower that will constantly change throughout the season.

It continues to amaze me how rapidly the Sandhills can change. During May, the hills were so dry I wondered if we'd have grass, say nothing of wildflowers. Then came the rains. Overnight, it seemed that blossoms of every size and color were heralds to the season of renewal.

Soapweed buds are swollen and pregnant with the promise of an ivory floral display for the prairie. Some buds are creamy white, while others I've seen are a deep rose-blush.

Willowy leaves and inky-blue blossoms of the spiderwort share the sand with the towering soapweeds and brambles of the fragrant wild rose. Golden clusters of gromwell and groundsel add enticement to insect pollinators, which dart from large blossoms to the tiniest fragile ones.

Another colorful native to the Great Plains, the Lambert crazyweed, is now in full bloom in clusters of deep purple that will sun-bleach to blue as the season progresses. The beauty is a bit deceptive because locoweed, as it's often called, is toxic to all grazing animals if enough is eaten.

Last week I mentioned having seen a shooting star for the first time near Oshkosh. Thanks to Bud and Gayle McGooden of Stapleton, I'm able to positively identify it. They sent me a book of wildflowers native to the Great Plains, which contains information and 225 colored photos, the nicest I've seen and a treasure.

I found in the book why I've not seen the shooting star locally. It is considered cordilleran or, "of the mountains," growing in marshy soil along streams.

The penstomen, often called bluebell or beardstongue, ranges in color from white through blue and lavender to purple and is a member of the snapdragon family. Although there are some 250 species of penstomen, I know of only five commonly seen in our area. Of these, the shell-leaf is my favorite because it is showy, graceful and regal. The prairie Indians are said to have used the stem and roots of the penstomen for extracts and treatment of fevers and toothaches.

The plant which has me really excited is the penstomen heydeni, or blow-out penstomen. It is extremely rare and hasn't been included in wildflower books, but I have taken photos of it, a Sandhills' native. It is included on the U.S. Fish and Wildlife's list of candidates for the endangered species declaration.

Last June, I had the privilege of visiting one of the very few known sites of the plant with Dr. Ron Weedon, Chadron State College biologist. Dr. Weedon is conducting research and exploring for new locations because the plant has been officially charted only a few times within the past century. Very little is known about the heydeni.

A few days ago, I revisited the heydeni site so that I could report to Dr. Weedon. The favored terrain is at the brink of a steep, choppy Sandhill and the lip of a blowout. When I reached the spot, I was breathless from the steep climb and the sight of the magnificent flowers.

In comparison to plants on another lower site, the stalks were extremely vigorous and about the size of my forefinger. Where I had counted 30 blossoms in a clump last year, there were more than 100, with about the top five inches in solid blossom. The air was heavy with a sweet fragrance.

Some things gain a certain beauty merely by rarity. The heydeni beauty extends with abundance. The hillside was peppered with scattered clumps. While plant foliage at the lower site was insect riddled, those on the sandy hill were unmolested by wild animal or insect, except strange looking wasp-like bugs busy with pollination.

Dr. Weedon will spend a couple of days here doing research, collecting insects and exploring for new sites and asked me to join him. I'm excited!

This is much different, but somehow I can relate to the excitement that pioneer explorers must have felt while trekking into unknown lands. The Sandhill mystique enshrouds the penstomen heydeni but just possibly I may watch as the mystery unfolds. For me, that anticipation is a real "high."

I'll share visits to the site as I act as "eyes" for Dr. Weedon. And I promise that all I'll take from that hill are my photos and all that I'll leave are my footprints in the sand.

S R O Y W

SANDHILLERS AID NEIGHBORS
IN FIGHTING FIRES
- August 7, 1980 -

There is nothing like a prairie fire to arouse dread in the heart of a Sandhiller. We've gotten to view each thunderhead with suspicion during this hot, extremely dry summer.

Those clouds have delivered minute spatters of rain and powerful lightning bolts. A carelessly flipped cigarette could have devastating results.

Gordon McLeod, our neighbor five miles to the west, said while flying two weeks ago, he saw evidence of six fires in two pastures, which had apparently been ignited by lightning but had been extinguished by a rain shower before they could spread.

The mere geography of this area makes the fire hazard an explosive situation. Often, 10 miles separate neighbors and the rough hills restrict the view. A fire can burn for hours before sending enough smoke skyward to be seen.

Last Friday, we had a brisk wind and a lightning display shortly after lunch. The hay crew kept an eye on the horizon and I kept an ear to the radio for any fire report.

By late afternoon, I decided to take some photos of the hay harvest and then drove down the road to the popcorn field. At the crest of the first hill, I saw that dreaded smoke which appeared to be in the first valley north. I sped back to the ranch.

Like most ranchers, we keep a 250-gallon cattle sprayer filled with water in the back of an extra pickup and ready to go. Ours is bolted down because it was thrown out while driving through rough hills at the last fire.

Before going to the field to get John (G.R. was gone), I went to the shop to get the fire fighter and the phone was ringing. The sheriff's department said Jon Davenport, who runs the Merritt Dam Trading Post, had reported the fire I saw.

Kathy started hoses to top off the sprayer and I flew to the field. John saw me coming and shut down his swather, knowing full well the reason for my speed. I knew that throughout the area, hay crews would shut down and rush to the fire at the first report. I would go with John and drive while he ran the sprayer.

The fastest way to the fire is hard to determine. Smoke is so deceiving that it appeared to be across the first range of hills. I hung on for dear life and we headed out across country crossing cattle trails, rough hills and even a creek while trying to hit fence line gates.

The fire turned out to be on Bud Reece's property, adjacent to our Snake River pasture, and nearly four miles further than we had thought.

Miraculously, an isolated shower extinguished that fire after it had burned some 100 acres. Members of the rural fire department told us they had radio reports of fires all over the country, and we could see billowing smoke in several directions from our vantage point atop the range of hills. Leaving others to watch the smoking soapweeds at the Reece fire, we took off again.

After driving some 15 miles across rough country to the Hanna fire, we were told by the crew of the Valentine tanker truck that winds had re-ignited the Reece fire and it was burning out of control. The crew refilled our sprayer and we retraced our path at breakneck speed.

"Are we glad to see you!" the blackened fire fighters told John when we arrived. They were out of water and were fighting the roaring flames with burlap sacks — trying to beat out fire from soapweeds and tall grass in the rough hills. An additional 100 acres had burned.

The effectiveness of the "wetter water" provided by the rural fire department became very apparent. A wetting agent is added to make the water penetrate and go farther. The base of soapweeds were glowing coals and exploded in sparks when the blast of water hit them. The intense heat even kindled fresh cow chips and both will smolder for hours unless completely drenched. Cattle sprayers really pay their own way at a prairie fire.

It was midnight when weary fire fighters headed for home, leaving land owners to keep vigil for a hidden spark.

The effect of fire on those drought pastures will be severe. It took the heart out of the Reece pasture and cattle will have to be moved out much earlier than anticipated.

Greater damage was prevented only because everyone in the area immediately dropped what they were doing to respond to the fires.

S R Ō Y \─/

LOOKING AT NORTHERN RANCHES
- September 25, 1980 -

G.R. and I left the ranch for five days last week, but I doubt if it could be called a vacation. We covered about 3,200 miles, half by air, and visited two ranch operations that were a distinct contrast to the Sandhills.

We drove through eastern and southern Montana to Billings and then flew north half-way across Alberta, Canada, to Lac la Biche.

Traveling north by airline is an experience all its own. We left Billings to land at Great Falls, Calgary, and Edmonton, and had to change airlines at each stop. G.R. grumbled his way through the airports and said he had enough of "hurrying up to wait" to last a lifetime. We went from Edmonton to Lac la Biche by private plane.

I was intrigued by the vast, flat country of Canada where golden barley fields have replaced dense stands of poplar forest. Rain was delaying the harvest.

We saw huge fields where the trees had been recently bulldozed, winnowed and burned. The Canadians told us they plant grass between the winnows, which can be grazed the following spring. In about three years, a crop can be planted.

The pastureland at Lac la Biche was lush and green as a lawn. Their pastures are handled similar to alfalfa ground; land is plowed and planted to fescue, which must be replanted when the density diminishes.

The thing we found incredible was that three acres will run a cow the year round ... one and one-half acres for summer grazing and one acre will produce enough hay for winter feed. We figure about 14 acres per head in the Sandhills.

It seemed strange to see 100 cattle in a very small area where there was abundant grazing left, although they had spent the summer there. The soil is black and we were told they've averaged an inch of rain a week all during the summer.

Our trip through Montana was a different story. Wheat fields splashed across the high plateau north of the Yellowstone River for as far as you could see in that big sky country. We were told, however, that wheat yield was practically nothing because of the drought.

We spent a day on a ranch which covers 300 sections of sagebrush country ... that's nearly 200,000 acres where 40 acres is needed to run a cow. Two married couples and a single man run the spread and G.R. was intrigued by the lack of overhead. There was no expensive equipment because they don't harvest hay and baled hay is purchased and fed from a pickup.

The ranch headquarters resembled a camp; a trailer house, a few sheds and pole corrals and not a tree for miles. They said wells for water were practically non-existent because the minimum depth was about 3,000 feet. They depend on a 2,000 gallon cistern to catch rain water and snow melt and their own tanker to haul water from Melstone some 30 miles distant.

Lawns or trees are considered frivolous in that waterless country.

They have been affected by the drought in that most of the earthen dams to collect water for the cattle are dry. Cattle often travel two miles to water.

I'm sure our finicky old cows would die of thirst rather than wade through belly-deep muck to drink the murky water in the dams with water.

The big Angus cows looked in good flesh, however, but the calves probably only weighed about 350 pounds.

Donald John, the foreman, told us he hires only a couple extra riders for roundup, which starts in a couple of weeks and takes 10 days.

He said the ranch had its beginning with sheep and, at one time, 20,000 head were sheared there each spring. Now, area ranchers run predominately black Angus cattle.

Our trip was a study in contrast and quite an education for me. It also made me view our Sandhills with increased appreciation ... I'm glad to be home.

S　　R̲　　ȯ̲　　Y　　\-/

CROSSBREDS IN WINNER'S CIRCLE

- October 2, 1980 -

While reading the results of recent Ak-Sar-Ben events, the world's largest 4-H livestock show, I can't help but notice how crossbred cattle continue to dominate the winner's circle. It wasn't always so.

I remember well, the late 1950s, when our youngsters showed calves at the county 4-H show. We had always raised straightbred Herefords and the youngsters always did well, although they never won a show.

About 1959, G.R. became dissatisfied with the weight of our calves, and we started crossbreeding with Angus bulls — the results were pleasing — Black Baldies with larger frames and heavier weights.

We were proud of the calves and the kids practically lived with their 4-H calves getting them ready. In 1960, we had the only crossbreds at the show.

I'll never forget that judge. He went down the lineup, and when he came to the black baldies he seemed to shudder and square his shoulders to ignore the insult. His attitude seemed to be "ignore the freaks and they might disappear."

The judge selected a small animal popular at that time as the champion and our crossbreds went to the foot of the class. I guess you might say we were ahead of the times.

In 1962, one of our black baldie heifers had a late calf, which was entirely black except for a dollar size white spot under its belly. G.R. said, "now that's a popping good calf," and since it was younger and smaller, Lorin chose it to show.

I remember the guilt we felt disguising that black spot so the judge wouldn't eliminate the heifer as a crossbred. It's a secret that I've kept until now. We bought some black Clairol hair dye, and "doctored" the spot. Lorin's calf stood reserve champion Angus heifer.

The next year saw Timmy Baker showing a beautifully stretchy black baldie steer, which again insulted the judge.

G.R. said, "I've got to raise cattle to stay in business, not win shows," and the youngsters concentrated on other projects until they outgrew 4-H.

The rest is history. When crossbred cattle started winning, they never quit. Now, a good share of the champions are of exotic blood — big, lean, stretchy calves that weigh 150 pounds more than those straightbreds of the 60s.

The consumer demands leaner beef and the economics of cattle production have made it plain that, if the cattleman is to keep his head above water, he must produce heavier weaning weights and cattle that finish earlier.

We made another transition this year which possibly should have been made sooner. Our Angus cows were bred to Chianina bulls and the results of the calf sale last week speaks for itself.

Although we delivered the steers a month earlier than last year, they averaged 74 pounds more. The difference would have easily been 100 pounds had the delivery date been the same.

The price per pound was about a dime less than last year, so it becomes apparent why calves must weigh more.

During these rapidly changing times, one thing seems to remain the same: The cattleman's annual payday is at fall roundup time. The banker, however, might decide in late summer that you've reached the end of your credit.

I have to chuckle when some folks continue to view ranching as an easy, romantic way of life. I wonder if J. Paul Getty might hold the formula for "easy" success: "Rise early, work hard, strike oil."

S ℞ �) Y ⊢/

FARMER'S PRAYERS FOR PATIENCE
- October 30, 1980 -

I read something in a livestock magazine, which was written by a farmer's daughter who was anonymous. I thought it was quite thought provoking, so I'd like to share this Farmer's Prayer.

"Dear God: As farmers and ranchers, give us the patience and wisdom to understand why a pound of steak at $1.80 is "high," but a three ounce cocktail at $1.50 is acceptable.

Lord, help me to understand why $3 for a ticket to a movie is "not bad," but $3.50 for a bushel of wheat that makes 50 loaves of bread is considered unreasonable.

And a 50-cent coke at the ballgame is "OK," but a 20-cent glass of milk for breakfast is inflationary.

Cotton is "too high" at 65 cents a pound, but a $20 shirt is viewed as a bargain.

And corn is "too steep" at three cents worth in a box of flakes, but the flakes are sold for 50 cents a serving.

Also Lord, help me understand why I have to give an easement to the gas company so they can cross my property with their gas lines, and before they get it installed, the price of gas has doubled.

While you're at it, dear God, please help us understand the consumer who drives by my field and raises his eyebrows when he sees me driving a $30,000 tractor which he helped put together (at a higher wage) so he could afford to drive down that right-of-way they took from me to build a road on so he could go hunting and fishing.

Thank you, God, for your past guidance. I hope you can help me make some sense out of all this ..."

104

Now, in my opinion, that prayer could go on and on and I might add a few of my own. For example:

Help us understand why $1.40 for two packs of cigarettes is a necessity when that amount spent for a pound of hamburger which could feed four people (more in a casserole) causes people to say, "We can't afford beef?"

What is the reasoning behind passing over a $5 roast because "It's too high" to pay the same amount for a six-pack of brew?"

Only a divine revelation might explain the philosophy of hunters when it comes to expenditure of money and time; for example, deer hunters.

There seems no limit to money they'll spend for equipment: $10,000 four-wheel drive vehicle; $300 gun; $10 a box for shells; $2 to whatever for fluorescent garb; bottled beverage and who knows the extent of the list.

And if they bag a deer, it might take a $25 knife to field dress it so they can have it processed or maybe a trophy head mounted for $250.

It may take days to track down just the right deer, but the hunter doesn't begrudge those hours. Why then do many neglect the short time needed to ask a simple, "May I?" to traverse private property?

And, added to the expenditures if I understand it correctly, is a hunting license at $15 and a habitat stamp for $7.50? Too many, however, forget that added expenditure of a "thank you" which costs them nothing but common courtesy.

Thank you, Lord, for sending us conscientious, courteous hunters who appreciate the tax dollars we spend for the privilege of owning our land which supports their game...and our constant efforts to maintain a habitat which domestic and wild animals share.

May I suggest, dear Lord, that you have a talk with a few of your hunters who seem to think a hunting license is an unlimited passport to the entire state.

As farmers and ranchers, we ask most of all that you send us large portions of patience, tolerance, understanding...and rain.

S ℞ ⚥ Y ⊢/

RANCHERS 'CAN HANDLE IT' TOO

- November 20, 1980 -

Last week was almost a comedy of errors, but it turned out all right, so I think we might borrow the Union Pacific's motto, "We can handle it." G.R. had made innumerable trips to Montana, where he was dealing on some big, black Angus cows that were being sold to settle an estate.

He had finally put it all together and left for the 500-mile trip by small plane Sunday. He wanted to be there ahead of the trucks and then beat them home.

John joined the trucking crew, so just us "peons" were left to run the ranch.

Now, when G.R. gets on a cattle deal, he wants everything to move fast and smooth as silk, but it just didn't happen that way. Those Montana people are the greatest, but they don't get too excited.

That ranch covers nearly 200,000 acres and those cows were at home on a drought area where their diet was mostly salt sage. They often traveled six miles to water at earthen dams, and there is no prairie hay stacked in that area.

G.R. had taken his saddle and was going to join the ranch crew to round up the cattle Monday in a huge pasture. But ... the crew got sidetracked and didn't show up with the horses ... so ... G.R. got the cows to follow his rented car to the north end of the pasture.

Five trucks were supposed to load at daylight Tuesday, but the roundup was delayed, and then the brand inspector didn't show up until nearly noon. I'll bet the air was blue.

The first I heard about this was Tuesday night about 7:30 when John called. He said they'd had a terrible time loading because the cows stopped at the truck gate to eat the bedding. Then he dropped the bomb. They had made it only 100 miles when one truck quit and they couldn't get it fixed. I was to send a rescue truck.

Thank God, other truckers are so helpful. I called Bud Philamee in Valentine, who couldn't go, but he gave me the name of a trucker in Kadoka, SD. Within an hour, I had that trucker "bob-tailing" it to Broadus, MT to pick up the trailer and reload the cattle.

If the cattle were that hungry, we'd better have hay waiting. I got our ranch hands, Dan and Vicente, out in the dark to haul bales into the corrals. There was a crockpot of stew simmering for the truckers.

It was nearly 2 a.m. when the first two "pots" came in and G.R. was with one. (He had been returning by plane, hit bad weather at Interior, SD. and flew back to Rapid City. He grabbed a cab and, by sheer luck, caught one of our trucks at the truck stop just as they were leaving.)

Within the next hour, G.R. and his trucker had unloaded, eaten and headed back to Montana, trying to beat bad weather moving in from the West Coast.

Another pot came in about 4 a.m. and the "rescue" truck about 10 a.m. About that time, John called from Valentine to say he had a cow down and to send a horse trailer to transfer her.

John's Kathy made the trip and they were home by noon. John went to bed for the first time in two days, and the men and I drove the cows out onto a meadow where stacked hay was scattered. We wanted them located before night and the predicted storm.

G.R.'s truck was delayed by icy roads and they got in about 4:30 a.m. Thursday morning. John started on a return trip about 9 a.m.

By Friday afternoon, we all were flaky from lack of sleep. G.R. asked if I wanted to help drive the cows in the corral out with the rest of the herd, so I said, "OK."

Driving cattle in a sleet storm is one fast way of waking up, but the ride was refreshing and I wouldn't have missed it for the world.

The Montana cows were thirsty and never in their life had they seen a windmill. They'd move toward the water and stop, and I laughed as I watched them lift their heads high to inspect the windmill from bottom to the very top. They'd take a couple more steps and repeat the inspection until finally they drank.

I had seen those same cattle wade belly-deep in mud to water in Montana, so I'll bet now they think they're in heaven.

The last loads came in about midnight Friday night, so now about 400 head are acclimating themselves on our west meadow ... enjoying "the good life" of the Sandhills on stacked hay and "easy water."

They are still a bit homesick, so watching them adjust will be interesting.

S R Ö Y ⊢/

FOREIGN CRITTERS COPE
- November 27, 1980 -

For the past two weeks, we've gotten quite an education while watching the Angus cows we transported from Montana adjust to life in the Sandhills. It has taken awhile. The difference of feed and water alone has been quite a change.

I was with G.R. when we first looked at the cows, and I thought the droughted range didn't look like it could support a jackrabbit, but the cows were in good condition. We were told it didn't take a large amount of Montana grama grass and salt sage to sustain the cattle.

Limited amounts of baled hay were hauled in during the late winter calving season.

The ground there is nearly as hard as cement but Donald John Cameron, the foreman of the Big Timber Cattle Company, told us that if you could get through the first 18 inches you would find moisture sealed beneath.

So when there is rain, there seems to be no bottom to the ground. Cattle and horses sink to their knees in mud.

This was true around the earthen dams where the cattle must drink murky-looking water. Stock wells would run to some 3,000 feet if they could hit water.

G.R. commented that our Sandhills cows would die of thirst before they would brave that hardship to drink.

By the time the cows had been corralled for several days in Montana and trucked 500 miles they were stressed. So they received tender loving care.

I couldn't believe the huge mouthfuls of hay the cows grabbed from the first stack fed them. And I laughed as they viewed our windmills with suspicion. Now they prefer to water from potholes along the creek, but they don't have to wade belly-deep in mud.

Scattering cake cubes during the first week was something else. G.R. sat on the tailgate and I drove like heck so the cattle would slow down at the line of cubes. They literally "in haled" the cake.

It took nearly a week before they quit running and settled down at the cake line. Now G.R. strings a continuous line from an automatic caker, but he still maintains a fairly rapid speed. This morning they seemed content and didn't seem too interested in coming for cake.

Although the grass in Montana tastes like salt, the cattle are apparently salt-hungry. G.R. said a four day supply only lasts one day.

The cows found a piece of low ground where G.R. said our cattle refused to graze because it's saltgrass. The Montana cows seem to congregate there, so G.R. moved a salt box to the center.

We've found they have the disturbing habit of trailing single file and are cutting trails into the meadows. By the end of the week, they'll have been sorted and moved to pastures or cornstalks. As an experiment, I tossed out several ears of corn and the cattle didn't know what corn was...just ignored it.

I've enjoyed watching the cows. Besides their large size, I'm impressed with their feminine heads. G.R. laughed when I said they were pretty...but I think some Angus have coarse, ugly heads.

G.R. was allowed to reject about 100 head that he didn't want, so he spent three days in Montana sorting for conformation, sound udders and "good heads." Myndi took her horses and skipped college to help him. "Couldn't have done it without her," he said.

Having the cows is kind of a new adventure. We wonder if they won't weigh even more in a year's time on plentiful Sandhills feed. We are thankful for the clement weather we've had for their adjustment period.

We are also thankful for our little portion of the good life in Nebraska... our beloved Sandhills.

On this day, thank you, Lord.

S ᛦ � Y ᗐ

THANKS TO MOTHER NATURE
- January 15, 1981 -

I almost hate to mention the good weather we've had so far this winter. As sure as I write this, by the time it's printed, the weather can change. But ... we have November and December behind us which can traditionally be classified as severe winter months. Each nice day has made the winter just that much shorter.

You might wonder just what an open winter means to a cattleman. I could say money in the bank, except the only ranchers I know operate on borrowed money, so I'll have to say it means less money borrowed at a high interest rate.

During the past two months, we've been able to fully utilize corn stalks and winter grazing which, for the most part, eliminates the need to feed stacked hay. We've been feeding the cows about one pound of cake each, which is less than half what is needed during adverse weather.

I put a pencil to just a few of the essential costs involved in feeding 100 cows, for example, during a cold snow-covered winter.

Each day the cost of feeding 100 cows could include $100 for hay, $20 in supplement protein we call "cake," and about $10 in fuel and electricity needed for the feed equipment. Just those few items total $130 a day ... or $3,900 for a month without figuring labor, interest, and repairs, which are not minor items.

Thanks to Mother Nature, you might say a man with 100 cows has been spared about $6,000 in the past two months. He spent about $1,200 on cake which would double during severe weather.

Then, of course, a hard winter means cattle lost or weakened. So far, there is a big difference from the winter of 1978-79 when Cherry County officials estimated there was a cattle loss of $3.9 million in the county and ranchers spent 50 percent more than usual on feed and repairs.

Some of us are still trying to "heal up" from a couple of those winters. I'm sure it is difficult for the consumer to understand when they buy beef over the counter. Back in 1979, the USDA reported that ranchers received only 31 cents of the food dollar while 69 cents went for marketing. During most of the 70s, the farm value of food products went up very little but the marketing sector of food cost went up 38 percent of which 47 percent was attributed to labor.

Now we see current prices of choice fat steers at about 67 cents a pound or about 2 cents lower than a year ago, but feed costs are some 20 percent higher. It's easy to see why cattle numbers are down in feedlots because the profit picture for feeders is not good.

Farm commodities have responded to the inflation spiral the least of any other living cost although the prime rate soared to 21 percent as compared to 10 percent only short months ago.

December market quotations rate a choice quality stock cow at $100 less than a year ago and that's only $100 more than 10 years ago. Choice quality steer calves are bringing $22 a hundred weight less than a year ago. Although the current price for steer calves is double what it was 10 years ago, the price of oil has jumped from $4 a barrel to $40.

It would seem to me that the administration is totally insensitive to the cattle industry which currently is in a severe cost-price squeeze. Why else would they propose to suspend meat import quotas?

Not everyone will agree with me, but I feel president-elect Reagan might be filling his cabinet with some "real people" instead of just politicians. I like the sound of an "aggressive, articulate hog farmer" for the secretary of agriculture post ... and I'll shed no tears when Carol Foreman departs Washington.

In my opinion, the man to fill the Commerce slot can't be all bad if he finds enjoyment in being among animals and roping a few calves for relaxation. Malcolm "Mac" Baldridge, Reagan's candidate for Secretary of Commerce is scheduled to compete in the team roping at Denver today and Sunday.

Possibly the new administration will be sensitized to the problems of agriculture. So far, Mother Nature has been kind to the cattleman, and I hope she sends moisture to the wheat farmer soon. We're all in this together ... this job of producing food to feed the world. I'd like to think that 1981 will be brightened by a "dawn of understanding" between the administration in Washington and the world of agriculture.

S R ♂ Y ⌐/

SLOWLY COOKING ONE'S GOOSE
- *January 29, 1981* -

For some reason, I've been remembering bits and pieces of stories I learned long ago on a South Dakota farm. Reading was a favorite pastime and Aesop's Fables, a well-worn book.

As I remember, Jack (a nickname for John) was the farm boy who climbed the beanstalk in search of the goose which laid a golden egg.

It would seem to me that farming hasn't changed a bit since the time of Aesop. If a farmer wants adequate compensation for his time, he has to find a pot of gold at the end of a rainbow or a goose to lay gold.

Anyway, that's the way it seems to us with only about 180 acres of popcorn under irrigation. By the time we figure the price of custom farming, fertilizer, seed and fuel against the return from the corn, all we realize are the cornstalks ... if we're lucky.

Last year while delivering popcorn in Iowa, John bought a pair of geese. He didn't tell me, but I wondered if, subconsciously, he was looking for the magical pair to lay those golden eggs. We all knew we could use them.

John's three little boys watched anxiously for goslings to waddle from the nest the goose built in the barn ... but the eggs failed to hatch. Not even one was flecked with gold.

Added to that, G.R. reported in thundering tones that what the geese left on the shop floor in no way resembled even a golden egg yolk.

"But I've read that guano is gold on certain islands," I told him. "It's just a matter of allowing it to collect in sufficient quantities." A disdainful smirk was his only response.

John had all the joys of farming last summer. He planted popcorn with a contract fixing the price at harvest ... more than the previous year. The dry summer boosted expenses and labor, and he broke even — if he didn't figure his time. To add insult to injury, there was a shortage of popcorn and the contracting company doubled their earnings.

But he still had the geese.

In November, the gander apparently flew into the side of the barn during the night. He was found there with a broken neck. His mate was desolate in her sorrow, and her forlorn cries shattered the darkest of nights.

John brought home three more to ease her sorrow. G.R. was ecstatic. We've been told, however, that geese mate for life: So the lonesome female ignored the strangers, and they refused to stay near the buildings at night.

John and his boys had a "goose roundup" each night but we have to assume that some coyote had a goose for Thanksgiving dinner. Now there are three — the widow and the remaining wanderers.

The original female remains aloof from the others but she has developed a new pastime in imitation of our dogs. G.R. says she hisses and chases his pickup each time he drives through the yard.

The other day when it was about 25 degrees, John noticed the curtains blowing in the wind from the north side of the bunk house where a hired hand sleeps. He sent the man to investigate.

Possibly the goose had been looking for a place to nest. Just like a queen on her throne, she had perched royally on the couch, after flying through the window.

I'm afraid I've lost faith in that quest for a golden egg, but I find credence in the age-worn cliche, "All that glitters is not gold." Anyway, the men said what glistened on the floor among the shards of broken glass was not gilded.

Who knows. Under different conditions in another environment, the goose might lay eggs of 24-carat gold. If you're interested, contact G.R. He just might be coaxed into a negotiation.

S R ̊ Y ⊢/

RANCHERS TAKE ADVANTAGE OF WEATHER
- February 19, 1981 -

Our Nebraska weather gets more incredible all the time. As I write this, the thermometer stands at 60 degrees. Just a week ago, the same numbers indicated the wind-chill except it was below the zero mark.

The warm days certainly make it easier on the calving crew and they can relax a bit from their constant vigil. Baby calves bask in the sun on the hillsides where six inches of snow has melted and soaked into the thirsty sand.

Yesterday, one man was out harrowing cowchips ... unusual for this time of year because they are usually frozen or covered with snow. It's a job we usually work at in April.

I'm beginning to wonder if the hot dry weather of August will advance into June for the beginning of another drought. It scares me that recent highs and lows broke records set during the 1930s.

We're not letting the warm weather go to waste: we're fixing fence, repairing buildings, fixing fence and fixing fence.

We spent the weekend working the cows that will start calving the middle of March. The animals are put down an alley and given shots to help prevent scours in their calves. Modern technology has certainly given us additional tools to improve management.

We have used Norden Laboratories Calf Guard with very good results for the past two years.

In a recent telephone conversation with Dr. Bob Stear, who is manager of veterinary services with the company, I found they had some recent problems with the product in spite of extensive quality testing. Stear said their serum, bearing two serial numbers, had come under scrutiny and he felt, a victim of unusual circumstances.

Stear said the serum in question was tested in 1979 before it was put on the market last fall. Tests were normal although Stear said their equipment more recently has been even more highly refined. Further testing can be done by the National Disease Control Center at Ames, IA.

For some reason, the Center missed testing serial No. 103 and 98 in 20-dose vials according to Stear. Several instances of cows aborting their calves in northeast Nebraska were blamed onto the scour prevention serum, serial No.

103. When tests were then run at Ames, an insignificant amount of contamination by BVD (bovine virus diarrhea) was found, Stear said.

"Further tests at the universities at Brookings and Lincoln have not isolated the cause of abortion and we don't feel the vaccine was responsible but we've recalled serial 103 and 98 from the market," he said. "It is possible that some cattlemen have a home supply and should return it."

"Rumor has distorted the facts," he continued. "Ironically, and I can't explain it, calves are found to be born completely healthy, yet carrying small amounts of the BVD virus. Slight contamination of the serum was possible during the natural process of production carried through the cow's fetus, not through carelessness. The serum is actually produced from the blood of unborn calves which is extracted and highly refined."

"We take a great deal of care to produce a superior tested product and this is the first recall during the 10 years I have worked here," Stear said. "We are certain that contamination was in insufficient quantity to cause a problem, but we simply can't prove what did."

S R ŏ Y \—/

BEEF COW STATE MAMMAL PICK
- March 12, 1981 -

Hear this ... the Cornhusker state ... the state which ranks third in production of corn for grain and the number of all cattle and calves ... has an official state mammal; the white tail deer. I'm surprised deer hunters allowed that to happen. You know what happened to our national symbol, the bald eagle. Shoot it and you're in a world of trouble. Eventually, maybe the deer.

Frankly, I think Telegraph Editor Keith Blackledge had the right idea when he suggested the beef cow become the state mammal. After all, we are one of THE top states of agriculture. We ranked first in production of alfalfa, popcorn, and beans; second in number of cattle on feed and commercial cattle slaughter; third in production of corn and sorghum for grain and all cattle and calves; and fourth in winter wheat, according to figures of 1979.

If I remember correctly, our state seal proudly represents agriculture.

I admit to being partial, but can you think of a single animal which affects more people's lives than the beef cow? Can we overlook the fact that she is the most efficient factory converter of solar energy into digestible protein? What contributes more to our nutritional good health than a beef cow?

Right here in Cherry County, a total county population of slightly over 6,000 people, produce 310,000 cattle of which 136,950 are listed as beef cows. That means a few people are producing a lot of good eating for much more populated areas.

Had I been the teacher for those Lincoln school youngsters who pushed for the deer as state mammal, I possibly would have made an attempt to point out the plausibility of a beef cow. Oh well …

It makes me wonder how the goldenrod got to be our state flower when it makes so many people sneeze.

My second choice for state mammal was the saddle horse. At some time during our lives, most of us have yearned for a saddle horse, especially when we were very young.

The status as state mammal would have given all saddle horses a certain dignity ... even those of questionable heritage but are well loved. You know, the ones often called "dinks."

I have a solution for owners of such horses that I read about in the Western Horseman magazine. For $5, the "American Dink Horse Association" in California will send a "beautiful" certificate of registration.

Even a few registered horses might feel more comfortable included in a group with the following qualifications:

– Hard to catch in a box stall.
– Thinks "whoa" is a foreign language.
– Bucks when you're a dozen miles from home.
– Draws laughter from horse placed at the bottom of a halter class.

If an owner can relate to the following questions, it means automatic qualification. Is the horse broke or does he keep you broke? Which is higher, your vet bill caused by you or your hospital bill caused by your horse?

Where would we be without a saddle horse? Kids couldn't learn to ride before learning to walk, ranchers couldn't wrangle cattle, and cowboys couldn't rodeo.

Even some of the most "dink" horses might have a unique reputation.

Some years ago, a spooky horse nearly tore a Rapid City auction ring apart when a stirrup on his saddle caught on a fence as he entered the arena. He had fire in his eye during the auction and sold for only $400, as the story goes.

The cowboy who bought him said he "was going to hunt coyotes on him." The horse had kind of a mean streak and an unrefined "Roman" nose.

Well, that cowboy happened to be Paul Tierney and the horse named Jeff was retired after Tierney claimed the World Champion Cowboy title at Oklahoma City in December, 1980.

Tierney racked up a lot of points on that great rope horse named Jeff and a lot of stories have been written about that pair.

S 𝈄 ☩ Y \—/

CURTIS SCHOOL SET IN LONG TRADITION
- March 18, 1981 -

It's the first of March and I left the ranch in a cloud of dust because it was so dry. But two weeks later, when I turned east off Highway 83 towards Curtis, it was as though the Lord had said, 'Bless this area'. Nearly a foot of snow had turned the Medicine Creek Valley into a wonderland.

I'm always grateful for an excuse to spend a little time in a different community. Because G.R. graduated from the Nebraska School of Agriculture, he has many fond memories of Curtis. Now I have some of my own. I considered it an honor to be the first woman asked to address the annual Farmers and Merchants banquet in Curtis.

Two charming young Curtis women hold responsible positions there; firsts, I'm told, for women in the history of Curtis. Joyce Peterson is mayor and Pam Hazen is president of the Chamber of Commerce, sponsor for the banquet.

I have an idea that the capable and poised manner in which Pam handled banquet matters is indicative of the way both of the women manage their jobs.

It was easy to see how people of Frontier County feel about their veterinarian, Dr. Everett Stencil. When he was recognized by the Small Business Association, the crowd awarded him a standing ovation.

The Stencil family roots run deep in Curtis. They built their beautiful house on the highest point northwest of town, where they can view the valley and canyons in each direction.

Sandy Stencil's mother, Elna Kibben, told me the youngsters are the sixth generation of the Kibben family to live on that farm. It was founded before Curtis became a town in 1872.

Horace Crandall's roots also are firmly established in Curtis. He came there in 1920 and served the School of Agriculture for 44 years as teacher and superintendent. It seems fitting that the new high school was built across the street from the neat, trim house where he now lives in retirement.

The School of Agriculture, which was a high school, has now been converted into an agricultural technical college. One native has watched the transition and earned the rank of "outstanding employee" after 37 years of consecutive service.

Margaret Green Ringstmeyer graduated from the high school in 1942. In October of the following year she returned to work there. It was at "43 cents an hour", she remembers. "And six-day weeks with work on Sunday morning quite often ... long before the 40-hour week."

During his first two years at Curtis, G.R. stayed with Margaret's parents, Dick and Cecile Green. Cecile says she is now 81, but her youthful appearance and energy can be envied by women who are many years younger. Me, for one.

I found out her family, the Wilkins, had the first furnace in the area back in 1908. And that her son-in-law, Don Ringstmeyer, is a "jazz freak" with a fantastic record-tape collection of all the great jazz artists.

With the aid of Crandall, Don wrote the history of the Curtis "Aggie," which was printed in the fall edition of the state historical society's "Nebraska History."

It seems the idea for the school was a 1910 political ploy to please the rural vote. Governor Shallenberger failed in his bid for re-election, but his idea caught on.

In spite of controversy, Curtis was selected as the school site and area people raised $29,733; a sacrifice because of a series of dry years during the early 1900s. The school opened in 1913 and during the next 55 years some 3,000 young people graduated with a good foundation in agriculture.

In 1968, the transition to an ag-tech school was made. Many of our rancher-neighbors are graduates of Curtis. It's reassuring to know that a tradition, although altered, continues.

S ℞ ☥ Y ⊢

CALF-CAMP MEMORIES LINGER

- March 26, 1981 -

The Telegraph is celebrating its Centennial this spring; I'm going to celebrate my fourth year as a columnist for the Telegraph, and my 32nd spring in the Sandhills.

Most of all, I'm celebrating because we no longer use a calf-camp where G.R. and I used to go each spring to care for calving cows.

Four years ago, I told you about the Old schoolhouse we lived in down on the Sawyer meadow after the '49 blizzard. From that harsh initiation into ranch life, we moved to a little shack on Duck Lake about mid-March of that same year. While the Sawyer had only one room, Duck Lake had a lean-to bedroom and a lean-to entry. Never mind that the bedroom ceiling was so low that you could never stand erect.

Whoever used that camp before we arrived did a lot of cooking. I could tell from the rivulets of grease that I scraped from every surface and wall before I could move in.

It resembled a homestead claim-shack but it was cozy; furnished in ancient attic and early relative but with a propane heater and running water ... that is, if I ran to the windmill spout with a bucket. An earthquake couldn't knock you from the bed because the mattress touched the floor in the center.

The water smelled like rotten eggs which only intensified your thirst. We carried drinking water from the ranch in glass gallon jugs and also used the same type of jugs to hold white gas for the Coleman lanterns.

We were caught in a storm, couldn't get to the ranch and resorted to filling the drinking jugs at the mill. We'd take a deep breath and hold it so we couldn't smell the awful water.

Somehow, the jugs got mixed. G.R. took a breath, gulped and then thought he would die because he had gotten the gas jug. He didn't, of course, die, I mean, but he did refrain from smoking for quite a while.

He thought it was exceedingly funny when the same thing happened to me.

I had a two-burner Skelgas hotplate and an automatic dishwasher, but I could never get him started. The huge refrigerator was merely the cold water of the stock tank where I suspended food in tightly sealed jars on a string.

118

In spite of the cramped quarters, we had plenty of company ... baby calves warming in tin washtubs, skunks bumping against the underside of the floor and mice running between the walls.

Our view was of a beautiful meadow that we had to cross to go anywhere. The snow-melt from the severe winter turned the lowland into a quagmire and our car was usually stuck there. G.R. was never in a hurry to pull it out with our team of horses: said it was easier to keep me "home" that way.

The next spring, we returned to Duck Lake when our firstborn, Lorin, was four months old. Believe me, you haven't lived until you've washed diapers by hand and used the barbs on a fence line for clothes pins.

By then, we had a little engine and electric lights so I made my first purchase ... a sewing machine to put my spare hours to use.

The following spring, with a busy toddler, I thought I was going to die from a lingering case of the flu. The smell from the water jug and "refrigerator" made me deathly ill.

What I thought was the flu turned out to be warning signals that John would be born the following December. When I returned again to camp, I used one hand to rock the cradle and the other to pluck a runaway two-year-old from the calving lot where pawing mother cows resented his curiosity.

I refused to go to calf-camp in 1952. I was afraid it could result in filling a dormitory with boys.

Times change and the camp was abandoned. As I write this, I can hear the hum of my dishwasher and G.R.'s TV. Those two boys are taking their turn on the night shift in the calving lots.

They have no memory of the calf-camp and no reason to celebrate its abandonment. I do ... and I am.

S ʀ ᴓ Y ⊢⟋

THIRSTY SANDHILLS GUZZLE RAIN
- April 2, 1981 -

You might say the angels of heaven looked down upon the Sandhills and wept at what they saw.

What they had seen was sand turned powder-dry with the tops of hills starting to open, blasted by persistent winds. Cattle had been crazed by dry, itching hides and pawed sand onto their backs in their torment, hoping for relief.

Dust billowed skyward from a single animal trailing to water at a stock tank.

The Sandhills had spent the winter of 1980-81 without its usual snow cover and was exceptionally dry. We were at four inches below normal precipitation when we went into the winter.

Friday night, when the first scattered "tears" fell, they "pilled" in the powdered sand; each droplet remaining isolated and repelled by the dust. Slowly and cautiously, the sand finally accepted moisture.

As if planned, the rain came in short bursts until the top soil was dampened and then like a thirsty sponge, the sand drank in each life-giving drop for two days. We measured more than an inch; other locations received more.

We became impatient waiting for this rain and more aware of how dependent our plans are upon the weather. As my dad used to say, "Weather we do or weather we don't."

We're not out of the woods yet, but this morning I can see relaxed, freshly bathed cattle in the lots and a tinge of green has responded to the rain. Grass has appeared as if by magic, but is sure to be set back by one more hard freeze.

Ranchers and farmers have been doing a lot of "pencil pushing." If the spring remains dry, will herds have to be trimmed because summer range will be short? Can a farmer squeeze a profit above the cost of production if increased irrigation at escalating fuel prices is needed?

I talked with friends in the eastern part of the state who farm and feed cattle. They told me they've lost more than $100 a head on their fat cattle; more than $12,000 since the first of January.

Their loss hurts all of us. Right now, during calving season and the time most charged with tension, we wonder who will purchase these same calves in the fall — the feeders who are losing their shirts on fat cattle? And will the price go even lower?

It's a strange system. When people in agriculture encounter financial losses, they are unlike other industries that merely tack their loss to their price and pass it on to the consumer. Agriculture can't name its own prices, but must combat adversity by becoming more efficient and more productive.

Government figures back up what I say. In 1950, 15 percent of the nation's population was involved in agriculture but today there is only three percent. Yet, while our national productivity has decreased at an alarming rate, the productivity per farm worker has increased 200 percent during the past 25 years.

During the mid-70s, each farmer fed himself and 54 other people in our nation and abroad; today that figure has risen to 65.

We, the farmers and ranchers, are the stewards of a legacy that burgeoned from barren prairies into the nation's fifth largest agriculture state. That agriculture base maintains the economic viability of our state and its cities, towns and villages. Much of the credit and technology can go to our agriculture institutes.

Sometimes, I offer an 1896 quotation by William Jennings Bryan for people not involved in agriculture to consider: "Burn down your cities and leave our farms and your cities will spring up again as if by magic, but destroy our farms and the grass will grow in the streets of every city in the country."

I pray that angels never weep because of grass growing in the streets of our cities.

SOME BEAUTY OF ITS OWN
- April 9, 1981 -

Have you stopped to listen lately? Have you paused to savor the delightful sights and sounds of spring? We, who live in the Midwest, must be the luckiest people in the nation. With very little effort, we can exchange the harsh concrete for prairie carpet and experience the fresh country air, to relish all the wonders of nature's world.

Too often, we take our natural environment for granted. I, for one, am so grateful that I am not jailed by the confines of the inner city. I feel surely that it would smother my soul because my deepest peace is always found in a communion with nature.

Early morning in the wilderness is the time most precious. Before senses have become contaminated with common odors, while they are still aware and receptive, is the time to go hunting.

Experience the exuberance of morning air before it is adulterated with the winds and the full blaze of sunlight, and, no matter where you happen to be, you will find something worth remembering.

Charles Dickens said it best, "Nature gives to every time and season, some beauty of its own."

I'm always grateful for an opportunity to travel a different and lightly traveled road far from the monotony of an interstate. Last week, on a day when heavenly skies moistened the grasses of seasons past, and softened the outline of towering hills, I drove deep into the heart of Grant and Garden counties.

History was made there and deep grass-softened scars are all that linger from the historical cattle drives. Legends were made and history was recorded, but all has been erased by the fast pace of progress.

Yet surely, as they did a century ago, a group of antelope rested that day among soapweeds and knee-deep grass of a sandy hillside. Geese and ducks frolicked on a meadow lake, while a turtle slid into the privacy of a pond.

Graceful shore birds danced along sandy beaches, while a curlew, usually accepted as a harbinger of spring, voiced its haunting call and winged its way to another meadow. Dark clouds of cranes called their regrets from lofty heights on their unerring journey north to those of us who are earth-bound.

For some of us, the opportunity to see a falcon is more important than television ... and the chance to find spring's first flower is a right as inalienable as free speech.

The wild things that live in our country are reluctant to tell us how much of our land is within their daily or nightly realm. Can the size of their universe continue to overlap that of ours?

Of one thing I am certain, there are many forms of life which make up our world and each contributes in its own way to the balance of nature. Whether a prairie is cloaked in night or the hush of winter and seemingly void of life ... of any animal trace or sound ... I know they are there. The air is electric with their presence.

And it all can be enjoyed. Now is the season when grouse and prairie chickens perform their daring song and dance of spring that fills the air with throbbing sounds unlike any you have ever heard.

Entire battalions of birds seem to burst with the gaiety of song; some in a raucous pitch or with a muted elusive tone.

The first tender blade of wheat grass is a promise that, very soon, bright flowers of every height, color and fragrance will create a prairie mosaic.

Rabindranath Tagore wrote elegantly of nature: "The world speaks to me in pictures, my soul answers in music," and "Nature leaves no room for loneliness."

Have you paused lately to notice?

S R �уy Ⅵ

GIFTS FROM HEAVEN AND EARTH
- April 16, 1981 -

I 'll remember April 12 as a most unusual day filled with an assortment of new experiences. It started with space craft, involved wild birds and wild cattle and ended with a celebration of color overhead.

We all watched the early morning and awesome launch of the Columbia. The magic of television brought sophisticated genius into our rather homespun world. It boggled my mind to watch a product of man's ingenuity lift and soar with incredible perfection.

Later in the morning our son, Lorin, was excited about a product of the Lord's ingenuity. Wild turkeys could be seen strutting along the ridge of a hill to the north of our buildings. This time, binoculars took us in for a close-up.

That sight might be commonplace for those of you who live along tree-lined canyons. It was an exciting first for us here in open range country.

By mid-afternoon, the birds were leisurely picking their way through the hills of our east pasture. We guessed they were feeding on grasshoppers, because we've seen many of the dratted pests already.

I took my camera and G.R. eased the pickup to within 200 feet of the six big birds so I could "shoot" them. They seemed quite nonchalant about our presence but we didn't linger and "spook" them.

It was nearly noon when G.R. challenged me to a horseback ride. "If you think you can keep up," he said, knowing full well that I'd take that kind of bait.

We had to round up six young Brangus (Brahma-Angus cross) bulls that we had raised for fun with the thought they might become rodeo bucking bulls. A representative of stock contractor, Jim Sutton, was coming to look.

Well, that ride was a first for me as far as cattle drives go. Usually, cattle line out at a slow pace and you merely follow. When we got those lanky bulls headed in the right direction, it took us three miles of hard riding just to keep them in sight.

Our horses seemed "up" for the run; G.R. on Hi-Ho and me on Kilbars. Thinking of their names, I chuckled, remembering what a very Irish rancher had told me last week. It seems that the Irish like to put royalty into servitude roles so they give their horses names such as Queenie, Duke, King, etc. "Makes us feel good to order them around," he said with a laugh.

During the ride, we passed several tree groves which are memorials to the homesteaders who planted them. Each is named for that homesteader, but the McCoy Grove is the most unique; a large grove of ash trees.

Our prairie was devoid of trees until they were planted, which makes Arbor Day, April 22, an important observance for all of us. We have a tree-planting heritage but the state has lost 200,000 acres of forest land during the past 20 years, according to the Extension Service.

It's up to all of us to plant trees and can you think of a longer lasting memorial which says, "I was here." I'd like to think that some day our cedars, pines and cottonwoods will be known as the Beel Grove.

Sights and thoughts of the day whirled through my mind when John stopped from a trip through the calving lot to alert me of an unusual sky.

It was close to midnight and until my eyes adjusted, the night appeared quite normal; with a half-moon over head and a film of clouds lower on the horizon.

All at once, it came into focus; rouge-red streaks arched out and down from the moon almost like streamers. As we watched, the pattern changed. The color intensified and widened across the clouds to the south and then in the east. At one time, the entire heavens seemed blushed with rouge. Finally the color, like the clouds, disappeared.

I wish I had an explanation for that colorful display. Could it be possible it was reflection from the sun on the icy northland ... or what? The Lords stamp of approval to launching the space shuttle?

Sunday was an exciting day and all of the unusual aspects of it will linger for a long time in my memory.

S　R　Ŏ　Y　ᗺ

SPRING DRAMA ALWAYS THRILLING
- April 23, 1981 -

I often speculate about the dramatic Eastertide when we celebrate the mysteries of the Resurrection and Ascension of our Lord. Did he plan, in his infinite wisdom, that most animals would renew themselves during this season to celebrate His victory over death?

Into an awakening world of spring, a multitude of babies are born to fauna and fowl and each perfect birth is a miracle. That becomes very apparent during our intense vigil over our domestic animals because complicated births are impossible without assistance. I can't help but sorrow for those mothers in the wild that become a sacrifice when an impossible delivery decides her fate.

Ironically, the mild winter has seemed to cause more assisted deliveries because the cattle had less strenuous exercise; at least that's the philosophy of many ranchers. Anyway, it has seemed that we had to double check each and every cow.

Only about 50 cows remain in the "maternity ward" which I can see from my east window, so while the men are feeding, I keep watch with binoculars. When a problem arises, I go to find the men.

I never fail to thrill at the vigor of a newly born calf; the short time before it gathers those ungainly limbs to stand erect; and the unerring instinct which directs it to nurse.

We've been favorably impressed with the Angus cows that we bought last fall in Montana. It would seem those animals raised in that vast open country have a keenly honed sense of motherhood which many of our Sandhill cows have lost. They are exceptionally protective mothers.

We watched a little drama which might be hard to believe, but I swear it is the truth.

One of the cows lost her calf and for days refused to leave the spot where she had given birth, even though the men had disposed of the calf's body. G.R. said she was determined to find her calf.

A week went by and another cow delivered twins and did a good job of taking care of both, but G.R. thought it was worth a try to transplant one calf onto the first cow. However, eight days had elapsed since she lost her calf, so it might not work.

Because the cow was rather wild, G.R. put two other cows in the barn, leaving an empty stall between so she wouldn't be alone and try to tear the barn down. He put the twin in the empty stall.

He had a little difficulty driving her in but she entered the barn like a race horse ... head up and just a bit snuffy. Now I swear the following is true. As she charged into the stall and saw the calf, she froze in her tracks and didn't move while the calf circled her. Still not moving, the cow reached out and licked the calf, accepting it as hers. By mutual agreement, the calf started to nurse and by the next morning, they returned to the pasture.

Ordinarily, when we transplant a calf, we have to remove the hide from the dead calf and tie it onto the transplant to make the cow accept it. Sometimes, she never will. It seems the cow marks her calf with the scent of her saliva and in that way can single it out from a pasture full of look-alikes.

I always marvel at these little dramas of bovine life.

Speaking of drama, it was just a week ago that G.R. predicted we would see a dramatic change in our healthy calves. He had observed the first flock of crows and contends they always bring scours (a serious diarrhea which causes rapid dehydration, weakness and often death).

Prior to the crows, we had treated only a handful of calves for scours but now the disease is sweeping the herd. Neighbors report the same problem.

So, the pressure continues. Right at the time we could see the end of such constant vigilance with the cows, our attention has become concentrated on the older calves. Each one showing signs of the disease has to be caught and treated and those Chi-cross calves take a fast horse and a long rope ... even when they're sick.

Scours is one springtime drama we could easily do without.

LEARNING THE HARD WAY
- May 7, 1981 -

The first weekend of May was a great way to begin the month. I had my batteries recharged by spending the time in Lincoln with enthusiastic friends who belong to Nebraska Press Women. At the same time, our Sandhills were recharged by needed rain.

It was a wide-spread rain; one to three inches across the state and it brought a big smile to the collective face of agriculture.

As a writer, I'm just like the sand. If I go for long periods of time without learning from others, production declines. That blank piece of paper never fills with type by magic.

Because I'm an "orphan" and live so far from others who share my interests, our NPW meetings are very important to me. The weekend was crammed with workshops for learning and rap sessions for sharing.

And, of course, we couldn't be in Lincoln on Saturday night without seeing the latest "in" place, the P.O. Pear. It was so "in" we actually had to stand in line on the sidewalk, which was a first time, as well as a last time, experience for me.

The place was incredible and your senses of sight and sound were accosted in every direction. The entire floor space was decorated in wall to wall young people while an assortment of antique objects crowded wall and ceiling space. The throb of the music might have registered a seven on the Richter scale.

However, I thought a device to circulate the air was a bit ingenious. A huge windmill head hung from the ceiling horizontally and was most effective in clearing smoke. Near the door was a huge painting which showed the state capital building tilting to the right just like the Leaning Tower of Pisa.

You could probably return to P.O. Pear, 100 times and see something new and amusing.

During my trip home, I had a lot to think about.

I was excited about the rainfall knowing the vigor of the Sandhills' grasses would return and sandy roads would be stabilized. Six miles of road to the west of our ranch had become so dry that semi-loads of cattle would become stuck in the sand time and time again.

Sometimes, Sandhillers forget that all soil doesn't stabilize with rain. Near Broken Bow, I remembered the hard way.

I was tired and irritated by the detour sign on Highway 2 at Ansley. It was Sunday night and usually road work has stopped and thru traffic can flow.

I didn't detour.

Miles on down the highway, I was stopped by another sign — bridge out. But I could see a track lead off into the ditch, down the steep bank of the dry creek and up the other side. It looked fairly dry. I couldn't bear the thought of back tracking and besides, hadn't Professor Robert Reilly said during a workshop "If you want something badly enough, you will find a way."

I eased off the highway, down into the ditch and creekbed, and then gunned the car over the steep opposite bank and right into the middle of disaster. What had been hidden from my view was water and black, sticky gumbo as slick as axle grease and another steep bank to the highway.

I was mortified. Here I was in the middle of where I shouldn't be. I knew retracing my path was impossible, and I would be embarrassed to walk for help. Why did the war cry of "Damn the torpedo's and full speed ahead" pop into my head while I was glued to the mud? I'd back up three inches and gain only four inches forward and two sideways.

I finally made it and had saved miles, but time, — no. Later, telling G.R. of my brilliant driving, he said it was merely dumb luck. The road crew probably agreed with him Monday morning when they saw the creative designs I had left in the mud with tire tracks.

I learned many things over the weekend, and the one I might remember the longest is to heed detour signs.

S R Ŏ Y ⊢

A LONG DAY'S WORK IS DONE
- June 4, 1981 -

Most of us are familiar with the Boston Marathon — that endurance race which tests the mettle of everyone involved. As it turned out, we held a type of marathon last week, but we simply called it "Branding Day."

I knew better than to schedule a large party at this time of year. It was scheduled for Monday. At the last minute, I was informed we would brand on Tuesday. There was no time for leisurely cooking but I've had 30 years training for short notice. My teachers have been G.R. and his father, L.C., before him.

A portion of the crew spent the night, so they'd be here to leave for the roundup at dawn in a pasture near the Snake River. They returned for a noon meal which John's wife, Kathy, had prepared and dinner at my house at 8:30 that night. It was a long, hard day.

The logistics of the operation were rather complex this year, because we had five herds of cattle that couldn't be mixed. Animals were gathered from five pastures and branded in four locations spread over the ranch.

The men had portable corrals set up in two locations to begin the day. When branding was finished at the first spot, the crew split with some riders finishing the roundup while other men moved corrals to a third location. By the time the corrals were set up, the herd was gathered at the second location, and so it went throughout the day.

There is much more to the day than merely slapping a brand on a young critter, and it is possibly not as romantic as television would portray. It's hard physical work.

After the roundup, when the cows, bulls and calves are secure within the corral, they are sprayed for flies. Then the adult animals are sorted from the calves and the noise is deafening as cows bawl in frustration at the separation. Riders wait near the sorting gate because an occasional calf will escape. A fast horse and a faster rope is needed to snare that calf and return it to the pen.

Finally, the branding begins and it's a study of efficiency.

Ropers drop a loop on a calf's heel, drag it to the wrestlers who flip and hold it to the ground. Some of the crossbred calves weighed more than 100 pounds at birth in February and had doubled their weight ... testing a few "flyweight" youngsters who wrestled.

Castrating, vaccinating and branding each calf took less than a minute, but burning the horns on calves that weren't polled extended the time.

G.R. and our youngest, Myndi, wore out two sets of horses because they did the bulk of the roundup in each pasture while the branding was going on. I have no idea how many miles they rode as they gathered cattle from far corners and held them near the corrals until they had help corralling them.

The spraying, sorting and branding was repeated at each location. Moving corrals and horse trailers was the most time consuming.

I suppose 700 calves were branded during that marathon day, but if they could have been mixed in one location, it might have taken half the time.

The crew saw a lot of country between the four locations.

I guess they were going to call it a day after the fourth bunch, but someone said, "We've got the crew together so let's get it done."

I expected an exhausted, disgruntled crew for the meal I'd kept on the "back burner" for hours, but they joked while they ate and no one complained, saying the day "wasn't all that bad." Maybe some were too tired to complain.

When I heard of Jerry Adamson's idea, I decided we had really missed the boat. The first bunch of calves were branded very close to Merritt Reservoir which was lined double deck with vacationers. Adamson said we should have advertised and charged $50 a person to participate in a "real live western branding" complete with having their picture taken while holding a calf.

We should have done it and found a way to subsidize our way of living. At least it would have helped pay for the meals. When I hear people complain about the price of meat, I'm always tempted to invite them to help at a branding and then figure the cost of the meal we put out to feed those hard working men.

An abundance of food is a necessity, plenty of meat a must and branding crews often range from 25 all the way up to 50 hungry men. We certainly don't complain. It's merely one more hidden cost that goes into producing beef for your table.

S R O Y W

SANDHILLS ROOTS GROW DEEP
- July 16, 1981 -

In case you haven't noticed, I might be considered partial to "my" Sandhills. Although I wasn't born here, I've studied them and with understanding has come a very strong and deep affection. The Sandhills are unique to the world. It's a fragile land that responds to careful management.

It's always exciting to me when I am able to introduce someone to the hills for the first time.

It was my pleasure to have as my guest over the weekend an enthusiastic and delightful young woman who lives in Virginia. We experienced a colorful sunset along Gordon Creek, and on Sunday rode through the hills on horseback.

Our area was ranked among the land considered desolate and uninhabitable until late in the 19th century, so I asked my guest to fantasize while we rode; to pretend she was an Indian riding through when it was their domain.

We found huge pockets where a band of Indians could hide undetected from even a short distance and a deer emerged from a blowout to watch our journey. It would have made an easy hunt.

From the top of a ridge, we could see for miles; the creek to the west and lake country to the east. Cattle stringing single file to a windmill took on the form of Calvary in our fantasy. As Indian scouts, we had plenty of time to evaluate the situation before we were noticed.

When "Custer," which we called the red lead-bull, finally saw us, the column came to a halt in apprehension. We were peaceful on this day and all of us mingled and drank the clear water from the windmill.

She was interested in the vegetation which has stabilized the dunes of sand and was amazed at our huge underground reservoir and of the native grasses which may send down roots to a depth of 28 feet. Our native switchgrass can do just that, which explains the force which holds the sand together.

I think I've found another convert whose shoes took home to Virginia a bit of Nebraska sand.

The next day, I wished she could have been with me when I took dinner down to the hay crew. The crew is camping out near the heart of the refuge, about 14 miles from the ranch and within a couple miles of Highway 83.

130

That area gives you a completely different perspective on the Sandhills. It's lake country and the blue water dots the area to support wild fowl, as well as the surrounding marshes. It's a complete contrast to the steep rolling hills, but very much a part of the system. I'm told that bluestem and switchgrass can grow to six feet in that area.

I stopped along the sandy trail to check on a small colony of Penstomen Heydeni, a rare Sandhills flower, which was found several years ago. It's in an area where cattle don't graze.

Anyone climbing that sandy hill might understand why, at one time, the Sandhills were soft moving sands. Without cattle constantly tromping the ground in their endless search of grass, the sand becomes soft and bare spots appear between soap weeds and bunch grass.

Climbing was a tremendous exertion in the 103 degree heat, but it was made a bigger effort by what was underfoot. Rodents had undermined the bare ground so each step sank into the unstable sand and made climbing extra effort.

I have been told by "old timers" that saddle horses sank to their knees in the loose sand when settlers first came to the Sandhills. I could see how it could happen. Prairie fires raged uncontrolled and the exposed sand shifted with the wind until moisture could revitalize new growth. Meadows, however, were choked with many years of growth.

It's interesting to me that ranchers have actually improved the land by stocking it and with careful management. Research goes on at the same time while some refuge meadows are left uncut for several years in rotation. It seems when meadows are rested, there is a return of more native grasses in comparison to introduced specimen such as bluegrass, smooth brome and other species, which are basically cool season and of little value as stacked hay.

S R ठ Y \-/

QUIET EVENING REVIVES
THE COUNTRY SOUL
- July 16, 1981 -

In mid-July 1980, when the thermometer teased 100 degrees, I ventured outdoors to watch a drama of nature. G.R. had told me a family of ducks were on a windmill pond, so I went to catch photos. A mallard hen and her seven little ones went into hiding in the tall grass along the bank after I had captured only one picture.

It was midday and the herd of cattle were trailing to water, so I just sat and waited to watch. I knew the cows would wade in up to their chins to escape the flies and heat.

Before long, the mallard hen came swimming out to meet the splashing cattle, quacking and scolding. In-and-out she wove, but the animals paid her no heed.

As the cattle moved farther into the pond, the hen swam back to shore and the urgency of her calls intensified. Two little balls of fluff came swimming out to join her. A little farther down, a third came out from shore with the propulsion of a torpedo, just as a big bull walked into the grass.

Back and forth, the hen swam. When the seventh duckling joined her, she immediately took them to safety on the opposite shore. My question was: how could she count? I'll always find the instincts of wildlife to be fascinating.

I don't, however, appreciate being dive-bombed every time I step out my front door. Barn swallows have built a nest on the light fixture, and I don't have the heart to tear it down until the chicks have flown. The protective parents zoom at me and miss me by mere inches.

I love to watch a killdeer mother when she thinks you are too close to her babies. She feigns a broken wing so convincingly, as she tries to lure you away.

That same day, the rest of the family had gone their separate ways to escape the heat, so G.R. and I were left with only our two Doberman pups. We loaded them and picnic gear into the pickup and drove to a small dam we've built along the Gordon Creek where I used to take the kiddos.

I think the half-grown pups thought they were water spaniels and splashed and swam in the cool clear water. They have a thing about birds, and when gulls flew overhead teasing, the pups followed in hot pursuit. If the gulls flew over the water, the pups swam the lake. When they flew along the shore, the pups expended their energy in a powerful race merely for the love of running.

It was reminiscent of the days we took the kiddos out to the creek on hot days. They ran and splashed until they dropped. Hamburgers cooked on a hibachi were shared with the pups, and they finally settled down to lie at our feet.

It was so peaceful there on our private lake as the western sky turned to a burnished rose, while thunderheads billowed upward to the east. Squadrons of dragonflies patrolled the water. Some were single wing jobbies, while others were equipped with aerobatic biwings. There was sufficient breeze to eliminate any bothersome biting insects.

132

A bullfrog maestro called upon his chorus and we were entertained without background interference of highway traffic or trivial human chatter. It was as though a bullfrog prince was giving a command performance in the heart and privacy of our domain.

As the dusk deepened, however, we came to feel we were intruding on another's private pond. Ducks in pairs flew over, scolded, and continued on because we were invading their privacy.

The bright stars made headlights unnecessary and we slowly retraced our path along the edge of the meadow back to the house. A coyote noted our passage with a sharp yip.

Somehow a quiet evening such as that diminishes problems, recharges the batteries and refreshes the soul. It also renewed my gratitude for country living in the "isolated" Sandhills — where if you once stop — sand is certain to sift into your shoes.

PRESS CONVENTION BUSY PLACE
- July 25, 1981 -

There's absolutely no better way to appreciate living in the country than to spend time in a big city ... at least for me. Of course, a national convention isn't the most relaxed time to be in a city because there is so much to be accomplished in a short time. I've just returned from Philadelphia and the convention of National Presswomen exhausted but grateful for the opportunity.

During one workshop, our area was called the "buckle of the Bible belt," to which I silently said amen. We have problems but they seem very small when you talk to people who live in a large city. Freedom of the press, however, is just as important an issue here as in the city and is a freedom which should be a vital concern to all of us.

It was especially inspiring to listen to Victor Riesel, who writes for 357 daily papers with a total circulation of 23 million in spite of being blinded 25 years ago. Acid was thrown into his eyes when he was doing investigative reporting and the people involved were determined to stop him.

He didn't give up. Once printers' ink had entered his veins, he was committed to "telling it like it is."

The credibility of journalism, in general, and women journalists, in particular, was damaged by the unfortunate incident of Janet Cooke winning a Pulitzer Prize for a fabricated story. I feel better that her paper has criticized itself for allowing that to happen.

In contrast, it was my distinct privilege to have as my roommate, Hazel Brannon Smith, a Pulitzer Prize winner of the highest caliber. Her forceful and forthright brand of journalism earned her a Pulitzer for editorials that caused an economic-boycott to her paper, threats on her life and property, but she didn't weaken in her philosophy:

"Truth is the most powerful weapon in the world." The responsibility and privilege of the journalist is to seek and find the truth ... and tell the report that beef was served during most of our convention meals and I made a point of letting the hotel manager know that the beef industry was appreciative.

I think we're remiss when we are proud of something and don't say so. Today, I have to tell you I'm proud to be involved in two industries: that of producing beef for your table and copy for your newspaper. I take both very seriously.

A portion of the Philadelphia convention, however, was traumatic for me, a coffee-holic, because each cup of coffee cost 85 cents.

It was late Sunday when I returned to the ranch but the first thing I did was make a pot of coffee to enjoy while I caught up on the news in the stack of papers that had accumulated.

It is very good to be home!

My trip east has made me even more humble for the space I'm allowed each week in this publication and proud to be associated with a newspaper, which in my opinion, would not allow a "Janet Cooke" story to be printed.

I'm also very grateful to be associated with the National Federation of Presswomen and its Nebraska affiliate, which are devoted to professional growth of its members. Its exciting to me that a woman from the Midwest, D.J. Cline, journalism professor in Brookings, SD, was elected NFPW national president.

I was able to do a little industry promotion of my own during D.J.'s campaign social hour by supplying snack food representative of our area —beef, of course. With the help of Ruthie Harms, immediate past president of Region 17 Cow-Belles, we prepared homemade beef jerky.

The jerky proved to be a huge success and I was flooded with requests for the recipe which I'll furnish in our national magazine.

S ℞ ☿ Y ⊢/

MISHAP BRINGS ACTIVITY TO SCREECHING HALT

- September 17, 1981 -

Blood-red sun rose this morning and eventually kidnapped the frosty white glaze from the grasses. It's that time of year. The summer seemed to pass so rapidly that only a contrail memory remains. The fall looks as though it will be the same. Autumn is our annual, once-a-year payday so the pressure intensifies. It's a time of sorting cattle, weaning calves, and then trying to find a buyer on a market that seems to be 10 cents a pound lower than last year. It also seems to be a time when our banker gets the most impatient.

G.R. is usually geared to his fastest pace during the fall, but his activities have come to a screeching halt. Our daughter, Myki, the nurse, has given him a little wall plaque that has fingers and toes clutching a square, "Lord, help me hang in there."

The plaque is most appropriate and G.R. can see it from his hospital bed and his bed is equipped with metal bars and hand holds so he can change positions. He is truly hanging in there.

He has been in the hospital 10 days.

On Tuesday of last week, he and the crew abandoned the hay fields to gather bulls in the Snake River pasture, which lies about six miles north as the crow flies. They took saddle lunches.

Shortly after lunch, daughter Myndi, who works as an aide at the hospital, telephoned and was really upset. "What happened! The ambulance was just called out for Dad."

My heart stopped. Had his horse fallen with him or had a bull gotten him down in the corral? I knew that John must have gone to Jon Davenport's store on Merritt Reservoir to call for help. That line was busy.

Where in that big pasture had he been hurt? I could get to the north gate by going around 15 miles on a road and just hope I could find them when I got there. I left in a cloud of dust.

Luck was with me at the north gate because I could see someone standing by a horse trailer off in the pasture. It was John.

135

John had moved the trailer to break the burning sun from G.R., who lay on the ground with his knees held in a bent position by sacks of salt. He said the pain was excruciating and he couldn't move.

"I feel like I've been split," he said.

He had been chasing a big bull when his horse jumped a trail and then started to buck, catching him totally unaware. Instead of getting bucked off, he came down hard on the pommel of the saddle. Later, the X-rays showed a 1 1/2 inch gap in his pelvis.

He was determined that we not blame his horse, Freddy Rabbit. I found a cactus lodged in the horse's belly, near the back cinch, which was possibly the answer, having been kicked there by his hind feet.

More than a week of total inactivity has been a new experience for the workaholic who ramrods this outfit. I'm so grateful for painkilling medication, which has eased his discomfort somewhat.

He's done a lot of thinking, he told me. "I'll never try to make a cow get to her feet after she's had trouble having one of those big calves. I feel like I've just given birth to a 160 pound one," he said, and grinned.

His injury, it seems, didn't fracture his sense of humor. While I was repositioning his legs, he said "Wouldn't I be hell to live with if I were a cripple?"

"Forget the 'if' business," I said, "you're hell to live with when you're moving 100 miles an hour."

He'll be home soon with a walker and then crutches. I'll put his 'hang in there' plaque on the wall right beside one given to me by John's wife, Kathy. Mine reads, "Lord, I pray for patience but I want it now!"

S　R　♀　Y　\-/

SANDHILLS FENCE REPAIR
PROVIDES SETTING

- June 3, 1982 -

There is no sense in waiting for opportunity to knock. Opportunities are ever present and waiting. It was midmorning. Clouds jogged leisurely across the sky and birds sang joyfully to the sun. G.R. stopped at the house.

"Want to go fencing with me?"

"Only if you'll give me time enough to brew a thermos of coffee and load my cameras."

Within 15 minutes, we were bouncing over the hills. Barbed wire, posts and other supplies shared the back of the pickup with G.R.'s doberman named Ted.

Spring fencing is a ritual of taking fallen barbed wire and turning it into taunt steel threads. Winter snows weight the wire until it sags or breaks, especially in the pockets. Now, those depressions in the land are filled with lakes formed from torrents of rain during May, so hip waders are added to fencing supplies.

While G.R. traded his boots for waders, I carried supplies to the water's edge. I try to do a lot of his walking for him because he still walks with pain from his injury. He doesn't think he can yet take time to have something done about it.

"This spot will take an hour," he said. "Go take a hike."

Ordinarily, that advice would make me bristle with indignation. Not when I'm out in the remote serenity of the Sandhills, however.

I walked to the banks of the swollen Gordon Creek where curious yearlings watched me from the opposite bank. We all spooked when a tiny teal duck exploded from the water and mallards made their splashing takeoff. Shore birds rose into the air but then returned to share the sandy shore.

I sat on those banks pretending that the cattle were buffalo and I was an Indian of days long past. I knew I was safe in my little private world because hadn't the calvary turned back when they reached the Sandhills calling them "uninhabitable and foreboding."

Foreboding? Never! Peaceful and private, yes.

The green of the towering Sandhills was broken with splashes of golden brown; little bluestem of the season past resembling daubs from an artist's brush. The signs in the moist sand told me that a deer had stopped for water and a badger and coyote had passed through.

I looked with sadness at willow trees that had flanked the creek.

Beavers had leveled all of them during the winter. New growth, however, had started on those trunks that weren't completely severed. The indestructible willow, I mused, knowing that a branch thrust into moist sand will take root and grow.

With my boot, I kicked loose the hardened cowchips on the prairie so that smothered grass could know the sun, watched a toad emerge from the sand and admired the first wildflowers.

Sweetpeas, locoweed and narrow-leaf penstemen mottle the green carpet with blue. The first two plants have a toxic effect when eaten by cattle but the latter was used as a medicine by the Indians.

Mimicking the gold of the sun were colonies of gumweed, groundsel and gromwell. Clumps of snowy pussytoes stood like a regiment of soldiers at inspection. The blossoms on the five-inch stems resemble the soft and fuzzy toes of a kitten.

The flowers that now dot the prairie are only teasers of some 450 varieties that will bloom until winter sounds a retreat to underground haunts.

G.R. and I traveled to many locations on the fence ritual but never saw another person or signs that they existed. We had been gone five hours but it seemed more like only one.

We had not taken a lunch, but I felt no hunger. Perhaps, because I had feasted on the unique beauty which visits the Sandhills each spring.

"Beauty seen is never lost, God's colors all are fast." Tennyson wrote it and I believe it. I'm so humble with gratitude that there is so much unspoiled natural beauty in our little chunk of this good earth ... our little piece of the virgin prairie that is the Sandhills.

'TENDERFOOT' RIDER ENCOUNTERS SIGHTS
- June 23, 1983 -

Myki and I talked G.R. into going on a trail ride Sunday for Father's Day. Vinc Morabito organized the ride, followed by a "steak-out" at his ranch south of Kilgore to benefit the cancer fund.

I hadn't been on a horse for some time...knee problems, mostly stiff. Myki loaned me Fibber, her 4-year-old mare that she says is "all heart." Only a short year ago, however, a local cowboy had said Fibber bucked every morning, just as a matter of course.

The ride began at the Niobrara River and wound through McCann Canyon, site of a ranch on the open range during the 1870s. I was excited about retracing historic trails.

We trailered our horses about 65 miles to the canyon, where about 30 people were saddling their horses. They ranged in age from three young Galloway

138

boys, who rode bareback, to Herman Lind, 85, from Tilden. My confidence grew. If Mr. Lind could ride all day, so could I.

Fibber spooked when I swung into the saddle. "She thinks you're nervous," Myki said.

"Smart horse," I gasped.

We trailed up the densely wooded canyon, along winding McCann Creek, which the horses crossed on banks sometimes gentle and some times very steep.

Bud Pavlik owns a portion of the land that we crossed and was an interesting guide. We stopped at a lone fence post and he told us the great great-grandmother of the Galloway youngsters was buried there, but later moved to a cemetery. Farther on we viewed a stone foundation hidden in brush. Steep canyon walls rose on either side and disappeared skyward into the pines.

I tried to reconstruct those days of the open range. The area was named for D.J. "Sugar" McCann, early rancher whose nickname was said to result from the theft of sugar ... 80 barrels. Moonshine, maybe?

In 1879, James Williamson, a McCann cowboy, was riding a bronc to gather stray horses when he was killed by Indians. The hand-carved wooden marker has been replaced with a tombstone and the original preserved at Fort Robinson.

I could see why the secluded canyon was attractive to Indians...and to the bandits who hid out in caves. Our horses climbed to the outer rim and we examined a cliff over which Indians were said to stampede the buffalo on a hunt.

Early history also notes that McCann cattle drifted over the cliff edge and perished during the Blizzard of 1888.

We saw the depressions of old dugouts along the canyon walls, where some 20 families lived and made brooms from the broom corn which settlers grew. Wilhelm Anderson and a Mr. Gunderson had a steam sawmill along the river near the Anderson Bridge. Four yoke of oxen were used to transport the boiler from the railroad. The first bridge was built in 1886 and the present one in 1913.

After riding about six miles, we left the canyon for a broad plateau overlooking the Rosebud Indian Reservation seven miles to the north. The highlight of the entire trip was there, an old fort standing proud above the plains. Measuring about 10 by 12 feet, it was built solid from canyon stone except for a door and gun portholes and it remained untouched by vandals. The roof was long gone, but many of the supporting logs remained. Wild roses grew along the inside where stones made steps up the wall.

The fort must be almost a century old, or older, because the Indian scares ceased after the 1890 Battle of Wounded Knee.

The return ride was filled with mental images...of hardy settlers, cattle and cowboys...of Indians wearing war paint and feathers riding those hills covered with yellow and lavender flowers, while puff-ball clouds rimmed the horizon. We had, indeed, retraced historic trails.

We rode into camp and I asked someone to hold my horse while I dismounted. My aching knees refused to bear my weight and I crumpled onto the ground.

I watched Mr. Lind. He swung from his horse and unsaddled, apparently rejuvenated by the ride.

I chuckled while I sat on the ground and rubbed my knees. What else could a "tenderfoot" do'?

S ⟀ ⟀ Y ⟀

COWBOYS ARE HEROES FOR KEEPING MUM
- October 25, 1984 -

There has come to be a hero in my life; in fact, several of them. Not celebrities like Robert Redford or Tom Selleck, but "real" heroes. Perhaps, instead of getting the cart before the horse, I'd better start at the beginning.

Last week, I made detailed plans to intercept an 80-mile cattle drive at several locations. Cliff Andre and his Doubletree cowboys were moving 500 cows, some with calves, from the Arabia Ranch to a ranch west of Merriman.

I would meet them on horseback as they crossed the Snake River and then ride with them for a time. I would photograph them from the air while they trailed up Steer Creek. Then I hoped to be in position on the crest of a canyon when the herd forded the Niobrara River south of Eli.

The cattle were headed out on Thursday, caught in a storm, and faced the forecast of a second storm that would catch them in open country. Andre had to change his plans. After the second day, trucks would transport the herd. I had to be satisfied with Friday only.

G.R. loaned me his four-wheel drive pickup. "You might need it," he said. "Those meadows east of 83 can be pretty wet."

140

It was 30 miles to where the herd spent the night, but I was there shortly after dawn.

Now, there is one thing I know when men are moving cattle. You stay out of their way! In doing that, and keeping at a vantage point for photos, I paid little attention to where I was driving. That is until the wheels started sinking into the mud of the soft meadow. Water was hidden in the tall grass. There was no hope of backtracking. Aim for the ridges and full speed ahead!

I seem to have a knack for seeing parts of my beloved Sandhills that I have not seen before. But some of those places do not treat an interloper kindly.

There was no trail. I opened several gates and angled northwest. Finally, I was back following the herd that could cross wetland where I could not.

Then we came to choppy hills. There too, they had little trouble. Blowouts or lob-lollies filled with water turned me back time and again.

Finally, there was a road ... a trail. I was safe now. I'd pass the herd and meet them at the highway.

I felt safe on the trail, but my peace of mind was short-lived. Wheels dropped through a bog in a wet gulley. I was hopelessly stuck and more than a little embarrassed. I hadn't been stuck in 20 years.

The herd was a half a mile behind, the highway more than a mile ahead and the closest ranch was God knows where. It would be hours before the riders could send help, and injured pride made durned poor company.

Cattle started passing the pickup. Young John Andre stopped his horse by the open window.

"Stuck, huh?"

"Yup."

"Did you know that you took a picture of my last bull ride during High School Rodeo?"

I had found a friend.

"We'll get you out," he said while hailing two other riders.

I was skeptical. But the three young men dismounted, tightened the cinches and loosened their lariats. Each of them attached the loop to the trailer ball of the hitch and wrapped a dally around the saddlehorn.

Now understand, saddle horses are not draft horses. It is not their duty to pull. But pull they did and the pickup was free within seconds.

Can you understand why I say that John Andre, Marty Blocker and Chuck Oliver are my heroes? But so are their three good ranch horses.

Best of all, not one of those nice young men made any snide reference to women drivers. Heroes they are!

S ℛ ♄ Y \⊢/

CHERRY COUNTY WOES NOT SUDDEN
- November 29, 1984 -

S ome people still don't understand. Recently I was asked this question: "Why did the economic climate in Cherry County deteriorate so fast? What happened during the past three years?"

The question was in reference to the recent failure of three financial institutions reportedly caused from loan losses and a three-year decline of land prices.

I'm no expert, but let me tell you the situation has been fermenting for the past 10 years, according to information in my files, which I obtained from county officials. Cherry County comprises only a small portion of the American scene, but it's where my familiarity lies, specifically in the cattle industry.

These are a few reminders of what occurred in Cherry County during the past 10 years:

1974: The price of calves dropped from 80 cents to 30-40 cents a pound and stayed there for four years. Precipitation totaled 10.57 inches. It was the first of the three driest years in succession ever recorded in Cherry County including the drought of the 1930s.

County officials estimated loss to the cattle industry in depressed prices, and loss of hay and grain production to drought totaled $47.6 million. Many producers thought land development was essential for survival.

1975: A March 27-28 blizzard caused an estimated death loss that included 15,500 newborn calves and 800 cows. Death loss and loss to production was estimated at $3.5 million. Annual precipitation, 11.2 inches.

1976: Precipitation 11.21 inches. A 50 percent drop in yield of wild hay and summer range was estimated at a loss of $14 million. Lower crop yield, $3.9 million loss.

1977: Cattle numbers down, prices depressed, but precipitation totaled 32.68 inches. Speculators moved in cattle from out-of-state.

1978: Fed steer prices rose to 52 cents a pound. (The 1975 average price of 45 cents a pound changed to 39 cents in '76 and 40 cents in '77.)

1979: Much of the county was declared a winter disaster area in January. The death loss, livestock lost to production, and 50 percent higher feed, fuel and repair bills was an estimated $9.4 million loss to the cattle industry.

During a six-year period those items alone caused an estimated $79.6 million loss to rural residents, less than half the 6,757 county population.

During those same years, the beef industry nationwide was plagued by negative effects from the president's price freeze, a beef boycott, tripled fuel prices and the grain embargo. Inflation pushed land prices to false values that increased borrowing power and some producers went deeper into debt just to remain in business.

In 1979 lightweight calves brought up to $1 a pound on an unstable market; small compensation for five years of prices below production cost.

May 15, 1979, headlines in the National Enquirer read, "Cattlemen Roping in $Billions in the Big Beef Rip-off." The story alleged that cattlemen had systematically created a beef shortage.

Choice grain-fed steer prices of 70 cents a pound in April dropped to 57 cents a pound by June 6.

Lenders traded "horses" in midstream. They abandoned financial statements for cash-flow projections and interest rates doubled. While trying to keep producers in business, some lenders found themselves headed for trouble.

Profit on a stable market predicted for the 1980s didn't materialize, but inflation continued.

One banker recently explained the cattle business this way. He said if everything was comparatively priced at $1 in 1980, beef today would cost $1 and most other items would cost $3.15.

The current situation was not created just within the past three years.

But I have a firm faith in our heritage. The so-called "uninhabitable" Sandhills were settled a century ago by strong-willed people who failed to buckle under adversity.

S　R　ठ̄　Y　ᗉ

BANKER JOKES RELIEVE RANCH STRESS
- December 6, 1984 -

Time spent with one certain rancher friend is always an uplifting experience for me. He seems capable of maintaining a droll, dry sense of humor even when he's experiencing stress.

I'll try to pass along portions of a conversation I recently had with him, but I think I'll preserve his privacy by calling him "Jed."

While we were visiting, Jed complained that his boots were so tight he hardly could stand to wear them. I suggested that he have them stretched.

"Are you kidding me!" he said, while feigning indignation.

"Every morning, I squeeze my feet into those tight boots and go round up the cattle that busted through the fence during the night. Then I hobble along and fix the fence that those cattle tore down.

During the day, those boots squeezing my feet help me forget that my banker holds a mortgage on most of those cattle ... and probably even the barbed wire and staples.

At the end of the day, I spend the evening listening to my wife nag me about quitting the business and moving to the city.

Finally, it's bedtime and I can pull off those durned tight boots. Why, that's the only real pleasure I get all day!"

The twinkle brightened in Jed's eyes and I knew it was story-telling time. He was going to vent some of his frustrations.

"My banker drove out to see me yesterday," he said. "I was still fixing fence, so I just leaned on a post while we talked.

He reminded me that my notes would be due in a couple of months, and he told me he wanted me to sell my calves immediately. I said I wanted to feed them to a heavier weight. Then he told me I ought to sell some cows, but I said I wanted to wait until the market improved."

Jed said that he knew his own cattle, and that they would bring more money only when they were in the right condition. The more money they brought, the more he could pay on his note. He rejected all of the suggestions until his banker became angry and said, "There's very little separating you from a fool, Jed!"

"I didn't say it very loud," Jed said, but I answered: "Only the fence, sir. Only the fence."

I could tell from his broad grin that Jed was just getting warmed up on the subject of his banker. Remember that I told you in the beginning that Jed had a unique way of handling stress.

"The minute I borrowed money from that young city-raised man, he thinks he should tell me how to run my business," Jed continued. "But I remember one time when he wanted some on-the-ranch experience. He worked for me one spring before he became a banker.

I had to go to town one day, so I left him with a list of things to do. One was to file the horn buds off a small calf. I told him to be careful and not file too deep.

When I got home I asked about the calf, but the young man said it had died.

'You didn't file the horn too deep?' I asked him."

Jed said the young man told him he didn't know that the calf "was dead when he took its head out of the vise."

Now, I have no idea if part or any of those stories were really true. Perhaps they were merely stress-relieving jokes. Perhaps the stories are merely a result of the times.

You know how it is. We've had farmer-rancher jokes for years. We have an increase of political jokes when there is an election. We have ethnic jokes. We have celebrity jokes.

Perhaps 1985 will be the year of banker jokes. It just might be the best way to handle difficult economic times.

Raymond Hitcock (whoever he is) perhaps said it best: "A man isn't poor if he can laugh."

S 𝑅 ☿ Y ⊢

'YOU CAN'T MISS IT, WE'RE EASY TO FIND'
- January 17, 1985 -

Recently Lloyd Synovec asked me, "Just exactly where do you live?" North, I said. "North of Tryon?" I said yes, even north of Mullen. "Sometime why don't you describe to your readers just exactly where you live," he said.

Lloyd's job is beyond my comprehension because he is a computer expert at the gigantic Gerald Gentleman Plant near Sutherland. Our environment here in the heart of the hills is far less complicated in January 1985.

We're easy to find Lloyd, but you'll need a pencil and ruler. Open the Atlas to the map of the United States.

Draw a straight line between Salt Lake City and Lansing, Michigan. Then draw a line between Fort Worth, Texas, and Moose Jaw, Saskatchewan, Canada.

Right about where the lines intersect is the location of our buildings. If you fly by DC-10 from New York to Salt Lake City you will pass directly overhead. Ask the pilot to show you.

I direct you in this way because many people think we live at the end of the earth, out in the boonies, or in no man's land. I contend that we live in the very heart of the universe.

If you really want finer details turn to the Nebraska map and I'll give you more explicit directions.

I've charted the course for Sandhill cranes flying due north from North Platte to Murdo, SD. They pass three miles to the east. But crows flying from Merritt Dam pass directly overhead on their way to Halsey. Merritt is six miles by air — 12 miles on foot. Steep hills, you know.

But if you travel by vehicle there are several easier ways. Turn off U.S. 83 at Brownlee and take the narrow oil strip for 30 some miles north northwest.

But I don't suggest that. Potholes.

Or start from downtown Mullen and follow Nebraska 97 for 40 miles, then turn east five miles.

I don't suggest that. Thirteen miles of one-way oil strip and five miles of sand.

You might drive south from Nenzel on Nebraska 97, cross Merritt Dam and turn south on the road to Mullen, turning east on the graded road.

I don't suggest that. About 11 miles of "washboard gravel" south of Nenzel and the five miles of sand.

Or you might leave West Valentine on Nebraska 97, pass Merritt Dam, turn towards Mullen and find our turnoff.

I don't suggest that. You'll get lost.

The scenic route originates about 17 miles south of Valentine or 56 miles north of Thedford. Natives describe the distance as a "six-pack west and two cans south."

Head west from U.S. 83 on 16B. You'll pass one lake on the south side of the road and two lakes on the north side.

The highway turns south at a grove of trees and you'll see a large herd of cattle to the west unless the rancher moves them to his east pasture.

A "fair piece" down the highway from Hackberry Lake slow down where a windmill stands in the middle of a frozen lake. Tons of dirt were hauled in to raise the roadway above water. That stretch is narrow and rough and the rest of the highway has been undermined with muskrat runs.

Keep on driving down the road, but from there I lose my direction. When you come to an auto-gate on the right-hand side that went underwater and froze over there will be a windmill and tank that went underwater on the other side. Know that you're getting close.

Our sign blew down two years ago, but no worry. When the blacktop ends keep going just a teeny ways. Turn in where the barbed wire gate is hooked back on the fence.

You can't miss it. We're easy to find.

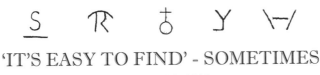

'IT'S EASY TO FIND' - SOMETIMES

- February 28, 1985 -

A few weeks ago I explained how Sandhillers gave directions that usually ends with, "It's easy to find. You can't miss it." You might be delighted to know that I got caught in my own trap. I followed a fellow rancher's directions and I failed the test.

Okay. It served me right.

I have the perfect excuse. I didn't listen closely, and I didn't ask the right questions.

When I called this man, it was for directions to catch a cattle drive enroute from one ranch to the other. You know, out in open ranch country where it's five miles between neighbors.

He told me to head west down the mail road and I couldn't miss them. He did say that he'd have to cross the creek to avoid mixing his cattle with other herds.

No sweat. He would be easy to find although I had not traveled that area more than a couple times and that was years ago.

I followed the mail trail west. When it angled south, I left the road and continued west over frozen cowchips, soapweed and steep sidehills. No cattle. I backtracked and headed south a couple of miles.

No cattle. I had missed them, but where?

I stopped to review the situation. Because I knew that cattle normally occupied the feedgrounds to the north, I was certain the man's cattle would be driven down the south side of the creek.

I studied a large herd far to the north. Instead of remaining scattered across the feedground, they had moved to the west fence. Aha! Being the super sleuth that I am, I knew this had to be the herd. Those cows had been recently moved there and they wanted to return home.

There was no excuse for the extra miles I'd traveled. I simply hadn't asked enough questions and crossed the creek at the right time.

Perhaps, that is why it's a challenge to follow directions from Sandhillers. It's a test of how attentive we are.

There are a jillion examples of how people give directions. I wish I could collect them all and record them for posterity.

Frank Lammers, longtime employee of the Ogallala Livestock Market, shared one with me that a traveling salesman liked to tell on himself.

The traveling man told Lammer that he carried a bottle, and if the trip and the day got too long, he might over-indulge.

On one such time he became lost and pulled into a farmyard to ask directions. He admitted that he was a bit inebriated.

The woman was very tolerant. "Drive past the corrals until you come to a "Y" in the road. Take either fork. It really doesn't matter which one because you're lost anyway."

Directions of "It's easy to find" also stirred memories for Irene Beaman of Lewellen that she shared in a letter.

She remembered an old rancher who lived far north of Oshkosh. He said the way to his ranch was: "Keep goin' 'til ya think you're in hell, then go 10 miles further!" I love it!

Most ranchers have their own unique way of expressing themselves that should be recorded. For example one rancher always describes dudes wearing a cowboy hat as, "All hat and no cow."

Yet another man had this way of describing the vast Sandhills: "It's so durn far across that no-man's land that even the jackrabbits carry a lunch."

If you have one of these little gems to share, I would love it.

S ‡R ‡ Y ‡

LITTLE CREEK HAS BIG IMPACT
- March 14, 1985 -

G.R. and I drove west on an errand during those hours before the dawn when most of the world remains sleeping. Hundreds of Canada geese rose in a restless cloud against the sky. Wild ducks scolded us for intruding before they also took wing.

Short days ago, there was no lake in the spot where they rested. It was meadowland; wet and soggy, but some distance from the creek. That was yesterday. Today, water has flooded vast areas of the lowlands.

The Gordon Creek is a mysterious body of water, so innocent that it's not even charted on many county maps. It begins from swamp ground near the very southwest edge of the county.

Perhaps long ago it didn't exist. Then spring water trickling out from the sand fed the creek, swelling and pushing the volume of water until it followed the course of least resistance.

It charted its own course down a vast east-west valley through the heart of the county. Then, like the Snake River and the Schlagel Creek, it veered north to empty into the Niobrara.

Through the years it has changed its course at different times.

In some places, the creek bottom has remained shallow and nearly undisturbed. In other places, the water angrily cut through the soil leaving deep pockets for prime swimming holes during the early summer.

On its journey through our north pasture, it has left steep sandy banks in its path. Years after the early Indian had disappeared from the prairie, strong winds uncovered vast numbers of arrowheads along its banks.

Walking the creek to gather the flint points was a favorite pastime for G.R. when he was a boy.

During the summer, the flow trickles to a standstill in that pasture and water goes underground for several miles before emerging again. It is a mysterious circumstance.

Early homesteaders, of course, staked their claims along the creeks. Tree groves are all that remain to immortalize the names of those early settlers: An ash grove in that northern pasture is still called the "McCoy Grove." Other trees mark the former Latta, House, and Rathenberg places.

Captain Davey Piercy, a Civil War veteran, was the first family man to homestead in our immediate area in 1883. Billy Piercy, his son, built a two-story house on the same ground in later years.

Somehow, Billy changed the course of the Gordon Creek so it flowed though the ranchstead.

It is the area surrounding those buildings that is now a lake where the geese were resting. I mean a lake that extends from the former creek bed across the vast meadow to the newer channel. Cattle there are left with only small islands on which to avoid the water.

The situation is the same on lowland meadows all along the Gordon. In some places, water surrounds stackyards that weren't emptied during cold weather. Frost has left the ground so meadowland is no longer firm enough to bear the weight of tractors.

In some places, those meadows have gone completely under water as the Gordon Creek pushed outward from its shallow banks.

What appears to be an unobtrusive little stream, not worthy of note on a map, can certainly exert a powerful influence given the right conditions.

ODE TO A BETTER NEW YEAR
- December 19, 1985 -

A few days ago at the ole water hole I heard an old man expounding.
He told of hard times, of nickels and dimes
With indifference that's downright astounding.
He bragged about running his outfit
On a worn-out old boot strap or less
Then made a disclosure of a heartless foreclosure
That left friends of ours in a mess.
"This farm credit crisis is foolish,
You durn fools all shoulda known better
It took a real dummy to borrow that money,"
(This man was a real goat-getter.)
I didn't reply, I just grit my teeth
Mostly because of his age
As he sipped on his beer, he was surely sincere

He just measured with an outdated gauge.
As long as we've been in this ranching
We took bad times when they came
This year might not pay, but if you can stay
In a few years you're back in the game.
But this year the business got tougher
Poor prices, low prices, bad weather
The checkbook is flat and boots full of holes
'Cause they're now made from triple-split leather.
Our notes we extended, got out on a limb
Shouldn't stub your toe more than once
But a summer gone dry and a real estate buy
Can change you from smart to a dunce.
We're guilty as heck like all that we know
Thinking good times would last past forever
Buy good bulls and cows and more real estate
'Cause our banker advised that was clever.
Well, I told that old man, our side of the tale
'Cause stories all have two sides
Our credit allowed, we bought "fat" Carter cow
Now we're paying with thin Reagan "hides."
But we'll not be defeated, we'll never give in
Especially with holidays near.
Keep faith my dear friends and may you know peace
And please Lord, a less tense New Year.

STRENGTH BRINGS A BRIGHTER END TO '86
- January 2, 1986 -

We said goodbye to "Old Man 1985" with mixed emotions. He was such a pathetic looking sight, that we had to feel sorry for him. Never before had we seen the old man of year's end so bruised and battered, so tattered and torn or so bandaged and bleeding.

Thank God that the poor old soul has been laid to rest. At least he is at peace.

The poor little New Year's child inherited a legacy that I fear he will, at best, find traumatic. The bruised and battered farmers and ranchers of the Midwest will be constant reminders of a year that was tough going. Then too, ag-related businesses have grown tattered around the edges from the domino effect.

Time and again we've heard the phrase, 'When the going gets tough, the tough get going, and we have seen examples of that in agriculture.

Very few extremely stressful situations in our area during 1985 made the news, but that doesn't mean they didn't exist.

We know of too many younger operators who experienced the misfortune of seeing their bank close. The lack of a new credit put them out of business.

We know of cattlemen who were forced to sell their herd because a drought cut their feed supply into half. When the brutal, early winter depleted that hay supply by December, some could not get financed in time to buy feed for their animals.

We've seen bred cows sell at auction for $375 that were purchased for $650 only two short years ago. It simply is not fair.

Animals cannot be put back on the shelf to wait for an adequate feed supply or a better market. When the owner reaches a point of no return, he is forced to sell. Then he feels guilty and takes it as a personal inadequacy that he couldn't continue to provide for his animals.

We know of a few instances when such men suffered indignities at the hands of callous officials who were in command. Thank goodness those instances were rather rare.

The reason we've mentioned the above is to explain the basis of a deep pride we feel for the people in our area who have come under dreadful stress. They've confronted their problem with quiet dignity, not violence or destructive protest. Some have drawn upon a strength they didn't know they had to maintain that dignity.

That doesn't say that they weren't torn apart inside from the frustration of helplessness. That doesn't say that unshed tears didn't choke away any attempt at speech. That doesn't mean that despair wasn't voiced within the privacy of their homes.

This does not present the situation of all who are in agriculture. This is just to say that so far, there has been a tremendous strength shown by a lot of people during stressful situations. We are extremely proud of those people.

Our few New Year's resolutions are very simple, but we'd like to share: Make a concerted effort to find the positive side of every situation; greet all whom we meet with a smile and a hello; deal logically with the real problems, and try not to manufacture imaginary ones; walk barefoot through the green grass of spring and pick more daisies; let the soothing music of singing streams calm our nerves; and amid confusion to seek calmness in the everlasting hills.

Most of all we intend to voice the pride we feel...pride in the strength of our people who chose agriculture as their lifetime business. It is that strength that will persevere and bring a brighter ending to 1986.

$$\underline{S} \quad \mathcal{R} \quad \overset{+}{\underset{\circ}{\delta}} \quad Y \quad \backslash\!\!\!-\!\!/$$

RANCH LIVING – HIS AND HERS STYLE
- May 29, 1986 -

I have a postscript about ranching being called "a way of life." There are definitely two sides to the story. And because Father's Day will be observed soon, I intend to show how the man of the house might reflect considerable influence on that "way of life."

Last week, I made two trips to Halsey as one of the instructors for a week long program concerning the Sandhills that was sponsored by Kearney State College. G.R. was home, so he cooked for the hired hand.

"Not to worry," he said.

Vacations are as scarce as hen's teeth around our place, so I've learned to take one in any manner or form.

The trips between the ranch and Halsey were my vacations. Early morning is prime time on the prairie. While some creatures of the wild are nocturnal, others are just beginning to stir, and the world of Nature is most visible during those post-dawn hours.

I left the ranch at 6:30 a.m. Ponds dot the prairie and everywhere there were species of ducks gently clacking about the brilliant pink of the eastern skies.

I stopped and let Canada geese lead their clutch of goslings across the trail toward a rain-swollen pond. (On my return the following night, the geese were eating tender blades of grass along the northern shore.)

Hundreds of Hereford cows and their babies were lying along the eastern slope of a sandhill. If there is a more beautiful sight than red and white Herefords against emerald green grass, it's when the scene is tinged with a rosey glow of early morning light.

153

And everywhere there were wildflowers: deep blue narrow-leaved pentsomen, prairie rose, puccoon, wild phlox and spiderwort.

I found it difficult to concentrate on driving while enjoying my "way of life."

G.R. had to be gone overnight, so I was to do HIS chores. This morning, during heavy rainfall, I experienced the "other way of life;" the business called country living.

I fed the dogs and fed and watered the chickens. Then I drove over the hill to grain Freddy Rabbit, G.R.'s saddle horse. There in the corral is what I call a "reluctant" mother, a snorty cow that refuses to claim her calf.

We have to drive her into the barn and snare her in a head-catch so she'll let the calf suck. Otherwise, she kicks the slats out of it.

I opened all the gates in the barn in readiness. Whip in hand, I went to drive her in, but she took one look at me, lowered her head and pawed the ground. Bravery isn't my best suit.

Remembering that G.R. said, "Don't wear that red jacket," I went to the barn and removed it. That ole cow apparently liked me better soaking wet, cold and jacketless.

I fed her cake, but she didn't produce enough milk to satisfy the calf. So, back to the house to fill a bottle with milk replacer.

I spent an hour checking the calves for scours and found three sick ones, but I couldn't catch them.

About noon, Tim Colvin stopped his work to help me. I drove the pickup and he jumped out to swing a lariat at the appropriate moment. While he held the sick calf, I brought the pills and the penicillin.

It's still raining, but the day's routine must be repeated before sundown.

Egads, I wish G.R. would get home. His presence would certainly improve the quality of this "way of life" that we call country living.

SQUISHING AROUND THE SANDHILLS

- June 12, 1986 -

Water is said to be one of our nation's most priceless natural resources. If those of us who live in the Sandhills area, where the economy has been depressed far too long, could market our water, we'd have no problem right now.

Since Sunday night, rainfall has ranged from an inch in some areas to more than five inches in others.

The heaviest rainfall occurred in an area south of Cody, a drought area last year where the hay crop dropped to half the normal amount. Rainfall up to six inches was recorded there.

I've heard ranchers say, "This will make our hay crop." I hope so.

Moisture this spring has been above normal. Wild flowers are blooming in clusters instead of single blossoms. Cool season grasses are vigorous, bright and tall. To view the Sandhills now is to view the beauty of spring in all its glory.

Here, on our portion of the Gordon Creek Valley, the ground is soggy. Our sandy road is now a lake, and a portion of our lawn went under water again.

Corrals that have always remained dry are now a quagmire. A calving lot is useless for little more than ducks. The ground apparently has reached a saturation point.

Water is up to the door of the chicken house. They have to walk a plank to get to their feed.

Some old timers predicted long ago that Merritt Reservoir might eventually affect our ground water ... would cause new lakes to form and turn meadows into swamps during wet seasons.

I wonder if that's the answer.

"Cool Hand" G.R.'s vocabulary recently has been limited: "I'm so !&*! ! tired of wearing these &$*** overshoes!"

Monday afternoon, when it quit raining, he left his muddy overshoes outside on the doorstep. By the next morning, another inch of rain had fallen ... according to the overshoe rain gauge.

Today he's griping about his wet boots. So am I.

G.R. sent me on an errand out behind the south bunkhouse. The ground is so wet the grass has gone unmowed. I felt as though I needed a machete to blaze a trail through the wild oats.

All at once, I dropped into water over one boot top. I had stepped on the rusty top of a submerged barrel. What the heck is this?

"Nothing to get excited about, just an old skunk trap," G.R. explained as I returned to the house with water squishing from holes in the left boot.

He thought it was funny. "We'd have it made if we could find a way to market this water or quit cattle and raise tanks, guns and bombs," he said. "Seems like there's always a market for those things in countries where there's a shortage of food."

I'm not certain, but perhaps he found a way to start a similar project. When he came back from fixing a windmill, the air was blue around his sweat-stained hat. "Dropped a brand new pipe wrench down the *%$!& well ... and do you know how much they cost?!"

"Who knows," I said with a smirk. "Maybe that little pipe wrench will grow into a tree and we can sell the baby wrenches to the government for $970 apiece. You saw that the 'seed' will be 'well' watered."

(I didn't stick around to hear his reply.)

S ᴦ ᵇ Y ⊢/

BROWNLEE RICH IN HISTORY
- July 17, 1986 -

The little village of Brownlee, located halfway between Thedford and Valentine, will celebrate its centennial August 10. I'll remember the 1980s as the decade of the centennials and I think it's marvelous. Celebrating has been acknowledgment of our Nebraska heritage, young though it may be compared to that of our nation.

In preparing for centennial celebrations, memories have been tapped and research has unearthed all sorts of marvelous stories and long-forgotten situations. I've collected community books published from most of the Sandhill area and I treasure them. It's an enjoyable way to learn of area history.

Unlike most inland, century-old towns, Brownlee still claims descendants of its originators. There are fifth-generation Lees ranching in Cherry County.

The town was actually named for Nancy Brownlee Martin, the grandmother of J.R. Lee, who with part of his family, emigrated from Ireland in

1850. Two brothers, Edward A. and John R., settled in the area that became the vast Brownlee community.

Prior to that, J.R. hunted with the Ponca Indians and fought with the Pawnee against the Sioux. In 1886, he built a store with living quarters above on the north banks of the North Loup River, where he sold pioneer needs from food to machinery.

Then his application for a post office was approved in 1887, his cousin was postmaster, and it carried their grandmother's maiden name. A school district was organized in 1888 with J.R.'s sister, Mamie Lee, as teacher. It was built of sod and called, "Mud Institute."

If memory serves me correctly, the current population sign reads "17 more or less." But at one time, Brownlee was an important and busy little town with three stores, a blacksmith shop, livery barn, drugstore, hotel, bank, church and community hall.

It also was a stage stop between North Platte and Valentine. People traded there from miles around and, during one year, Lee sold more mowing machines than any of his competitors throughout the state.

Celebrations drew hundreds, especially the Fourth of July, when circling the wagons was preserved as a tradition of the West. Wagons formed a circle for the baseball diamond and another for the rodeo. Other entertainment included horse and foot races, dancing, singing and games for the entire family.

Important to Brownlee was the black community of DeWitty, established to the west by 1904. The industrious and musical blacks also had a baseball team that seldom was defeated between 1910 and 1920.

A favorite story originated during Prohibition, when a state liquor agent heard an elderly black man was producing and selling illegal brew. The agent found a witness and bought four bottles at 50 cents apiece. The old man sadly told the judge that he did it in order to eat and was fined only $1 and costs. But the judge knew he'd been had when Sam Hood cheerfully pulled out a fat roll of bills to pay the fine.

Don McGuire tells me that the celebration will be a "good old-fashioned get together like the old days, but without a rodeo." The Lees will be well represented because many of Edward and J.R.'s descendants continue to ranch in the community.

J.R.'s grandson, Marion, was born in a soddie in 1902 and you can bet he'll be there. Then I understand that Marion's son and his wife, John and Kay Lee, are a couple of the prime planners for the celebration.

What could be more fitting?

STORY

PAINFUL REACTION OF SANDBUR ALLERGY
- September 11, 1986 -

G.R. may unknowingly start a new fashion trend, if he's not careful. If he doesn't start wearing his pantlegs inside his boot tops, I'm afraid he soon will be wearing denim pedal pushers. The bone of contention at our house right now is sandburs. Sandburs travel indoors on the bottom of his jeans and scatter like an Army regiment, armed and ready for attack.

I'm usually in my stocking feet around the house, but the bottoms of my feet seem to have a knack for finding all loose sandburs. The hardy stickers created a new type of a dance, if you know what I mean: step, one two, ouch; step three four, ouch. Then I sit out the rest of the dance while pulling stickers.

In self defense, I've started eliminating the burr-laminated bottom seam of G.R 's Wranglers with scissors. If I don't, they spread to all else in the washing machine and then we pick hidden individual spines from unexpected places.

G.R., poor soul, can't understand why his pants keep getting shorter. "The easier to stuff them into your boots during sandbur season," I say. "If this practice keeps up, your pants soon will be at your knees and you'll set a new trend for the teenage set."

When I first saw young men in high-topped tennies with shoestrings dragging, I thought the poor dears were underachievers who had never learned to tie a knot.

Then a neighbor told me that was the new teen fashion trend...a trend that wasn't at all popular with him in the hayfield. "The kid kept walking out of his shoes and spent most of his time putting them back on. But he never would tie them."

The field must have been void of sandburs ... and/or cactus. Sandburs this year caused the design of a new cut for long-haired dogs. A friend told me that she spent most of her time plucking sandburs from the coats of two miniature Schnauzers. In self defense, she instructed the groomer to trim the long hair short, even the muzzle, and called it the sandbur cut.

Makes sense to me. I imagine that's how some standard trims for various breeds came to be. I wonder how an English sheepdog would look in a burr-cut.

158

Burrs and pollen try hard to drain enjoyment from the wonderful autumn season. Both grow in overwhelming surplus.

Speaking of pollen, I appreciate being challenged by Dirlene Wheeler, whom I'm told is an avid student of native plants. Last week, I said, "ragweed and goldenrod are both spelled sneeze."

"Goldenrod pollen is waxy ... it is not a hayfever culprit," she wrote.

I mispoke Dirlene. Goldenrod is high on the allergy list for many people, my daughter included, but it may not cause hay fever. I checked with a range specialist who confirmed this and who is highly allergic to the plant. "It produces an incredible amount of pollen," he said.

Tom Dill, extension agent, said that pollen from dozens of plants, including trees, cause allergic reactions. Our daughter is allergic to pollens, barn dust, wheat and other things, but goldenrod is high on her list.

Ragweed pollen is, indeed, the barbed wire of the pollen set and nearly impossible to escape, because it will drift hundreds of miles on the air currents.

Some air conditioners have become a breeding ground for some mold spores, which bring allergy suffering indoors. Myself, I'm only allergic to indoor sandburs.

APPRECIATION OF OUR FASCINATING PRAIRIE
- September 18, 1986 -

That the mysterious prairie constantly reveals its secrets to the curious has been my longtime philosophy. Quite appropriately, I thought during this prairie appreciation week, I viewed for the first time some longtime residents of the prairie.

Fog lay heavily on the ground when I found the two wild flowers quite by accident in a pasture that was mowed this year for the first time within my memory. Both are small species growing perhaps 4-6 inches tall and both were easily identified when I relied upon my book, "Nebraska Wild Flowers," compiled by Robert C. Lommasson.

Nodding ladies' tresses was the most unusual and resembled small white flags from a distance. I learned that the fragrant blossom is a member of the orchid family; the tiny white flowers winding down the stiff, upright stem, in from 3-4 spirals.

The book says, however, that they are found in Pierce County of northeastern Nebraska. Somehow, these dainty beauties made their way to the prairie of Cherry County. I counted about 50, but quite possibly there were more.

Growing among the native grasses also was the slender gerardia, a tiny, delicate plant with fuschia, cup-shaped blossoms. The tip of my little finger was about the size of the blossom.

Referring to my book again, it said the flowers are produced in late summer and each lasts but one day.

I've collected books and brochures to build my reference library on Nebraska vegetation. I've also taken slides of many flowers and was honored to have my photos of the rare Penstomen haydeni included in Claude Barr's hardbound book, "Jewels of the Plains."

The more I study and the more I learn, it seems the more I appreciate the prairie, its grasses, flora, fauna, and its moods. But isn't that true of most things?

At one time, I looked at grass as something cows ate and men harvested; something I fertilized, watered and mowed. It grew during the summer and went dormant in winter. That was it.

So, during this week of prairie recognition, it seems appropriate that I also recognize the people who tutored me about those earthbound residents of the prairie and taught me to stop, to look and to observe.

First in line were a group of neighborhood youngsters who wished to enroll in the 4-H range management project. They elected me as their project leader. "What do I know?" I asked and they replied, "Learn along with us."

So we studied the manual. Then extension agent, Harry Stokely, and his assistant, Keith Redinbaugh, agreed to help us identify an incredible number of plants. At first, our brains bogged down with the wealth of information. The men shook their heads and I'm sure wondered if we'd ever get past prairie sandreed.

When we became familiar with unique identifying features of each plant and on what range site each grew, the project became an enjoyable challenge.

There were many more people who willingly helped us learn; Soil Conservation Service personnel such as Bob Lowe, Willie Joe Holmes and John Sautter, to name a few.

The more we learned, the more curious we became about water, soil conservation and nutrition for animals the prairie grasses supported. That information came from such professionals as Jim Nichols, Don Clanton and Jim Goeke at the University of Nebraska North Platte Station.

I became a student of our environment and have remained so for the past 25 years. Thanks for an introduction to the real prairie, however, goes to a host of fine teachers.

S ᴿ ᴼ Y ⊢/

JOURNEY HOME GOES THROUGH HISTORY
- September 25, 1986 -

Sometimes a sentimental journey to explore new areas and retrace old steps can refresh the soul and charge the batteries. At least it does for me.

Last weekend, I left Columbus after turning the Nebraska Press Women president's gavel over to longtime friend and fellow writer, Judy Nelson. My two-year job was finished and I had no reason to hurry as I headed west along Nebraska 91.

The rolling countryside was lush, with fields of corn and soybeans turned golden. Oh beautiful for spacious size, this rich Nebraskaland.

A church tower at Humphrey reached high into the sky; a towering steeple of unusual height that caused me to turn off the road for a closer look. And at Spalding, I stopped to visit the old Catholic Church whose echoing interior made me very aware that I truly was in church. The ghosts of worshipers past welcomed me to pause in prayer.

The basketball team from Spalding Catholic, the name forgotten to me, was a long-ago rival of St. Mary's in O'Neill, my own alma mater.

A sign loomed at a highway corner: "Fort Hartsuff, 9 miles by county road." Strictly by reflex, I braked the car and headed south to the fort that was in existence from 1874-1881 along the North Loup River, south of present Burwell. At one time there was a little town nearby, Calamus, an Indian name meaning food for the muskrat.

While scanning the register in a building that once was a granary, I counted 191 pages with nearly 5,000 entries during 1986, some from France, Spain, England, etc. Most were from Nebraska, which I found rather nice that we enjoy historic...sites. The comments were favorable, all except one from California: "Very dull."

Too bad for the Californian. I found the restored history of our pioneer prairie very fascinating as I visited the officer's quarters, post hospital and guardhouse of the nine-building complex.

My favorite stop was the bakery, where Buck Newberry, longtime Burwell baker, plies his trade on Sundays at the old-fort bakery. A slice of his delicious, freshly baked bread needed no butter or jam.

Buck explained the huge thick oven that was built from scratch using authentic blueprints by Roger Frink of Ord. All of the metal components were hand-forged by Frink. Newberry had found the four and five-tin bread pans in California and donated them to the fort bakery.

"We fired up the oven for the first time six weeks ago," Newberry said. "We burn the wood fire a day and a half and then bake the bread, usually about 10 loaves."

Newberry settled down with his pipe for a chat. Interesting fellow, knowledgeable historian and map collector. I was accepted when he dropped the name of James Mackay and I recognized him as a 1700s Scottish explorer.

Newberry explained that there were two bakes a day, of 36 loaves each, during days of the military infantry post. While one batch baked, the other bread rose in the large proof box to one side.

I stayed long enough to learn that Newberry's great-grandfather was an early settler in the Burwell area, and that his son, Dan Newberry, is an actor appearing in movies such as the Shootist and Maverick.

Newberry, himself, was honored by the Pawnee with a name meaning, "good man."

Reluctantly, I left the fort after standing in awe before the 97-foot pine tree flagpole brought to the fort by an NPPD helicopter.

S ℞ ☌ Y ⌐/

ACROSS THE STATE;
A SENTIMENTAL JOURNEY
- October 2, 1986 -

During my leisurely trip across the state, it was dark when I left Fort Hartsuff after one last admiring glance at the 20-foot garrison type flag flying from a 97-foot flagpole. The original pine tree in 1874 was cut by soldiers at Long Pine Creek, just south of the Niobrara River .

Alyria is a tiny village just south of the fort, where an old bank building now houses the town watering hole and gathering spot. Friendly folks there, just like those in similar small communities, give meaning to the pause that refreshes.

Twenty miles down the road, Nebraska weather turned from pleasant to typical; stabbing spears of lightning accompanied by vibrating thunder. The approach of severe thunderstorms caused me to seek shelter at the little motel a mile south of Taylor.

I was glad I did. The friendly young woman said she and her husband were buying the motel, but were struggling to rebuild the business because it had been closed for a time by the FDIC.

The area had been hard-hit, she said, when the bank and then seven businesses had closed at nearby Sargent. "Now we're worried about our schools," she said.

For a time the storm kept me awake, but gentle rain was falling when I awoke to a soggy dawn. Farmers, unable to pick corn in muddy fields, gathered at Bridges Cafe in Taylor for breakfast.

Conversation was solemn as they discussed agriculture and its future in their economically-stressed community. Time and again, however, the comment was repeated with that eternal optimism: "But we're hanging in there!"

Those words rang in my ears on the way to Brewster, a tiny inland town I had visited some years ago. Since 1967, the townsfolk have hosted an annual barbecue the first day of grouse season; this year for 450 people.

The visiting bench, resting against a building front on Main Street, stood vacant and lonesome. Only a few cars were parked along the unpaved street. Activity was apparent at the courthouse, a filling station, and a new cafe.

I was disappointed to find a door knob had replaced the latch string on the cafe where I had drunk coffee at round, oak tables. Now the cafe was closed. The fire marshall had demanded the door knob replace the rope I later was told.

Happily, I found the old oak tables at the Doc Middleton Saloon & Steakhouse, opened in a remodeled store building by three young area men; three young men plus a lot of help from the community, I was told.

Jim and Betty Hannah were having coffee. "We all helped," Betty said. "We hammered and sawed and painted and papered. We all got behind those young men and helped because we didn't want to lose the cafe. It's sort of a community center."

Lyle Zeigler, 73, said that he had helped, too. Zeigler said he worked 15 years in the building when it was a store. He said his temper sometimes was hard to control while working for the public. "My anger would boil up into my throat, but I stopped it there. I shut it off before it got to my mouth."

Zeigler said he left the Mullen area in 1930; said he remembers working on the Great Plains Highway. "We used to fix the road with soapweeds ... smashed them until they were like ropes binding the dirt together."

None of the people were the same ones I had talked with before, but they all made this stranger feel welcome. Retracing the trail of some years ago was, indeed, becoming a sentimental journey.

S R Y

SHOT IN THE FOOT WITH A ONE-WORD BULLET
- February 19, 1987 -

When a professional makes a mistake they say, "I'm sorry, but I'll correct it." When an amateur makes a mistake they say, "It wasn't my fault." I found that quote written in my notebook. I remember taking those notes while someone was speaking, but I no longer remember who was the speaker.

I share that quote only because no matter what we consider our position in life it never hurts any of us to admit to an error and to say "I'm sorry."

Writing is considered a profession ... or perhaps in my case, an obsession ... whatever. And writers are mere mortals who are capable of mistake. At least this writer will be the first to plead guilty to errors, and errors are errors even though they may be unintentional.

But, although column writing might be less formal than a news story, it is no different in that what's written must be accurate. Sometimes it's hard to believe that one little word can shoot holes in a writer's credibility.

Case in point is the SIMS column I wrote a couple of weeks ago after Francis and Caryl Crowe fell through the ice on Hackberry Lake.

I talked with Caryl and she told me the story I passed along to you ... how she had carried the buckets and followed Francis who pulled the sled ... how they fell through the ice when their combined weight was too much in the same spot.

164

All of that was reported accurately. But, I'm not a fisherman and I wasn't thinking logically when I wrote the story. When I thought of fishing I thought of minnows ... and that little word was my undoing.

This is what I wrote: "Caryl carried the minnow buckets ..."

Now the Crowes are law-abiding people and minnows are illegal bait on Hackberry Lake located on the Valentine National Wildlife Refuge. Can you imagine how they felt when they read the story? I can, and I'm sorry.

Caryl said she tried to call me to explain that what she carried were five-gallon buckets on which they sat while they fished. She tried to call me, but I was gone. She said she called the game warden to assure him that she didn't have minnows ... that I had made a mistake.

Thank heavens we live in a sparsely populated area where most people know everyone else. It would take more than my column to convince our Conservation Officer that the Crowes would even THINK of breaking any law.

But see what one wrong word can do?

Had I thought twice, I would have known that minnow possession on the refuge carries a $100 fine. The logic behind that is to keep undesirable fish from infesting lakes that have been renovated.

While attempting to correct my mistake, I learned that the Nebraska Game and Parks also made a mistake some time ago through their information and education press release. It said that good fishing results were reported on a refuge lake with minnow bait.

There it is, again. That one little word ... minnow ... leave it out and we're okay.

We're seasoned writers ...but sometimes we shoot ourselves in the foot with a one-word bullet.

<u>S</u>   𐤓   ☥   Y   ⊢/

AWASH WITH SEASONAL FEELINGS
- April 16, 1987 -

Time does make a difference. While researching history, I consistently found a phrase that described the Sandhills as "The Great American Desert." And I'm certain it was true at the time.

Soldiers avoided the area and homesteaders sought land along the creeks. Houses were built on the lowlands so that blowouts wouldn't form around the buildings. Roads avoided the hills and followed the valleys for the same reason. There seemed to be little water in the dune area.

That was a century ago. If you want water, I'll show you water.

Many of those building sites on lowlands are now surrounded by moats without a drawbridge. The surface water has become incredible. Shelterbelts of cedar and pine trees standing 30 feet tall are drowning.

Trails through the Sandhills that have been traveled for decades have been abandoned because water now stands there. We're thinking of holding straightaway boat races up the valleys.

Longtime stack yards on higher ground at the rim of meadows will have to be abandoned. Water now stands around the stacks. Any hay left on the wrong side of creeks remains there. Meadows are too soft to transport the hay out.

Duck potholes have turned into sizable lakes. At least three windmills along U.S. 83 south of Valentine now have wet feet. Water has risen half way up the tower.

But, I guess they have to leave the wells pumping even though the lead pipes are well under water. Otherwise, sand filters down into the well.

Muskrats are homeless and sleeping in the streets under newspapers for blankets. They were drowned out of their reed-built huts. Gophers abandoned the meadows long ago, but they are throwing up mounds like crazy throughout the sandy hilltops.

Those industrious gophers are real innovative. They can't stay in one place long enough to call it home, but they have a great rent-a-mound business going for them and tourist gophers from 40 states are taking the rentals.

God only knows where all of the water comes from. Son John grinned as he took off soggy boots and said I missed a newsworthy event the other day ... said he saw gray whales migrating south down the flooded road ditches.

I won't even talk about the disgusting situation in my basement. But what can I expect when there is a lake in my front yard.

The Sandhills are either too wet or too dry. In spite of growing webs between our toes, we prefer the former. At least grass is shooting upwards during the days too hot for April.

Cattlemen aren't done feeding yet, but already they look at the green tinge of the land and say, "Think this moisture is going to make a hay crop."

A traveler told us that Montana and South Dakota already are green with grass. I suppose grass tetany poisoning will be a problem in cattle earlier this year.

But why am I so crabby? This is spring ... the Easter Season ... the time of new life, rebirth and renewal. The calving lots filled with baby calves, and more on the way, should be adequate reminders of renewal during this Holy Season.

Do celebrate a happy holiday, dear friends. I'm sure the Easter Bunny will make his usual rounds. I just saw 10 whiz by on water skis, pulled by 10 fat muskrats.

S ᴿ ᵟ Y ᴡ

FAMILY RANCHES:
DIFFERENT FOR MANY REASONS
- April 30, 1987 -

R ecently, a city dweller asked me this question: "Why is a family ranch different from others?" I'm sure there are hundreds of reasons – both pro and con – depending upon the point of view.

For starters, I explained that members of a family unit operating a ranch might learn certain methods together and there is continuity. Youngsters learn through hands-on methods — learn by association with animals while growing up.

For example, when one of our daughters was quite young, she accompanied us in the pickup while we checked a pasture of yearling heifers one wintry day. We found a heifer had fallen on the ice of a lake and she couldn't get back onto her feet.

G.R. tied a lariat onto her hind feet, tied it to the pickup frame and pulled her off the ice. We worked with her until we forced her back onto her feet, and then kept her walking until the bloat diminished.

When we were finished, our daughter was full of "why's." G.R. explained that a beef animal has several stomachs, and when the animal gets into a certain position the passage from their stomachs block. When they can't get up, the gases in their inner mechanism that digests their food continue to build, but can't be burped. So they'll bloat and die if help isn't almost immediate.

She never forgot that lesson.

In a few short years that same daughter saved several cows that had laid down in a ditch or with their back enough downhill that they couldn't get to their feet. This happens especially with cows heavy with calf.

No one seems to know just how long they can survive in this awkward position, but ranchers agree it isn't very long. But, if you don't know the result, you don't realize there is a problem.

As a youngster, that daughter learned to constantly look for signs of sickness in newborn calves as she rode horseback through the herd: drooping ears, signs of eating sand, depression, or a red and feverish muzzle. She also learned that "easy does it" is the motto for moving cattle.

She also knew that after a calf nursed, its mother selected a spot to "hide" the calf, and that's where it stayed, flattened to the ground in the grass or hay until the cow returned. Try to move such a calf without its mother might cause it to run in fright until it dropped from exhaustion.

We've had hired hands who tried to move those hidden calves because they thought their mothers had abandoned them. Others have put cattle through the wire fence time and again while trying to corral them. They didn't know about easy does it. Rather they yelled, pushed and crowded until the frightened animal went through anything in front of it.

Watching the boisterous and noisy roundups on television is not a proper training vehicle for the real cattleman.

Kiddos riding with their dad usually learn early-on to check for empty salt boxes, downed fly rubs and a jillion other insignificant, but important aspects of animal care.

Why is a family ranch different? Perhaps one reason is that by working together for so long they have learned to read the signs of what needs to be done without being told.

Or perhaps the answer is more simple ... as in the words of G.R.: "I can't get fired and I can't quit. I've got a tiger by the tail and I can't turn it loose."

S ℞ ☿ Y ⊢/

A FARMER'S LAST WILL
- April 30, 1987 -

Did you hear the story about a rancher who had worked his place for 50 years and was able to retire at the age of 70 with $100,000? His neighbors were curious and asked to what he credited the ability to accumulate such a savings.

"To my uncle who died six months ago and left me $95,000," the old rancher answered.

I don't know if that uncle was into Arabian oil or gold bullion but I've been looking around for a surrogate uncle and the supply seems to have been exhausted.

I read of a more realistic situation in the Farm Bureau Spokesman recently of a farmer's last will and testament. It read:

To my wife — my overdrafts at the bank. Maybe she can explain them.

To my son — equity in my car. Now he'll have to work to meet the payments.

To my banker — my soul. He's got the mortgage on it anyway.

To my neighbor — my clown suit. He'll need it if he continues to farm as he has in the past.

To FHA — my unpaid bills. They took some real chances on me and I want to do something for them.

To SCS — my grain bin. I was planning to let them have it next year anyway.

To the farm advisor — 50 bushels of corn to see if he can hit the high market after years of telling me why I never did.

To the SCS people — my farm plan. Maybe they can understand it.

To the junk dealer — my machinery. He's had his eyes on it for years.

To the undertaker — a special request of six implement and fertilizer dealers for pallbearers, please. They've all been carrying me for years.

To the weatherman — rain, sleet and snow for the funeral. No sense in having nice weather now.

To the grave digger — don't bother. The hole I've dug for myself over the years should be a big enough thank you.

G.R. and I had our will revised the other day and it didn't take too long. It was similar to that of the farmer's. We did add a couple of items:

To the lawmakers — a plea for legislation to take young ranchers and farmers from the endangered species list.

To our children — an unshakeable sense of humor. They're certainly going to need it.

S R Ö Y W

REMEMBERING THOSE WHO CAME BEFORE US
- May 28, 1987 -

Memorial Day is for remembering, and Mount Hope Cemetery at Valentine probably never has been more beautiful. Light rain all during the weekend was not what vacationers had ordered. But the moisture, always welcome in the Sandhills, brightened the broad expanse of cemetery green. Hundreds of bright fresh flowers placed at graves remained upright and beautiful during the cool weather. It was a beautiful sight.

Something I couldn't take lightly was the number of flags that marked the veteran's graves...veterans who served their country in the Armed Forces ... some making the supreme sacrifice.

Two of those flags marked the graves of my father and my uncle, veterans of World War I. Another flag, I hope, marked my brother's grave at Belle Fourche, SD, a World War II veteran.

We don't consider Memorial Day as a vacation weekend, rather only as a special day to remember our loved ones and to visit their graves.

Because we had weekend company, G.R. did take the day off for a change.

We visited the cemetery and decided to drive along the scenic north side of the Niobrara River south of Kilgore where reminders of life a century ago remain. An open-range ranch was located at McCann Canyon in the late 1870s and a broom factory was operated at McFarland Canyon in 1889. Settlers raised broom corn, and stone foundations of their homes are still visible along the walls of both canyons.

Five years ago, on a trail ride up through those canyons, I was certain I heard the voices of long-ago settlers relating hardships of early life on the plains.

We now were distressed to find the roof had fallen in on the old McCann schoolhouse built of hand hewn logs. That's where Nelda Keller, who will be 97 on June 1, taught 34 pupils in eight grades for $40 a month in 1898.

But that area now is posted to warn trespassers, and padlocked gates close off access to McCann Canyon. An investor from Washington, D.C., owns the land, and since he doesn't know any of us, he must not feel neighborly.

We drove across the old Reimenschneider Bridge that was put back into service near the Hockenbary place about 1966. Until then, the Hockenbarys were forced to drive four miles to the Anderson Bridge and four miles back to visit neighbors living directly across the river. The bridge first was erected across the river south of Nenzel in 1918.

Our destination was an isolated burial site, high on a sidehill south of the Niobrara. That's where James Williamson, from the McCann Ranch, was buried after he was killed by Indians while gathering horses along the Snake River on May 6, 1879. He was 28.

A cowboy at Sharpe's Ranch, L.J.F. Iaeger (better known as "Billy the Bear" while traveling with Buffalo Bill), shaped a headstone from cedar to mark the grave. Sometime, after it nearly burned during a 1914 prairie fire, C.J. Anderson of the Diamond Bar Ranch, replaced the wooden marker with a marble duplicate. A fence now keeps cattle off the grave and the original marker is preserved at Ft. Robinson.

Perhaps it was wind whispering through the pines, but I thought I heard the words, "Thanks for remembering."

We placed wildflowers...spiderwort and penstomen...on the lonesome grave and retracted our steps. Memorial Day is set aside to remember those who came before us.

S ꞅ ☿ Y \—/

WIND, WATER PROVIDE EARLY GIFT
- June 1987 -

The boss man at this place says he got nearly all he wanted several days before Father's Day, 1987. Wind finally started turning windmills, and an inch of rain Tuesday night soothed hills parched by the heat wave. The hail we didn't need.

Water. We have it in abundance, a short distance below the surface, here in the Sandhills. Livestock wells need to be only 50-75 feet deep. But when the wind doesn't blow that underground water doesn't do us much good.

Until Tuesday, when it was 100 degrees, we'd had five days of calm weather 90 degrees and above. Water supply to the cattle became critical because adult animals consume at least 25 gallons a day, I'm told.

Say there are 500 cattle to be watered. Do you realize that means at least 12,500 gallons a day? Perhaps more in hot weather. Multiply that times five windless days and it seems like a lot of water when you have to depend upon pump jacks attached to windmills.

If you are fortunate to have a creek running through your pastures, the pressure is less intense. Our most critical area is what we call the Snake River pasture where we are entirely dependent upon windmills.

That wasn't always so. Through the early years of this ranch L.C., G.R.'s father, bought land parcels piece by piece until he owned a goodly stretch of the Boardman Creek and Snake River. There was no worry about water problems during the busy hay season.

When Merritt Dam was constructed, the government condemned that land and pushed our fences back into the hills far from any access to water. Of course they paid for the land, but the point is, a rancher simply doesn't sell his access to water for any price...if he's given a choice.

So be it for progress and recreation. Once again, we've bought an airplane, a small one that can be landed in a pasture if necessary. Nearly every morning, son John flies the pastures to check on water, salt and mineral, bull dispersement and for an overall check of the cattle.

How can we afford it? It cost less than half the price of a new pickup, and he can make his trip in about an hour. It would take all day in a land vehicle.

John has developed an eagle eye from the air. In addition to the above, he spots animals with hoof rot or a jillion other problems, and keeps check on fly control.

Perhaps, I should say fly population. Fly control has gotten to be a serious problem. As soon as an effective insecticide is developed, flies either become rapidly immune or the EPA removes it from the market.

Flies got an early start this year. We sprayed for flies, have dust bags distributed throughout the pasture and I believe they used fly control ear tags. None seem to be terribly effective.

This morning, John reported cattle in our pastures seemed scattered and content. But cattle across the fence were bunched together; a sign that flies were driving them bonkers. I suppose flies crossbreed and become more vigorous just like we breed for hybrid vigor in our cattle.

When cattle fight flies they lose the desire to eat and their weight gain diminishes or stops. In spite of modern technology, the age-old battle with flies still exists.

172

LEARNING 'GOOD OLD' SELF-SUFFICIENCY
- June 11, 1987 -

Today I learned the meaning of the word "good," when people refer to the "good old days." Life was simpler back then, but most of all, we were more independent, more self-sufficient. That was good.

Today our life suddenly came to a standstill because the electricity was shut down without notice. There were downed poles in the area near Alkali Lake, we were told. It makes me angry that we've become so durned dependent upon electricity.

I was working at my desk on the word processor. Everything that had been written disappeared in a flash. It was gone forever, because I was not finished, and I had not saved the copy on a disc.

The men came in from the shop where they had been welding a pipe to fix a windmill. "How long are we going to be off?" They asked crabbily.

For quite some time, I told them, and they changed their plans from fixing windmills to riding through a pasture. No electricity needed to start the four legs that powers a saddle horse, they said.

I was not so lucky. I don't have a manual typewriter anymore. It's been so long since I've written copy in longhand that the lack of mechanics involved causes a mental blank. Besides, it's impossible for me to decipher my own handwriting once it's two minutes old. Writing was put on hold.

So I'd finish preparations for a trip to Grand Island to attend the Nebraska Stocker Growers convention. All I had to do was prepare eight meals to leave for my crew, launder and press a few clothes and wash and fix my hair with a curling iron.

Confidently, I opened the door to the refrigerator, but then I realized that the dark interior taunted me. The light didn't come on. Of course not. There was no electricity and I literally was brought to a standstill. Without power there also was no water. Every job that I needed to finish before I could leave required electricity.

Ordinarily, the enforced inactivity would have been welcomed. I could have read a book, taken a walk or even a nap. And I could have enjoyed any one of those leisurely acts.

But when I needed to use every minute to its utmost throughout the day, I was not the least bit happy. In fact, it made me down right crabby.

As the hands turned on the battery-powered kitchen clock, my hope dimmed at each passing hour. Frustration deepened into anger at being so helpless.

I fixed the men cold sandwiches for lunch. But I could fix neither iced tea nor coffee, because there wasn't so much as a drip of water from the faucet.

For each hour I lost, I knew that I'd be working into the nighttime playing catch-up. I couldn't possibly leave without meals prepared ahead. My genius rancher who fixes windmills, pickup motors and anything else mechanical can't seem to figure out how to turn the control knob on the cook stove.

Finally, I postponed motel reservations. I'd just have to work into the night after power was restored and travel during the wee morning hours.

Sometimes I feel as though the devil makes plans to stop me each time I have a commitment to be somewhere other than home. But if we as individuals can be made so helpless by the lack of electricity, what would happen to us as a nation if an enemy destroyed a few key power sources?

Then, I guess, we'd return to being self-sufficient as in the "good old days."

<u>S</u> R ð Y \─/

CERTAIN HAZARDS TO QUIET RURAL LIFE
- July 3, 1987 -

There are certain hazards to living the quiet life ... a rural life far from the frantic traffic snarls of the inner city. Hanging clothes on the line to dry should be a quiet time. Most women I know who leave their automatic driers idle in the summer do so because they love the smell of line-dried clothes. They also use that time out of doors to meditate, while listening to a certain bird's song or perhaps watching clouds form familiar shapes overhead.

Sounds peaceful, doesn't it? Delores Colburn, who lives in the Beaver Lake area south of Valentine, finds time at the clothesline to be reflective and intimate.

At least she used to. One recent day, she said she was in sort of a reflective mood as she went to her clothesline. In a matter of seconds, that peace was broken so fast Delores said she hardly had time to absorb what was happening.

Wasp stings bring one back to reality in short order. Delores said apparently wasps had built a nest in the support pipe at the end of her clothesline. Or perhaps they were merely congregated there in convention.

Whatever their purpose of gathering, the yellow tuxedoed little hooters declared war with a quivering clothesline their only provocation. Sounds like the Persian Gulf with mines quietly lying below the surface.

We have to wonder if insects respond to intense heat in a manner similar to humans. It seems that tempers are shortened by hot weather. Violent crimes seem to increase and there seems to be a hair trigger on anger.

Did someone say hot weather? Ten days of temperatures 90 degrees and more and three days when the mercury passed 100 degrees.

Ranchers involved in the hay harvest here in the Sandhills turned "swampland," say they are grateful for the hot weather. It takes little time for hay to cure once it's cut ... unless it falls onto water saturated lowlands. In fact, I heard one remark that might qualify for Roger Welsch's tall tales collection, "It's so durned hot the hay burns up before it hits the ground, if the raker doesn't catch it on the fall."

We don't know about other areas in the Sandhills, but ours is inhabited by an unusual number of bumble bees.

One of our "hay waddies" came in for lunch Monday with an eye swelled completely shut. An unprovoked bee stung him on the eyebrow and again on the forehead.

The next day a man on the mower was stung.

Travis, our 15-year-old grandson, spending his second year on a hay rake, calls the hayfield hazardous duty this year. Says he frequently has to bail off the rake to avoid the angry bees.

Reminds me of my youth in the hay field on our South Dakota farm. I drove a team of horses on the rake. The worst run-away I ever experienced was when a cloud of bumble bees attacked my horses.

A definite advantage our grandson enjoys is that he can pull the throttle and jump. There was no easy shut-down with a team of horses.

The men say the bees are more aggressive this year. Someone mentioned the possibility that the killer bees have moved north earlier than expected.

Probably not. More than likely, the intense heat is straining tempers to a hair trigger release. In the case of bees, it's more likely a stinger release.

S ꓣ Ꝋ ꓬ ⱵⱵ
WINTER...SILVER TIME OF YEAR
- December 31, 1987 -

Somewhere today it is warm and winter creatures scurry. But here in the snow-enshrouded Sandhills, the pace has been slowed by winter. Short days ago, while winds and wildlife slept, snow sifted quietly and unannounced...fell gently onto bough and twig and fenceline post... and poised there to await sun's warm approval.

Giant flakes of beautiful and gentle snow, filled the sky and blanketed the earth below. It danced a slow-paced waltz and left behind scenes of infinite beauty.

Snow fell...and fell...and fell, and piled high on peaked roof of barn and shed. Rafters groaned in loud complaint from the burden of weight in 22 inches of snow.

To the appreciative eye, however, the scene resembled those reserved for Alaska, where wind seldom accompanies snowfall. Each filigreed flake rested where it fell until there was untold strength in numbers.

Shrubs were mittened in snow, pine trees wore ermine capes, and the giant arms of the spruce were weighted and folded against the cold like the wings of a giant bird. Rough bark of the cottonwood trunks, resemble rough-hewn stone in a sculptor's loft. Upper twigs snapped and cracked in the crisp cold air.

Wide-topped posts that support a plank corral wore elaborate caps of ermine... splendid cone-shaped headgear extravagant in its size.

Nature's wild ones...much in evidence during the snowless months...now remain hidden snug and warm in sheltered nook, in burrow deep, or tree trunk high.

Yesterday, the Sandhills wore tattered rags of winter brown. Today, winter has blanketed the land in a benediction of white that softly caressed all that it touched. One track in the snow seemed a blasphemy to that pristine beauty.

As if to preserve its handiwork, Nature filled the atmosphere between the earth and the sun with cloud cover to deflect glistening light and rays of heat. A flat light blended all objects into one mass.

But the persistent sun finally clawed its way over an icy horizon.

First, it tinged the hills with a soft touch of rouge, but then it threatened to shatter the ethereal beauty with the mere intensity of light.

176

Crystal beads shimmered from each stalk and stem that stood above the snow cover...the sun rays touched and danced across the hills and then the lowlands that seemed covered by a downy, sequined quilt.

Warmth from the cabin's open fire spreads upward. That warmth, and that from the sun, gradually caused icicles to form, cautiously at first, and then droplets of water flowed downward, extending the shafts of ice nearly to the ground.

Chimneys vigorously smoke their pipes and the land draws its white quilt up to its chin seeking warmth. Frozen ponds, now snow-covered, become autographed by tracks of foraging deer.

Intense rays from the noon-day sun give an illusion of warmth. A snowshoe hare leaves the tunnel it burrowed into the snow and hopscotches a short distance. Appearing to change gears, the leap becomes shorter, but higher into the air.

Squirrels leave their treetop nest to hunt their buried acorns. In rapid spurts they burrow into the snow until only their tails are visible, but their heads emerge often to check for possible danger.

Winter has come to this part of the country. Winds are on the rise and the thermometer is on the fall.

But beauty prevails, if only we have the eyes to see.

This is the silver time of year...silver veined, slender icicles dangle, and roofs are shingled with silver frost and silver snowflake spangles.

Perhaps winter's beauty may be best appreciated by people with short driveways, or by people who do not have animals that depend upon them for daily feed.

For those, my wish is that winter be as short-lived as most of my previous New Year's resolutions.

May your New Year be filled with peace and beauty, dear readers...a beauty similar, but not as deep nor as cold...as that which currently blankets our beloved Sandhills.

S ᚱ � Y ᚺ

TRIP PUTS USUAL SCENERY
BACK IN PERSPECTIVE

- April 14, 1988 -

I'm often guilty in the "take life for granted" department. A recent cross-country trip made me more aware. I saw nothing out of the ordinary, just the sights we've grown used to seeing.

Mallard, pintail, red head and numerous other duck species are plentiful on our Sandhills ponds. My favorite is the pintail, perhaps because of the male's long graceful body and colorful plumage.

Along the shores of one lake, I stopped to watch a pair of geese that ignored me as they plucked tender shoots of new grass. Each year I see one pair along the same lake. In fact, last fall I stopped while they leisurely led their gaggle of goslings across the road and toward the lake.

The fact that Canada geese now nest in numerous spots across our Sandhills is because of the efforts of the Game and Parks Commission that made releases of young geese in favorable spots. Those geese, I'm told, returned to nest and raise their young and following generations kept the tradition.

I've read accounts of a century ago, when flocks of migrating wildfowl "blackened the sky," they were so numerous. Then the pioneer hunted for the market to survive — killed birds by the hundreds and sold them to the Eastern market. And hunters traveled here to slaughter ducks, geese and game birds for the sport of it.

Game laws and closed seasons became a necessity when numbers dwindled. Now, most species are once again plentiful, but we must not forget and take them for granted.

There is something about the call of a wild goose that is especially pleasant to my ears. Sometimes, the nocturnal sound seems the joyous answer to the compelling call of migration, while at other times it seems a mournful question. Geese mate for life you know, and the lonesome calls are most certainly from those that have lost their mate.

During my journey, I saw the first curlew of the season and other bird species too numerous to mention. Eight turtles were lined up on a log sunning themselves above the water.

You have no idea how many times I've tried to capture that sight on film. But the turtles are too wary. They slip off into the water at the slightest sound.

Deer are no longer an unusual sight, but did you know that at the turn of the century they were on the edge of extinction in this state? Officials estimated the number at 50.

Only through game laws, transplanting and migration from other areas was our deer population rebuilt — certainly nothing to take for granted. My sympathy often goes out to our city cousins, who do not enjoy the daily contact with an abundance of wildlife as they travel the concrete jungle.

I'll have to tell you that one sight during that trip was unusual. I actually saw a four-wire pasture fence that was intact and taut as a fiddle string. This year, when snow drifts buried our fence lines, most of the wire went to the ground or snapped under the pressure. For most ranchers, the busy calving season has taken priority over fencing.

We've been working outward from the buildings as time permits. Most of our summer pasture fence lines resemble cobwebs with strands drooping from post to post ... or tangled among the grasses along the ground. A lot of man-hours will be involved before spring turnout to pasture can be made with any assurance the animals will be confined.

Tight fences, this year, are not to be taken for granted. But it was the weather, not man, that put tight fence lines on the endangered list.

CATTLE DRIVE CAN BE FUN, TOO
- May 28, 1988 -

Cattle ranching is a labor-intensive business, but if you enjoy animals, the labor involved with their care seems rewarding and fruitful. Like any other type of job, if you really like what you're doing the job is pleasant ... at least most of the time.

We seem to like animals, and I like to share amusing stories about their behavior. Sometimes animals share the story with a vehicle newly introduced to ranch work.

One such story comes from a recent cattle drive that several people told me about at separate times. Each one told it with a chuckle.

But this tale has its beginning last spring. Son John began riding a young paint horse during the calving season, considered a good time to break a horse to cattle. But the young mare really wasn't too interested, which made John disgusted.

This calving season, for the first time, we used a little four-wheeler part-time in the calving lots. John thought it was great ... faster than saddling a horse, but G.R. had reservations. He preferred his saddle horse.

Later in the season John was to rope a few calves in order to treat them for scours. For that job it was back to the paint horse. Sometimes it took him awhile because the paint seemed disinterested and often switched directions about the time John was ready to throw his loop.

Then one day John came for lunch wearing a broad smile.

"We picked out a calf, I dropped the reins and Spot kept me right there until I caught it," John said proudly. "She's beginning to show a little cow."

We all were pleased, of course, because we feel a horse doesn't earn its oats if it isn't good at working cattle.

Last week our crew faced a six-mile drive with 200 hard-moving cows and calves. G.R. trailered the horses, including Spot, to the pasture for the initial roundup, but John drove there on the four-wheeler. G.R. frowned on using it, but it wasn't long before he changed his mind.

"I couldn't believe the hard riding he saved us," G.R. said later. "He could travel back and forth across the pasture and move cattle out of pockets twice as fast as we could horseback."

However, John said later that his "steed" had bucked harder - over a soap-weed than any horse he'd ever ridden.

The drive was completed in record time, but about now you ask, "What about the horse?" Patience. I'm coming to that.

Since John couldn't ride both Spot and the four-wheeler at the same time, he tied the reins to the saddle horn and turned her loose. As the cattle and riders strung out to the northeast, Spot followed along behind.

But we think that Spot, perhaps, was bored and offended with a lack of duty. Remember, John said she was beginning to show cow sense.

Gradually Spot worked her way through the herd to the point ... the front. There she singled out a cow and calf and moved them out into the lead. Several times she disappeared over a hill, brought them back to the herd and then off again.

John finally had to catch and lead Spot behind the four-wheeler. He said she was building too much enthusiasm for the job she'd picked.

The riders came home laughing, each telling that John rode the drag on a four-wheeler while his riderless paint horse worked the point far ahead.

Another drive is scheduled tomorrow. Now that she knows the route, the paint is pushing for trail boss duties. By now she probably considers the four-wheeled critter as a threat to job security.

S ʀ ᵹ Y ⌐⁄

ASH TREE ON BANK IS LIVING MEMORIAL
- June 2, 1988 -

A 10-foot ash tree was planted along the north bank of Big Alkali Lake on Memorial Day. It was planted as a living memorial to a youth, who for the first time in 10 years, did not accompany a group from Omaha.

An ash tree grows rapidly, as does a young boy. Soon the tree branches will soften rays from a relentless sun and cool the camping space below. The tree will also stand as sentinel over the lake and the hills beyond, as wind whispers through its branches.

Sights and sounds of the Sandhills will surround the tree, and perhaps on a future Memorial Day weekend another young boy will come to camp beneath its branches.

Perhaps that lad will thrill at the sight of ducks and pelicans on the water, or the sound of song birds in the tree's branches. Perhaps he will come from the city to the Sandhills, learn to love the serenity there and thirst to investigate the land.

Scott Schultz was only 10 years old when he first came with his father to Big Alkali Lake in 1977. It became an annual pilgrimage for a half dozen Omaha men and their sons.

John Schultz, Scott's father, said the group camped at their special quiet site along Alkali and fished all of the area lakes. "We loved it. Scott loved it," Schultz said. "From the beginning, Scott marveled at the stars...said he couldn't believe he could see so many. Out here there were no city lights to interfere with darkness."

Schultz said that from the very first, Scott saw little things that others missed. "One time, while wading through the bull rushes along Hackberry

Lake, he found a redwing blackbird's nest and was excited with the find. He was intrigued with everything that surrounded him."

Schultz said his son was allergic to some weeds, which caused severe sneezing, but an allergy shot before the trip usually was effective.

"He was a good boy...a real outdoors man. We hunted deer near Mullen, where he downed his first deer two years ago," Schultz said, as his voice broke with the pain of memory.

"He died last November, when his lungs collapsed during an asthma attack over the lunch hour at Central High School. Scott was an honor student and band member. He and his best friend were goofing off in the music room. His friend said he lost his breath, sat down and collapsed. CPR was to no avail."

Pain fractured his voice. "He had just been accepted into the University of Alabama... our only son. It's been hard to accept."

Memorials to the lad were sufficient to offer two $500 scholarships annually at Central High. "Scott had made an impact on a lot of people," Schulz said.

"Each time we camped on our special spot, Scott had talked about planting a tree to provide more shade there...but somehow..." A tree was planted and a father grieves.

Perhaps comfort may be found in the words of philosopher, Kahlil Gibran: "When you are sorrowful, look again in your heart and you shall see that, in truth, you are weeping for that which has been your delight."

S R ȯ Y ↦

FOLLOWING THE SUNFLOWER TRAIL WEST
- September 6, 1988 -

An interesting postscript to the last column comes from Rachel Holmes of North Platte. It concerns sunflowers, the abundant weed that sometimes is called the yellow rose of Texas.

Rachel wrote that some years ago she saw a marker somewhere near Albuquerque, NM. The marker stated that when the Mormons traveled through on their way to Utah, the men who were with the first train scattered sunflower seeds. When the flowers took root, the later parties of older people and children could follow the route.

She thought that might suggest that sunflowers were more or less unknown in the west until that time.

We found that bit of information fascinating. A sunflower trail sounds logical to us and most imaginative.

We love to share information such as that and feel that when we quit learning, we quit living.

Another reader offered an addition to our what's in the name game: Indiangrass appears in the fall, often after a meadow has been mown. The plant that contains the seeds is soft as silk and bronze in color.

The explanation given for the name, possibly, was because it appears on the meadows stately and tall as if by magic...not unlike the quiet movements of an Indian hunting party.

Indiangrass is but one of 172 common range plants in Nebraska that includes forbs, shrubs, introduced and grass-like plants, and one among 47 important range plants in the state.

The maturing seed heads of those plants now have created a prairie mosaic in the colors of nature; colors that range from the purple of big bluestem to the earthy tones of switchgrass and the glistening bronze of Indiangrass.

Sunflowers of many varieties grow in profusion this year, lining the roadways and spilling over from pockets in the hills. Native vegetation grows in great abundance, creating a mood of quiet serenity this year. Moisture has been adequate and when that is true the sand is a fertile host.

It would seem that all animals, both wild and domestic, will add a thick layer of fat in preparation for the winter months.

We asked a question about a resident of the prairie some time ago, and Blaine Runner, whose ranch is located in the far western portion of Cherry County, offered a possible solution.

We asked of what purpose could be the porcupine, the rodent armed with barbed needles that often strips the bark from pine trees. G.R.'s Doberman came away from one encounter with hundreds of barbs in his mouth, tongue and muzzle.

Runner suggested that the porcupine might have been a meal for a starving Indian or isolated trapper during the early years of the frontier. He said a club would be a sufficient weapon. That's entirely possible, because it is a slow-moving animal that doesn't bother anyone. Only when attacked, does an enemy come into contact with the porcupine's miniature spears.

During the summer months, we had hoped to travel to the Runner Ranch and photograph trumpeter swans that nest on a lake there and raise their young.

Cooking duties have kept me somewhat chained to the kitchen sink, so that trip has joined the list of things that I delegate to "maybe tomorrow."

S ℞ ☿ У ⊢/

FROM COOK TO HAY MOWER IN 20 MINUTES
- August 13, 1989 -

Sometimes there's a good feeling from being tired. Hard work is unpleasant only when you hate what you're doing. As usual, I cook full-time for the hay crew, and, until recently, without a dishwasher. I'll not tell you that I loved washing stacks of dishes when the temperature was 106 degrees.

But there was a cool breeze Monday when G.R. asked his favorite question, "Would you like to get out of the house and get some fresh air? — You'd like to mow. It's the easiest job in the field."

"But I've never driven a mower. It scares me," I whimper in my best helpless female voice. Perhaps he'll reconsider.

He doesn't.

After 100 years of marital crisis that some like to call marital bliss, he knows he has me when he adds, "We need your help. We're short-handed."

Twenty minutes later we're in the field.

"At least show me how to run it," I say as he starts the tractor. Typical answer: "It's easy. Just get on it and go." He notes several hydraulic levers, none of which I recognize. "Drive. I'll ride around with you once," he says and pushes a lever.

The light turns green ... machine surges forward ... my head snaps back and we are off in the Indy 500, or so it seems for a few seconds. "Slow it down!" I cry above the sickle's clatter, "at least until I understand what I'm doing!"

Round one. Uneventful. Naturally, the sickle doesn't plug while he is along. I'll figure it out when the time comes. G.R. moves to a second mower.

Round two. G.R. pulls ahead. Says he can't stand the slow pace. He soon leaves me behind, but halfway around the field I find high gear and gradually close the gap.

Round three. A patch of sweet-clover is so tall and rank that it fails to fall once it is cut and I guess my way through behind him. His mower plugs. Mine doesn't. He leaves strips of grass at sharp corners. I don't.

184

Perhaps when you lack experience, luck comes to the rescue.

The hours tick by. Now more relaxed, I study my surroundings and try to isolate the many shades of green that range from emerald of prairie cordgrass to sand bluestem's subtle tones. Sedges have turned from green to brown. Timothy and foxtail wear the color of bleached bones. Pleasant is the smell of newly mown hay, especially that of wild peppermint.

Wishing we could leave it stand, I watch stately switchgrass and bluestem topple, and Indiangrass wearing bronze headdresses fall in battle behind the sickle.

It is certain that Indians once rode proudly across this very meadow before settlers built their homes and corrals from sod. Several flattened mounds on Duck Lake Meadow are evidence that such structures collapsed and native grasses eventually recarpeted the spot.

The tractor bounces over a long narrow ridge, once a fence built from sod. Many signs are evidence of the pioneer. Even the calf-camp shack where G.R. and I spent long ago springtime weathers on a nearby hillside. But the wood will rot away leaving no sign of our having been there.

The sun teases the horizon as we finish the meadow. "I'll bet that's the longest time you've ever gone without a cup of coffee," is G.R.'s only comment. It was.

Surprise comes while I serve a late supper and G.R. tells the crew, "She mowed like a pro. Didn't stop once. Crowded hell out of me all day."

That comment is called minimum wage. It takes the ache out of tired.

THE 1990s AND EARLY 2000s

Marianne recieves the Valentine Sweetheart
Award from the National High School Rodeo
Association in 1977.

Brands & Ownership

Brand: Bow and Arrow
Owner: E.L. Spencer, Jr.

Brand: Powder Horn
Owner: Powder Horn Ranch, Inc.
      J.B. and Will Fischer

Brand: Three Quarter Circle
Owner: Dick Ballard

Brand: Dollar Sign
Owner: Sunny Slope Ranch, Inc.

Brand: Bar Eleven
Owner: Bud and Judy Reece
      Kevin and Jenny Reece

PEOPLE FROM THE PAST
- June 2, 1990 -

Photographs and people from out of the past provided me with a lesson in Sandhill history on Sunday. Until then, "Tiny Town" to which G.R. often referred, was only the name of a wide corner along the county road about a half mile west of our buildings.

When Hugh Wilber brought members of the House and Lessard families to the ranch to visit their roots, their stories and photos put meaning to names such as Tiny Town and the House Pasture.

I've heard people speak affectionately of Mama and Papa House, who took a homestead in 1917, about a mile east of our ranchstead. In 1933, they sold their land to L.C., G.R.'s father, and moved to operate a little store and gas pump at Tiny Town, 40 miles from Valentine. Charles and Della House moved to town in 1938, and for the next 10 years, ran a little store and station to the west of town. Now, Tehrani Motors is located there.

Hugh is a Cherry County native. His mother, Gertrude, is one of the 11 House children. Her sister, Edith, married Frank; one of 10 children born to the Sam Lessards, who spent 30 years on a claim where the Boardman Creek joins the Snake River, six miles north of here. In June 1926, L.C. bought Lessard land when the families moved to greener pastures in California.

An October 1900 local newspaper item noted: "Sam Lessard shot 500 ducks in eight days and sold the birds for 20 cents apiece." At the time, market hunting was vital income to homesteaders.

Sam Lessard's daughter, Eva, now 83; Frank Lessard's three younger children, Ed, Frances and Ruth, all from the West Coast; and the former Gertrude House, were among the visiting group. Frank said he was 8 when the families moved.

Eva said she remembers stories that her dad once was a scout for Buffalo Bill Cody, but as of yet, she's not found documentation.

Frances and Ruth said they both were born in a small square house that once stood in what we call our "House Pasture." Their grandmother, Della House, was midwife for her daughter Edith Lessard.

G.R. remembered where it had stood, and asked if they'd like to see it. It now is used as a storage shed next to our calving barn. When I came to the ranch in 1948, it was used as a small barn at our Duck Lake Camp. It is now roofed with tin and kept in repair. So the Lessards were photographed in front of their grandparent's homestead house.

Ed showed us his album of old pictures that included Mama and Papa House, one of them standing by their little store and gas pump. Typical of those times, it was a small false-fronted building faced with tin. At last, I enjoyed a visual image of Tiny Town. We drove to the spot, which G.R. confirmed from memory and by hills in the photo's background.

The former Lessard/Beel land was condemned in 1960 by the U.S. Corp of Engineers for Merritt Dam and Reservoir. That's when we lost all of our access to live water along the Boardman and the Snake. The landscape was altered, but our visitors told us stories of their youth there along the river.

Eva said that as a girl she worked for G.R.'s mother, Sadie, while she cooked all summer for a 20-man hay crew. She also remembered that L.C. bought the Lessard family milk cows before they moved west. "We shipped the cows that weren't milking, and they each brought $12.50," she said.

Ed had visited the area previously, but it was a first in 64 years for the three women. "It's so beautiful out here!" they exclaimed. Abundant rain has blessed the Sandhills. Native grasses and wildflowers enhanced their memories. I'm glad they didn't visit their roots during the recent drought.

UNUSUAL COLORS, DROUGHT DAMAGE
- August 16, 1990 -

Much of the northern Sandhills appear garbed in unusual colors this year. From Mullen westward to Alliance, the hills exude an almost eerie atmosphere. They appear washed with a color that varies from that of bleached bones to ripened wheat.

The scene almost compares to one seen at midnight, under a full moon.

Creating the altered appearance is mile after mile of needle and thread, a tall, cool season grass that matured and dried by the end of June. Underlying the golden veneer is a ground-hugging green carpet.

Pat Reece, who is a rangeland expert at the Panhandle Station, Scottsbluff, said the plant probably increased as a result of drought that devastated warm season grasses last year. At least, he said, N&T roots help to keep the sand from moving.

Unless needle and thread is grazed early in the spring before the barbs mature, cattle make little use of it. It would appear, however, that few if any cattle now roam those pastures. Possibly they are reserved for winter grazing.

It will take several years of careful management for Sandhill rangeland to heal from the effects of drought, Reece said.

In the central portion, the Sandhills are tinged with yellow icing. The common sunflower, an annual, invades areas that have been stressed by drought or overgrazing. It seems strange then that the perennial sunflower, which is considered a decreaser, is also plentiful this year.

On a steep slope above Merritt Reservoir, I noticed a splash of bright color ... dozens of bush morning glory blossoms. You'll seldom find that plant in grazed pastures, because cattle seem to find its foliage a treat as they do the blossoms and seed pods of soapweed plants.

Moisture has been a godsend. So far, precipitation has been 14.34 inches compared to 12.42 inches total during 1989. We're nearly two inches above normal for this date and the country reflects the timely moisture.

A bonus to living on the Nebraska prairie is the marvelous network of caring people who share. Letters from Evelyn McCune and Lenore Crouse in Grant and Keith counties shared my appreciation of the wild prairie gentians which I recently saw for the first time.

Lenore, who has pressed three albums full of wildflowers, said she found a "miner's candle" in the hills near Arthur, an unusual find, because it's native to Wyoming and the High Plains.

She mentioned heart's delight, which I saw last year for the first time. But Floss Garner at Brownlee has spotted jewel weed, sometimes called "touch me not," which I've never seen. I'll keep looking.

Several suggestions to solve the gopher and/or mole problem in my garden came from North Platte, Broken Bow and Gothenburg. Thank you all for sharing! I think that I'll combine all combat methods because the rodents apparently went on a rampage. I think they've heard me complain.

There must have been several generations of gophers AND moles in residence. Now the mole runs are halfway above ground in the garden leaving behind violated carrots, beets and potatoes. A bite here, three bites there, etc. But the pocket gophers are really on a roll. All at once, sandy mounds are appearing all over our front lawn, so fast there are several fresh ones each time I look.

The enemy has "dug in" right in my front yard. Now the battle lines are drawn. In this war, however, it appears that "underground forces" do not aid the oppressed, rather the aggressors.

SANDHILLS GOLD LIES BELOW GROUND
- September 27, 1990 -

The crisis in Iraq has made us aware of the importance of oil, the same "black gold" that elevated many Texans to millionaire status. I noticed recently, that a full service gas pump here registered $1.62 a gallon. Oil might rapidly become as precious as gold.

Not to be outdone, we hear gold mentioned quite often here in the Sandhills. Just the other day, I heard a rancher say of his hired hand, "He's worth his weight in gold."

The hills of summer are caressed with golden blossoms of the spinney prickly pear cactus, the puccoons, cone flowers and more than 60 species of other golden blossoms.

Perhaps, we speak loosely of gold. It adds to our quality of life, but is it really a vital life-sustaining commodity? If we were left on the desert with a hoard of gold, could we drink it to maintain life?

The real Sandhills' gold surely is the vast water reservoir lying beneath our grass-stabilized sand dunes. A water shortage in high populace cities grows at an alarming rate. It is my firm belief that underground water has drawn absentee land owners to our sandy hills. They are investing in the future.

Take flows of the Snake River and Boardman Creek, as example. Water of the Snake percolates out of marshy ground south of Gordon and the Boardman emerges south of Nenzel on the Three Bar Ranch. After a few short miles, the Boardman joins the Snake and the combined flow over Snake River Falls measures 190 cubic feet per second. This phenomenon is an outflow from the Ogallala Aquifer.

Once that flow was harnessed behind Merritt Dam, available water in the reservoir totaled 74,486 acre feet, an amount that would cover that many acres with a foot of water. Reservoir waters provide fishing and recreation for a multitude of vacationers. Annual visitations, recorded by the Nebraska Game and Parks Commission, range between 100,000 to 200,000 annually.

In addition, reservoir water flowing down the Ainsworth Canal irrigates 34,000 acres of feed grain crops in Brown and Rock counties, according to Marvin Blake, superintendent at Merritt Dam for 12 years.

By mid-September, Blake said reservoir water had lowered 12 feet during the season leaving 45,217 acre feet in the reservoir. During the height of the irrigation season, 580 cfs flows down the canal, but one third of that amount is replenished daily by flow from the spring-fed Snake and the Boardman.

Although the Ainsworth Irrigation District holds full water rights and the right to shut down all flow from the river, the Snake River cannot be stopped. Numerous springs immediately below the dam, provide 16 cfs of flow and more springs closer to Snake Falls and maintains sufficient water flow for prime trout habitat.

The least water released this summer into the river through the conduits was 38 cfs, and in mid-September about 60 cfs, Blake said. By October 1, typically the end of the irrigation season, Blake said flow into the river is completely shut down for a short time during the annual conduit gate inspection.

The reservoir refills in six weeks and a full stream, once again, courses down the Snake and into the Niobrara.

Could it be that growing importance of water puts credibility to an old timer's words, "There's gold in them thar hills."

A READY CAMERA CATCHES NATURE'S BEAUTY
- December 6, 1990 -

It is my hope, that everyone throughout Nebraskaland notices and enjoys the glorious sunrises of late. The intense colors seem to herald the Christmas season. On Wednesday morning, the sunrise brought both pleasure and disappointment. In the predawn hours the horizon rim was free of cover, but the eastern sky was filled with the type of clouds that reflect the morning's drama.

There is a windmill about a mile from home where a long meadow ends at a break in the hills. If I hurried, I would be able to capture on film the windmill silhouette backlit by a sunrise in all its glory.

I drove to the spot and sat in awe as the colors from nature's paint brush began to appear. From a cold ice-blue color slowly transformed the sky to delicate pinks ... but only for a moment. Bold colors warmed a winter's world with such an intensity of light that shadows quickly retreated.

After I shot two frames, the film refused to advance. "Drat," I thought, "of all times for a camera malfunction!"

In my haste, I'd neglected to take a spare film, thinking that six frames were enough. I did, at least, linger and savor the sunrise as colors rippled across the clouds in dramatic display, and then were gone.

When I removed the film, I found the only problem was 20-exposures rather than 24 frames that I'm used to. Blessed relief.

I've carried the camera constantly, of late, and am excited about what I've "shot." Wildlife is much in evidence.

During one trip to town, I noticed something among a herd of fall cows and calves and slowed the car. Several hundred Canada geese waddled among the cattle, picking up corn scraps from the feedgrounds on Bud Reece's ranch. I guess the geese hadn't read, where some critics say, that domestic animals and wildlife are not compatible.

Tuesday, as I drove the same route, a skein of geese trailed across the sky above the same meadow. I stopped to watch as the formation spread through the sky and then tightened formation into an almost solid mass.

A short distance farther, several hundred gathered on the meadow adjacent to the cow herd. I shot some pictures on the set and then caught the flock as they took flight and winged off toward the north.

I never experienced such a sight that I don't feel shivers course down my back. Such pleasure is the bonus for those of us who live on and love the prairie.

A film recently developed, produced three photos of a coyote I saw among the tall grasses of a pasture. I pulled over to the shoulder and stopped the car. The animal was a young one that showed no fear, so I teetered on the wobbly third wire of the fence to get in the right position.

One picture was worth the effort. Charlie Coyote stood and looked back over his shoulder at me as if to say, "Whatcha doin' up there?" then trotted off on a sideways gait. The photo captured him looking straight at the lens. Tall, golden grasses touched with autumn's soft light, framed the animal in its natural habitat.

Not often does wildlife pose for a portrait, but when it does it's always a thrill. On Monday, I had my first shot at a screech owl sitting calmly on a fence post. I can hardly wait until the film is processed. Such photos are my way of celebrating the prairie.

LIVING AT COW CAMP BY NO MEANS PLUSH
- *February 27, 1992* -

A few ranches are nearly through calving. Weather has been exceptionally warm, and they've avoided the stress of saving calves from frigid weather or a snow storm.

Neighbor Bud Reece says they use a 60-day breeding period, but their herd is more than 80 percent calved after 45 days. That's efficiency.

Weather has been kind to the night riders who monitor the calving lots.

But March lies ahead.

G.R. remembers January-February of 1965. "It was unusually warm until the end of February," he remembers. A record low of -16 degrees on February 23, 1965, still stands.

At the time, we used a cow camp on Duck Lake meadow for spring calving. Camp was a shack, barn and corrals about three miles from home. G.R. and Sonny Dam were doctors in residence, so to speak. Sonny also did the cooking and specialized in popcorn. By that time I had four kiddos to care for.

"The weather turned nasty and stayed pure hell for the rest of March," G.R. said.

They had purchased an 830 Case tractor that year. It had a windshield, but no cab. When G.R. came to the ranch for supplies he drove the tractor and was one cold hooter. That was the year that snowdrifts blocked the road for weeks.

There was no protection from the wind at Duck Lake Camp ... no trees or no sheltering buildings. G.R. said he'd never calve there again, and he hasn't.

We now calve near the headquarters where shelter belts and two big calving barns provide shelter and working facilities.

Recently, G.R. decided to move the "house" from Duck Lake to near the shop which is some distance from the house. It will be a place for record keeping and the veterinary refrigerator, telephone and coffee pot. But there's a lot of work ahead on a shack abandoned for 25 years.

I entered the 14-by-16-foot building and found it hard to believe that I spent three months each spring for four years in that building ... along with chilled calves at times.

Words of a song that I related to while living at camp returned as I studied the crumbling shingles: "Oh, the hinges are of leather and the windows have no glass, while the board roof lets the howling blizzard in. And I hear the hungry coyote as he slinks up thru the grass, 'round the little old wood shanty at our camp."

Yes indeed, I know more than I ever wanted to know about living at cow camps ... hot and cold running mice above the ceiling and smelly skunks beneath the floor. Furniture was worn out cast-offs, the only refrigeration was in the stock tank and light came from a Coleman lantern.

Since 1965, the shack and a windmill stood as sentinels at Duck Lake. Now the lonely windmill is monument to a memory.

WOULD-BE MATADOR SURVIVES ATTACK
- April 9, 1992 -

Animals are listed as the top cause of farm injuries, according to a survey chart developed by the Institute of Agriculture and Natural Resources, UNL. But animals rank seventh as cause of farm fatalities with tractor overturns topping the list. There is no distinction made between farm and ranch.

Everyone rural is classified as a farmer. Farmers deal more with land and machinery. Ranchers deal more with land and animals. I'd be curious to know what the results would be if cattlemen were classified as ranchers instead of farmers.

I meditate over this as I repair and wash a man's down-filled vest that came to the house in bad shape. The vest had just survived the wrath of three cows with newborn calves.

Relating what happened, G.R. said that no matter how long he works with animals, their actions still surprise him.

G.R. and John were moving pairs out of a small lot. Both were on horseback. But a couple of the calves weren't very old and didn't want to be moved.

They seldom work on foot. But to move the animals, the men finally dropped their reins and walked behind the babies trying to push them along.

G.R. removed his vest and swatted the calves with it, thinking it would hurry them along.

The swinging vest brought results, but of the unexpected kind.

"Not one, but three cows turned on me and they were on the fight," G.R. said, "I was trying to get out of their way and John was trying to get there. He had a whip in his hand, but I was between him and the cows. I threw the vest at them and ran."

The story gave me chills. A cow or bull typically mauls its victim ... crushing it into the ground with its head and hoofs. Professional bull fighters are warned to jump up on the fence if need be. An enraged bull or cow can actually kill a person by crushing and stomping its victim.

G.R. said when it was all over he and John laughed about the unusual experience. "I didn't know if I was practicing to be a matador or a track star ... probably the latter," G.R. said with a grin.

The little calf, however, took the brunt of the cow's anger. G.R. said when he threw the vest it landed on the calf. "I thought the three cows were going to kill the calf before John drove them off."

The calf is OK and the vest can be mended. I'm not certain that G.R. would have fared as well had he stumbled.

Our cows are accustomed to men on horseback. But apparently they don't take kindly to a would-be matador.

AIRPLANE HOLDS SENTIMENTAL MEMORIES
- April 30, 1992 -

If we wait long enough, we often experience the true meaning of "what goes around comes around." Recently, I told you about the pair of M.L. Leddy boots that G.R. gave away nearly 10 years ago. Last month, they turned up as a "before repair" example in the Paradise boot shop. G.R. happily reclaimed them.

Now, I share a story about the sentimental attachment to an airplane.

Back in 1947, G.R. learned to fly after a stint in the Army. That year he bought his first airplane for $2,575, a 1946 Aeronca Champion 7AC. Later he traded for an Aeronca Chief and then a Cessna 182. He sold the Cessna about 1970 and bought a Piper J-3 which was much slower, but a perfect "pasture plane." Son John learned to fly it.

But, as time went by, G.R. yearned to own another Aeronca Champ. About five years ago he saw one advertised at Sturgis, SD, and John flew it home.

Built in 1947, the Champ had been restored, with a 100hp Rolls Royce engine. John flies daily during the summer months to check cattle, pastures and windmills.

Those small planes are no longer built and those that escaped structural damage increased in value about 600 percent.

Last summer, John got a call from a man named Jim in Minneapolis, who asked if the Champ could be bought. John's answer was no, but he filed the telephone number.

Circumstances changed, so John called Jim to ask if he was still interested. Jim said he was and we met him at the airport on Sunday. Ironically, he was flying a Cessna 182.

Jim said that seeing our Champ was like finding a long, lost friend. You see, he was 16 when he learned to fly in that very same airplane back in the mid-1960s in Clovis, NM.

Airplanes are registered with a permanent number. So, when Jim decided to locate the Champ, he contacted the Federal Aviation Administration in Oklahoma City. He found the N82113 was still in service and registered to people named Beel.

Jim called last night to say he'd return with his mechanic on Saturday to make the final decision. And he was excited when G.R. said we had in our files the original service manual for his first Champ. It's in mint condition.

I found other material in the file as evidence of how times change. For example, the metal propeller cost $100 in 1947. I understand a replacement today might be $2,000.

A 1949 statement listed 10 gallons of aviation gas for $3.30 and delivery of the plane 40 miles from Valentine to the ranch as $5. Aviation gas is now $2 a gallon.

The annual inspection in 1949 cost $41.66. This year two magnetos on the Champ were replaced at $400 a pop and pushed the cost to four digits.

If Jim takes the Champ back to Minnesota it is assured of a good home. A certain reverence enters the voices of men involved in "plane talk" especially when the subject is that very first airplane.

AIN'T NOTHING LIKE A WINDMILL HIGHBALL
- August 13, 1992 -

A mention of Poke Kidder last week, brought a letter from Doc Kloepping of Cozad who also remembers Poke. That letter also stirred a dormant memory for me, but we'll get to that later. For those of you who didn't know Milton "Poke" Kidder, you missed knowing a colorful personality of the Old West.

Poke was born in the Cherokee Territory of Oklahoma in 1894. His mother died when he was a lad of 10.

New territory was opening. Poke said his father told him they could go to Texas where they could sit in the shade of a cactus and holler "mañana," or go to Nebraska where he'd have to work to survive. They came by team and wagon to Cherry County in 1908.

It's been said that Poke had hair the color of fire and a temper to match. I never saw it. I didn't know him until his later years when his hair and beard were white.

Quite often, Poke stopped for the night at our house on his way to or from town. And each time we were treated to his clever ditties recited to rhythm as he "rattled the bones."

Through his poems and dittie, it was apparent that Poke Kidder had a keen sense of humor.

The Kidders and their eight children were a hard-working family on a small ranch surrounded by much larger ones.

He often told us of attempts to run him out in those early years.

One time, he told us that during a heated confrontation he shot a man in the shoulder and was charged with an attempt to kill. "Not so," Poke told the judge. "I'm a better shot than that. If I had meant to kill him, I would have."

A big, black hat and boots with high underslung heels projected an image larger than Poke's actual size.

Doc Kloepping remembers a time that Poke drove he and John, Poke's friend from Iowa, out from Mullen to the ranch in his Jeep pickup.

At the house, Poke went to a trunk and brought out a stack of poems that he had written over the years. Kloepping said one was the best he'd ever heard and he offered to buy it for a considerable sum. Poke declined.

John had noticed a nice, fat sow roaming around, followed by a litter of slick pigs and asked Poke what in the world he fed them out there in the hills. "They live on soapweeds and bunch grass," Poke said in a convincing manner.

Before they left for Mullen, however, Poke stopped by a shed and filled a self-feeder for the porker family. The laugh was on us, Kloepping wrote.

Kloepping said that on the way in, Poke stopped at a windmill to fill a burlap-covered jug with fresh water. Then he fixed, what he called "windmill highballs," in coffee mugs.

Mention of that jug stirred a memory for me. Back in the mid-1950s, G.R. and I made frequent trips to Omaha. But he couldn't stand the taste of city water.

So, on one such trip, G.R. raised quite a few eyebrows when he carried into the Regis Hotel a burlap-wrapped, glass gallon jug filled with Sandhill water.

Somehow, I think Poke Kidder would relate to that. But to this day I'm not certain of the specific ingredients needed for a windmill highball.

WINTER IN NEBRASKA
- January 3, 1993 -

Many country dwellers might relate to a poem titled, "Nebraska," written by the late Jim Mogle (1893-1966) of Cody. A grandson recently published a collection of Mogle's works in book form.

Mogle describes an eastern author who writes of romance in Nebraska ... young calves, colorful cowboys, tall grass, fat cattle and ... "azure skies, rattlesnakes and woodticks, porcupines and bottle flies."

Then Mogle explains that person has never seen the "other side" of Nebraska. "He's never stood at night guard when the rain was pelting down, or slept out with one blanket when the snow was on the ground."

Mogles advice was, "I've a tip to give you stranger, if you'll mind it not the least ... that's to spend the whole damn winter in some swell hotel back east. Just keep on writing poetry with your clean descriptive pen, don't come back to old Nebraska 'till it's summer time again."

Reading those words stirred memories of a situation 42 years ago. G.R. and I were at a cow-camp 15 miles from the ranch. In our care were about 300 cows and 200 big steers. We lived in a drafty shack, had a minimum of groceries, a saddle horse and a four-horse team to pull a drag sled. No radio at first. That was January after the Blizzard of '49.

The weather was brutal, but we had no way of knowing just how cold it was, or what the wind-chill factor was. When the pail of drinking water froze solid while sitting three feet from the pot-belly stove, we decided it must be v-e-r-y cold.

G.R. said it could have been worse; said he never did have to jump-start his feed outfit. Four head of Belgians.

Sometimes history repeats itself with certain similarity.

Son, John, is now 15 miles from home at isolated feed grounds that we'll call a winter cow-camp with 300-head. He has a tractor and bale-feeder with which to feed the hay, and a pickup. He also took his dog.

The motor home, equipped with a propane heater and a standby generator, was moved there for when he had to stay overnight. He also took a portable welder that would provide electricity for the tractor's headbolt heater.

Because the forecast predicted sub-zero weather, John stayed at "camp" on Thursday. But he was back by noon Friday, cold and just a tad-bit crabby.

Everything had gone wrong. The heater went out and refused to re-light, neither generator would start, heaters and radios in both the tractor and the pickup quit, and the pickup engine began missing. G.R. drove there and got things running, but it wasn't to last through Friday night.

Saturday morning the thermometer read minus 29 with a wind-chill factor of 77 degrees below zero. The heat went off again, so John plugged in a little electric heater. But the small generator fritzed...wouldn't take the load. Engines refused to start in the motor home and standby generator. The only heat to be found was from lighted cookstove burners.

John left the diesel tractor run all night so he wouldn't have to start it. Later, he was able to start the small generator and thaw out in front of the electric heater.

Here at the ranch, diesel fuel congealed and hydraulic fluid wouldn't flow. G.R. spent most of the day out in that bitter cold just to get equipment working and the animals fed. Later, some neighbors told us that they never did that day.

It's winter in Nebraska. The men agree that Mogle's words seem most appropriate: "I'm no pessimist or critic, kind friends I'll have you know. But who in hell thinks of romance when it's thirty eight below."

QUAKING BOGS MAY BE HIDING PLACE FOR JAKE
- August 19, 1993 -

Rainfall has been above normal throughout the Sandhills. Lowland meadows remain soggy and hay harvest is an on-again-off-again process; mostly off again.

Dense fog clung to the ground one morning, so hay in windrows surely wouldn't dry. Cowboys caught their ponies and rode out to move cattle.

Through the fog, a young cowboy noticed the crown of a felt hat sticking out of the grass on an abrupt mound. He dismounted and walked toward it, remembering that the boss had warned him against riding onto spring holes.

The hat was stuck in mud so the cowboy began to dig. He could use a new hat that was free for the taking.

As he dug, the cowboy's fingers touched something hard, yet soft so he dug deeper.

Imagine his surprise when a head appeared. The handlebar mustache could belong to no other than Ole Jake.

"Keep a diggin' sonny," Jake said. "I'm still sittin' on a durned good tractor and baler."

The young cowboy didn't claim the hat, but he took the cook a nice mess of fish for dinner. You see, as he dug down in the liquefied sand he kept tossing out sand trout, a species of fish that inhabits spring holes.

In case you think the sun has left me addled, know that spring holes are a fact of life in many parts of the Sandhills. Through the years ranchers learn to avoid meadow ground that rises in domes or ridges. The highest ground above peat beds is often the wettest. Pressure of groundwater pushing against the surface, results in a mound covered by a relatively thin layer of sod. Being fed by groundwater a seep usually appears at the center and stays open all winter.

Stories are legion of animals and machinery falling victim to spring holes during the early 1900s. One told and retold was of a team and a mowing machine being swallowed.

Perhaps those stories became exaggerated at each telling. But I well remember one winter when we lost 12 3-year-old steers when they became mired in spring holes along Dewey Lake. A blizzard drove them deeper into the swamp and their sharp hooves cut through the sod. We spotted their carcasses later when we flew over the area.

So if you see higher ground in the middle of a meadow that has not been mowed, know that the ridge possibly marks a spring hole – a soupy, mucky spot to avoid. One in western Cherry County is about a half mile long, 20 yards wide and six feet high. Quaking bog is another name that fits because walking across it might resemble walking across a water bed.

Spring holes are a rare problem in this particular area, but a lot of wet low ground cannot be mowed. Everyone, however, reports a heavy hay crop.

Neighbor Paul Young said he estimates native grass producing about 3 tons per acre and alfalfa about 4.5 tons. He usually starts about July 15, but this year it was August 3. The big plus, he said, was that the irrigation pivot on alfalfa went around only three times.

Another neighbor said he has covered only half the ground but has the same number of bales as the entire season last year.

Sandhill ranchers, however, are a bit skittish. They say that an above normal hay crop means they'll need every stem as feed this winter. They anticipate a severe winter.

GLIMPSE INTO HISTORY WITH A HORSE TALE
- March 9, 1995 -

Amazing, I think, what circumstance might stir a memory. "Have you ever heard of a cavalry remount stallion called R-Spot?" G.R. asked me. "I was just a kid, but call Ott Buechle and he can tell you," he said.

Ott remembered immediately. "The late Clint Anderson raised R-Spot," he said. "The stallion set a track record at Ak-Sar-Ben. The U.S. Cavalry at Fort Robinson bought him right off from the track and let me use him. I was just 21 at the time."

That was back in 1935. But from talking with Ott, I was given a glimpse into history.

Ott raised horses all his adult life with the last production sale held in 1989. He said he got his start when he was about 13 when he broke draft horses to drive for the late Johnny Buck Ormesher. Ormesher gave him a saddle horse for his pay.

"R-Spot was a red sorrel with a white mark on his right shoulder," Ott said. "At the time the cavalry put their studs out if they approved of your mares. Then they'd come back and buy the horses if they liked them," he said.

"He sired some good colts and I had four sales," he said. "Fuzzy Stilwell had a couple of good mares bred to R-Spot. Howard Lamoureaux bought one and rode him for years."

The cavalry was particular; wanted only solid colored, thoroughbred-type horses standing at least 15 hands and with no distinguishing marks, he said.

Ott said they wanted the horses broke to a snaffle bit and to hold its head low. "They didn't need to rein," he said, "just travel straight out."

Then he chuckled and said some of the soldiers had never ridden and that army saddles gave little protection should a horse buck.

Johnny Cronin was a young, Sandhill-raised cowboy who entered the army at Ft. Robinson. Ott said he was given the job of taming some of the horses that were inclined to buck.

"Johnny was a good hand," Ott said. "He broke his back there, but it wasn't from riding broncs. He had a runaway with a team of mules on a hay rake."

At one time, Ott said there were probably 1,000 mules at Fort Robinson that were sent out as pack mules. Probably 400 to 500 cavalry horses were maintained there, he said.

Ranchers could bring horses to his sale, Ott said. The cavalry might pay $175 when a horse was worth about $35 otherwise. "One Simeon rancher brought in a horse and said it was 8 years old, said he was sure because he kept track by the age of his kids."

"Colonel Whitehead told him he'd better check on his kids because that horse was 12 years old," Ott said with a chuckle. "You couldn't fool those guys about horses."

Ott also has a favorite story about one of the stallions he raised and sold for $4,100 in 1989. "Don Sterns of North Dakota bought him and turned down $7,500 before he got home," Ott said.

"Top Omega King has a wonderful disposition," Ott said. "King went to Martin, SD, after Don was killed in a vehicle accident. King was turned out with mares and hadn't been ridden for five years."

One day the new owner accidentally locked himself out of his pickup out in the pasture, Ott said. "He had some baling twine in the back of his pickup so he fashioned a halter. He was able to catch King and ride him five miles to get home."

"I don't know of another stallion that would have allowed that," Ott said. "Training will not produce a good disposition. It has to come through breeding."

WRITTEN MEMORIES OF 1870s CATTLE DRIVE
- June 8, 1995 -

We are following progress of 267 Texas Longhorns being trailed north to Montana with a great deal of interest. How different this drive is from those back in historic times. For one thing, I've not seen one mention of the cowboys eating hard tack and beef jerky stowed in their saddle bags or shirt pockets.

I understand that a Cowboy Choice brand of coffee will be added to the chuck wagon at North Platte.

Bill Drinkwalter, who owned a western store in Thedford for years, said he made the arrangements. And Bill says the coffee is just as good as the four different blends suggest.

There is the Bronco Buster Blend, Straight Shot Expresso, Rattler's Bite, and last but far from least, Decaf No Bull.

Cowboy Choice is packed in sizes from 2-ounce to 5-pound bags, either ground or bean, Bill says.

He wants the trail drive cowboys to enjoy the coffee in memory of his grandfather. Alvin Coleman was a pioneer who worked for a freighting company from Sidney to Fort Robinson in 1881. Later, he became a shipper for the Diamond Bar Ranch near Cody and traveled to Texas and Nevada for cattle.

I have to wonder if the ghost of Sam Hudson is riding with the present drive. Sam homesteaded in Cherry County in 1883 and his Bow & Arrow brand was one of the first registered in the county.

As a young man, Sam made several trips up the Texas Trail and his description was found among his papers following his death.

"I sure liked to hear the click of horns and rattle of their hoofs. When a herd moved up over a hill, they flowed down into the valley like a river swaying in and out between its banks," he wrote.

"With a herd of 3,000, there was a trail boss, 10 to 12 riders and a cook ... boss of the mess wagon. Each night, a 5-gallon kettle of beans and side meat was cooked over a campfire. Sometimes we had beef, but not always."

"The night that Otis Ivey, his horse and about 20 steers were killed by lightning was the worst I ever experienced. Lightning flashed so continuously that there was no need for lanterns."

"If you head up on a 2,000-mile trail with steers which have ranged free and unfenced through mesquite and prairie plains for 5-10 years, and if your drivers are mere boys, you are bound to have plenty of incidents along the way where houses are 200 miles apart. And where every man you saw had a pistol and Winchester and the children cut their teeth on cartridge shells." Sam wrote that it took three days to cross the Red River, and they lost several horses in the flooding Canadian. At Dodge City, he saw a gambler and a cowboy "mix-up in a six-shooter duel," and at another saloon, he said, "I saw a Texas fellow lose a herd of cattle in a game of stud poker."

"The first cattle were bought on credit and sold for cash ... gold and silver. We carried the gold in leather belts buckled around our waists, but the silver was placed in buckskin bags and loaded on the pack horse; $1,000 in silver weighed 62 pounds."

Those were Sam Hudson's memories of the late 1870s. Surely one of the present cowboys will record their memories of the cattle drive in 1995.

TRIP TO VET BECOMES LOST WEEKEND
- March 1996 -

S ometimes life can be a comedy of errors, but humor is found only in retrospect. Last Saturday morning, G.R. decided to trailer his saddle horse to an Ord veterinarian for a second opinion. We have two pickups equipped to pull a goose neck trailer; his red 1980 model on its second motor and 300,000 miles or the 1991 model that son John drives with 60,000 miles. He took the latter.

He left on the spur of the moment and I forgot to send the cellular phone. So through the day I answered collect calls. His language progressed to un-quotable color. Use your imagination.

Collect from Thedford: "Someone may have to get me. Alternator caught fire and I was towed in."

Found John. He said he could fly to town, pick up parts and fly them to Thedford. G.R. hadn't given his location so I took a chance and called Sandhill Oil.

"They had a new alternator and we took some wiring off from Allan's pickup to get me going. I'm ready to take off," G.R. reported.

Collect from Taylor: "Radiator leaking! Lost all the Prestone and there is no help here. Get someone from Burwell to tow me in!"

But who? I called Stan Klug. No answer. Called a truck stop. They said the only wrecker was at Ray's. But wait, Ray's building burned down so call him at Ed's. Called Ed's and a machine answered.

Garfield County sheriff's office: "I'm at Valentine. My husband has pickup trouble in Taylor and I'm trying to find help," I told the dispatcher. "I'll see what I can do," she said.

I called G.R. at Taylor. He said he was given empty milk jugs to fill with water. He removed the radiator cap to keep pressure down. He would try to make Burwell by adding water every few miles. "But I may get only part way," he said.

Collect from Burwell: "Send someone in the red pickup so I can leave this $#!! bucket of junk and take the horse to Ord!"

I called the sheriff to cancel the request for help and lined up our hired hand, showed him how to operate the cellular phone and told him to call me with progress. But before he could leave there was another collect call. "I have to unload this horse so I'll try to make Ord. Pick me up there."

Collect from Ord: "No one around so I just put the horse in the corral. I can't sit around here. I think I might be able to get back to Burwell. Call Howard and tell him that."

It was then I remembered that Howard turned off the power and said he would turn it on when he needed to call. I forgot to tell him to leave the power on and press "send" to answer on the cellular.

Collect from Burwell about 5 p.m.: "I've got a motel room. Haven't eaten all day." Grumpy was far from an adequate description of his mood.

Call from Ord: "This is Howard. I'm in Ord and there is no G.R." "I know," I said. "Go back to Burwell."

Call from Howard at Burwell, 8 p.m.: "We're going to stay all night. I'll pull the trailer and G.R. will try to get the gray pickup home. The fan belt broke during the fire and knocked a hole in the radiator."

Call from Howard 10 a.m. Sunday: "We've had to stop and add water about every 20 miles. We're now north of Thedford. But it's so cold the water jugs are freezing."

At home G.R. said they'd taken the old red pickup and trailer back to Burwell and picked up the horse. "I just wanted to get everything home because I'm never going back!" G.R. said.

Know what? He sounded like he meant it.

FAMILY MEMBERS FACE THE STORM
- *April 10, 1997 -*

If we thought we could fool Mother Nature, we found the lady still has the last word. Stressed out from the bitter weather during March 1996, we set our cows back to delay calving until the first of April 1997. So it seems that the fickle lady transferred the nasty March weather to April. Saturday was a wreck in more ways than one.

About an inch of cold rain fell Saturday morning while G.R. was on horseback moving out pairs. I suppose the weather affected the disposition of his mount that is normally mild-mannered.

Snuffy shied and spun hard to the left and G.R. landed hard on his right shoulder. He was in terrible pain and we worried because of recent heart surgery. No broken bones showed up on x-ray, but shoulder and chest pain was intense and lingers on.

Daughter Myndi was at the hospital when we got to town, having left her daughters with their paternal grandparents. She had her horse loaded and followed us to the ranch, ready to take over for her dad. By now, wind-driven, wet snow was falling and the storm was predicted to intensify.

Newborn calves were put into the calving barns and an eagle eye was kept on the cow herd in an attempt to bring them into shelter before they delivered. Even week-old calves were soaked from the rain and in danger of chilling.

Myndi spent the entire night in the calving lots and G.R. credits her with saving at least 10 calves. Son John, who had put in a hard day, was rousted from bed for a couple of emergencies.

To the uninitiated, a night in the maternity ward might seem like a piece of cake. Not when winds gusting to 53 mph drive heavy snow horizontal and the wind chill hovers at 20 below zero.

Mydni said later that it was a white-out most of the night. Only here determination kept her searching and found two older, white calves drifting under. They were among those picked up and moved to the barn.

At one point, she said she was disoriented. "I couldn't see anything and lost all sense of direction, but I knew if I kept in one direction I'd come to a fence wire."

After a couple hours of sleep at dawn, Myndi joined John and her dad who spent the day trying to reunite calves with the right cows which is seldom easy. Calves born and brought in during a storm are not tagged with a number that corresponds with it mother. And sometimes cows lose their maternal instinct during the storm.

G.R. called a grandson who is between jobs and asked him to come help until his shoulder mends. We're so grateful he is here. There is no one like family to respond during emergency situations.

Wednesday morning we woke to snow falling again. Thirty-five calves were born in the last 24 hours. The men were swamped, so G.R. gave me a job. "Can you possibly bottle-feed some calves?"

Of course. You do whatever is needed when you are part of a family ranch.

SUNSETS, OLD PICKUPS BRING FULFILLMENT
- January 4, 1998 -

The new year found me chasing holiday colors; colors in the sunrises and sunsets, that is. Friday morning the eastern sky was fantastic with blood-red colors spreading upward across the horizon and into the broken clouds. From red the sky gradually transformed to the most brilliant gold.

It is easier to capture a sunrise on film. Sometimes, I may drive to a favorite location and wait 10 or 15 minutes waiting for the climax.

Sunsets are a different matter. Quite often the color is so fleeting that I don't have time to get out away from the buildings.

I know that atmospheric conditions such as moisture and clouds are what create the magnificent colors. I prefer to think those colors say, "God's in His heaven, all's right with the world."

My early morning excursion acquainted me with the project that G.R. ended the old year with and continues on into the new year.

He spends long hours in his shop rebuilding pickups. He prefers Ford pickups of the late 1970s vintage; he says they're easier riding.

G.R. says he has no desire for a new pickup that may cost about $30,000.

"Doesn't pay. Never saw a pickup that had a calf," he says. "Besides, Detroit no longer makes 'working' pickups. They're too fancy for ranch work with velvet seats, plush carpets, CD players and everything computerized. Can't work on them, either," he says.

It would seem that pickups, like blue denim, have caught on with city dwellers. Once upon a time those two items were considered strictly country or "back woodsy." Prices, along with popularity, went sky-high.

In 1988 G.R. saw an ad in this newspaper for a 1977 pickup. He paid $750 for it, beat out the dents, replaced parts and drove it for the past 10 years. But the motor is weak, so he's started on a couple of others that he picks up as he can.

Table conversation has become filled with mechanic jargon which I don't understand.

"Called all over to find a steering column and then remembered I had a couple in a shed over the hill. Forgot that I had saved them from pickups that died."

I accused him of keeping our pickups running with baling wire and binder twine, but it's much more complicated than that. The man has infinite patience and know-how when it comes to old pickups.

Not all are a work of art; one won the ugly pickup contest at the county fair.

Friday, the only pickup available was one of his builders. It took both hands to lift the door latch and three tries to back it up and turn around.

Both the door handle and power steering need work. And a rusted hole in the floor board needs attention.

None of the modern options are found in our pickups, rather some burlap sacks, a brandin' iron, and a worn-out, coiled rope. A pair of holey western boots and a bar of Lava soap. The floor holds one old bridle, an ax, two pair of spurs, a head stall and two pop cans and a kerchief full of burrs.

A DIFFERENT KIND OF "WORK HORSE"
- Unknown -

Flight instructors drill their small craft students with a universal warning: "Go by air if you have time to spare." Translated that means if adverse weather is forecast, be content to stay grounded. "I believe that 99 percent of all small plane wrecks are from taking a chance on bad weather. I used to fly everyday, but now I look for an excuse," he said.

"I suppose, I've averaged about 100 hours per year. Another favorite slogan is: There are a lot of old pilots, but not a lot of old, bold pilots." Wood Lake rancher, Eldon Cozad, said he subscribed to both. He was 83 years young at the time.

During 52 years of flying, Cozad said his craft nosed over twice while taxiing; once when one wheel dropped into soft ground and once onto snow. Another time, after a forced landing, he found lint was plugging his gas line.

"Years ago, we leased McGinley land and calved in the hills. I flew everyday from the ranch near Wood Lake to check several herds. Besides the cattle, there were 49 windmills to check. It would have taken at least three days by pickup," he said.

Cozad said he bought the Piper Super Cub 115 in 1951 and always propped it by hand. "Just last year I had a starter and disc brakes installed. I surely do like that starter." Then he laughed to remember a near wreck. "I spun the prop from the front and realized I'd left the throttle wide open. The plane started off, but I was able to hang onto the wing strut until I pulled the wing down. When the plane began to circle I was able to get to the throttle. All I lost was one of my boots."

Another Wood Lake rancher said he has made 125,000 landings and walked away from every one. "But I've bent quite a few landing gears," he added with a chuckle.

Paul Hoefs was 17 when he earned his license from Bud Sheer, his stepfather and instructor/pilot of note. "I trained in a Piper J-3, but since Dad sold airplanes, I flew a variety, including stunt planes."

One stunt plane was a J-3 with an 80 horsepower, fuel injection engine. "I could maintain inverted flight for five minutes," he said. "I flew stunts in a lot of air shows, hopped passengers and did some crop dusting. But after we were married, Pat didn't take kindly to the stunt flying."

When he was 77, Hoefs claimed 60 years of flying to his credit. He said he used to log about 599 hours a year but now about 250. Neighbors say he wears an airplane like most wear an old Stetson.

After a flight, Hoefs lands on the unfinished Cowboy Trail, near his hangar at Wood Lake.

"The Super Cub 135 forgives more mistakes and gets off the ground in a short space," Hoefs said. "I keep a heat lamp on the engine during the winter which I feel increases its life."

Bob Kilmer, manager/instructor at Miller Field, said a lot of young ranch area pilots fly a Super Cub. He says they all know the drill: "Go by air if you have time to spare."

BOVINE MOTHER'S DAY
- May 8, 1997 -

We honor the matriarchs of the human race once a year, but we all know that everyday is Mother's Day for busy women with small children. If you are in the cattle industry, the bovine Mother's Day demands to be observed year-around. Those all-important ladies who roam the prairie provide the factory for red meat production. In a sense, we continuously pay homage to them. We visit them daily to fulfill their needs, especially now that there are babies at their sides.

By May, as grass emerges, one might think it is the end of management stress for the cattleman. That's not true, at least here in the northern Sandhills. It's transition time and difficult to keep cows in good condition so they may provide adequate milk.

Grass growth is not yet sufficient to support the cows, but they become dissatisfied with dried hay needed as supplement. For the past week, rain fell on the hay, which made it much less palatable. The herds congregate at gates, anxious to move into adjoining pastures.

Snow and cold rain all day last Saturday caused another delay. There have been reports of calves with enterotoxemia in the Cody area. A veterinarian explained there are many factors that may cause the problem, but usually over-eating. When a calf is cold and wet, such as on Saturday, it may not seek its mother to suck. Eventually, it takes on more milk than normal and that triggers an ever present bacteria in the gut.

Symptoms are the calf kicks its stomach and may die from toxemia in a very short time if not treated immediately.

We've not seen that problem, but did need to treat one calf for scours and one for pneumonia before we opened the gates on Monday. Our son, John, was helping a neighbor brand, so G.R. said he needed a "go-fer."

We've gone modern and bought another used ATV. I'd never ridden one, but G.R. said, "No problem. Just get on it and go." And I said, "Ye Gods! I'm getting too old for matching grandma and grandpa four wheelers."

He drove one and used a hooked rod to catch the calf's hind leg. I was to bring the syringe and medicine on the second machine. I gripped that seat with my legs like I do a saddle, but let me tell you, I prefer a horse when it comes to steep side hills. I definitely was not brave!

I really chickened out after trying to help G.R. corral a cow that wouldn't let her calf suck her sunburned udder. He said he and John do it all the time, but I'm not into high-speed figure 8s and wheelies needed while chasing a cow that won't cooperate.

Monday, I rode in the pickup with G.R. as he turned the west herd into the hills. It took about five minutes. They were waiting at the gate and ran for the length of a football field before stopping to graze fresh grass. He left the gate open so cows could return for calves left behind.

Moving the east herd wasn't so easy because they had to cross the highway. If the cows crossed leisurely with calves at their side, there would be no problem. But they were crazy for grass and crossed on the run, leaving calves behind.

Some of the calves ran back into the smaller area, but a lot of them took off running full bore down the road ditch. All the men could do was get ahead of them on the ATVs and turn them back, first from one direction and then the other. I was on foot at one side of the gate, but couldn't run fast enough to turn back scared calves.

Most of the cows grazed and ignored their motherly duties until their udders became painfully full by evening. Those with calves left in the original lot went to the gate and were let back across the highway to pick up their calves.

It got to be a very long day for the men celebrating just one more Mother's Day in the bovine world.

WRITER SPENDS A DAY TOURING SANDHILLS
- *November 9, 1997* -

The first mention in recorded history of the Sandhill area is that it was a place to avoid. Early explorers described it as "The Great American Desert," a land unfit for human habitation.

We now know that the hardiest of the hardy came and stayed on to endure untold hardship on the desolate prairie. For nearly a century outsiders, for the most part, continued to avoid the area. To this day, Cherry County is one of 15 Nebraska counties that retains frontier population of less than two people per square mile.

Perhaps when a few hard surfaced roads replaced Sandhill trails, the more curious ventured into the vast open spaces.

There are still those who feel that we, who live in the "boonies," or miles from nowhere, seldom receive a visitor. Some very interesting visitors have proved the exact opposite.

I look forward to reading a story about Nebraska that will be published in National Geographic next fall. Roff Smith, who is traveling the state to gather information, spent a short time with us on Monday.

The young man, born in a New England state before spending 15 years in Australia, is on a tight schedule. He was in Ogallala before coming to Valentine on his way to O'Neill, Columbus, Lincoln and locations he didn't mention.

Through the questions he asked, he put us at ease. He wanted an overall picture of the Sandhills ... the benefits of the life style as well as the burdens and what is causing change.

He arrived shortly before lunch. I invited him to join us and a bit embarrassed, explained that it was "stew day." He said he liked stew, and after his third bowl, I began to believe him.

He chuckled as he said, "It's easier to sit in the general's chair at the Strategic Air Command than it is to get an interview with Husker coach Tom Osborne." He said after lengthy negotiation he was granted 10 minutes with the coach on Tuesday. With that facing him, he didn't dare loiter along the way.

We found it awesome that the largest landowners in Australia are the Kidmans who control nearly 8 million acres, the largest continuous tract, 3 million. The headquarters, he said, resembled a small town. It was the sole duty of one crew to check all of the water facilities in a beat-up old pickup, a full-time job, he said.

Nicole Kidman, the actress wife of Tom Cruise, is a distant relative, he said.

He seemed so young (everyone looks young to me now) that I was curious how he came to write for the magazine. He said that National Geographic, contacted him when he was a senior writer for Time magazine. With those credentials we trust Roff to paint an accurate picture of Nebraska.

Many years ago I had fun driving Jody Cobb, senior photographer for NG, through the hills to capture the photos she wished for. At the end of the day I was filled with envy. She marked about 30 rolls of film so she obviously was not limited on film.

Another visitor at this ranch back in 1991 was Dayton Duncan, more recent co-producer of the PBS production, "Lewis & Clark: The Journey of the Corps of Discovery." At the time he was researching material for his book, "Miles From Nowhere."

We thought the book about the nation's 132 counties with frontier population was well researched and most interesting. We look forward to Roff's story about our state because his style much resembled that of Duncan's: sincere and objective.

COWS FAR OUTNUMBER HUMANS
- May 15, 1998 -

Last fall, I couldn't help but overhear a visitor asking questions of a local business person. "What is your most important industry?" the stranger asked. The answer came without hesitation.
"Why, tourism, of course."

I stored the remark on my brain's microfilm and thought, "I didn't know that."

Now understand that almost half the entire 6,757 population of Cherry County live in Valentine. It is a popular hub for tourists now.

But that remark kept simmering on the back burner. Finally, I did some research and put my calculator to work.

Among the largest in the nation, Cherry County claims 6,048 square miles in land mass.

Subtract the population of the small towns across the northern tier and the remaining 3,472 rural residents represent 1.74 people per square mile.

A few rural residents cater to tourists, but I knew of only a few.

Then neighbor Barb Gale gave me a beef cow inventory prepared by the U.S. Census of Agriculture and published in Beef magazine.

The 1992 census and map is the latest available, but I found the information fascinating.

The total number of farms in the census is 803,152 located in 3,057 counties.

The word, "ranch" is never used. And you must know that any rural place that runs cows is considered a farm, whether it be six acres or 20,000.

Some farms may have 10 cows and some more than 1,000.

The total number of beef cows listed nationally is 32,544,976, which, according to my files, is down from the 1974 total of 41.3 million.

Right at the top of that list of "farms" having 60,000 or more beef cows is Cherry County!

The 573 farms listed account for 169,536 beef cows, the most of any county in the nation. (The census doesn't include any other class of cattle.)

In second place, Elko County, Nevada, claims 74,061 fewer cows. That the government owns 83 percent of that state might explain the fewer numbers.

Figures for this county show there is a population of 27.8 beef cows per square mile compared to 1.8 people.

The average number of cows on each farm, small and large, is 295.8. I'll bet a lot of people didn't know that.

I was having so much fun I figured if there was a 10 percent calf loss, there still would be 152,583 offspring to sell; either as calves and/or yearlings.

Let us say that all the offspring was sold for $400 apiece. That total is $61 million, most of which is spent locally after the banker takes his share. Could this industry make a positive economic impact?

Four other Nebraska counties are among the 23 listing the most beef cows.

Sheridan and Lincoln counties are credited with 67,000, Custer with 90,000 and Holt with 92,000.

A total of 26 Nebraska counties made the list that began with 20,000 or fewer beef cows.

Although Arthur County has a population of about 500, 74 of their "farms" were listed on the census as having 19,833 beef cows or an average per farm of 268. Not too shabby.

Texas always claims the biggest of everything. So I was amused that Fayette County ranked 10th overall nationally with 70,034 but on 2,257 farms for an average of 31 cows per farm.

I estimate population there averages 57 cows and 15 people per square mile.

A few may overlook that cattle is a major industry in this county, but producers are still missing the boat.

If we'd just promote an "Adopt-A-Cow" to tourists at $5 for every cow in the county, some $800,000 could relieve much of our school finance problem.

Adopt-A-Cow just may be the only property tax relief in sight.

OLD NOT OBSOLETE; BENT NOT BROKEN
- February 20, 2000 -

Windmills and longtime ranchers just might have more in common than meets the eye. I look upon the windmill as a Sandhills sentinel. From its platform, 20 feet or more above the ground, the metal fans of the wheel scan the horizon.

I like to think it keeps vigil over the land and records history; if we only knew how to translate from wind language. But we know that during this century, it has watched livestock breeds change and greatly improve in quality. It also has watched as native grasses built sod over exposed sand through the careful management of longtime ranchers combined with increased precipitation.

Windmills mourned at the turn of the century as wildlife and wildfowl disappeared from the prairie from over hunting. Market hunting was a vital source of income for early settlers. Hunting seasons, set as early as 1879, were never enforced and mostly ignored.

In 1921, ranchers here called themselves the Klu Klux Klan of the West and organized to protect the prairie chicken from hunters.

Deer numbered as few as 50 in the entire state by 1902, so the Legislature prohibited deer hunting in 1907. Whitetail deer were transplanted into the state and mule deer migrated in from the west. Limited hunting was allowed in 1945 and an open season in 1961. Presently deer numbers exceed 100,000.

Now, the windmill celebrates an abundance of deer and their young that stop to refresh themselves with the water the windmill provides.

The windmill is a sturdy structure. Many have survived raging prairie fires and winds of 50 and 60 mph, at times accompanied by blinding snow. And some of those windmills have been quietly going about their jobs since they were erected in the 1930s. Some say the 1930 Aermotor is the best. And some were badly bent from the elements, but few remained broken.

For example, I know of one older rancher who sought permission to retrieve old windmill heads discarded in blowouts. In his shop, he rebuilt the heads and erected them onto towers, where they performed decades of faithful service.

That feat seems to prove that old windmills and old ranchers should be honored for their durability. Instead of looking upon their elders with respect, some young people may look upon the old as obsolete and overlook the experience and knowledge that can be shared.

Longtime ranchers, too, have suffered from elements beyond their control. I heard the late John Peters, a hardware dealer, say this about a Sandhills rancher during the Great Depression, "Money was terribly scarce, so I sent him a bill just once a year. I knew he was bent, but he was tough. I knew he wasn't broken."

Ranchers fought wildfires across their chunk of prairie and that of neighbors, survived the drought of the 1930s, blizzards such as 1913 and 1949, and the brutal winter of 1978-1979.

My father-in-law, L.C., once told me, "During the 1940s there was a beef shortage because we fed it to our servicemen. We made money in spite of ourselves."

Then came the 1970s when "do-gooders" and activists began a beef-bashing campaign that caused beef prices to drop by half. Here in the Sandhills, cattlemen reeled from below-production prices and the driest years in county history from 1974 to 1976. Beef bashing and a volatile market continue today.

While the windmill is the sentinel, the rancher is the steward. He may climb the tower for a broader view of his land, but he also religiously monitors range and cattle conditions from fenceline to fenceline.

218

Affluence seemed to create a throw-away mentality, but it appears that numerous old windmills and a host of old ranchers remain on the job and are doing it well. Bent in stature does not mean broken.

DOGS GIVE LOVE LIKE NO OTHER
- November 10, 2002 -

I think there is a reason for the expression "Fight like cats and dogs." Cats and dogs have distinct and opposite personalities. Cats remain independent, aloof and grudgingly show affection at mealtime. You may think it love when they brush up against your ankles. But that is just to trip you when you are trying to walk.

Most cats, but not all, dislike dogs.

When a dog bonds with his partner I doubt that you'll see anything less than unconditional love. At least I've watched that type of dedication bestowed upon G.R. during the past two decades.

Dobermans have a maligned reputation and portrayed as vicious guard dogs. Most must be trained to be such.

We raised several litters of Dobermans and found them to be gentle and loving. But the secret is regular hands-on contact from the time their eyes are open.

In 1979, I kept a male from a litter and we called him Ted. He was mine until he took the first ride in G.R.'s pickup. From that time on, the two were inseparable.

Ted grew to an impressive 100 pounds with a broad chest. His size intimidated strangers, but Ted wasn't aggressive. He thought he was "people."

Sometimes he'd run ahead of G.R.'s pickup just for the joy of running. He rode in the old Oliver tractor after G.R. gave him a boost into the high cab.

Ted stood at the open stack-yard gate snapping at the cows while G.R. loaded a stack or rode in the back of the pickup guarding the caker. But most of the time he rode in the cab.

If G.R. might be gone for a couple of days, Ted didn't move from the house and refused to eat. But he must have been psychic. From five to 10 minutes before G.R. drove in, Ted wanted out so he could meet him.

G.R. took good care of Ted and had him as a constant companion for 11 years. But that is very old for a Dobbie (about 77 in dog years) and he died in December 1991 with G.R. holding his head.

Son John built a steel casket and Ted was buried on the hill beneath a cedar tree. G.R.'s grief at the loss of his side-kick lingered.

Ted had been gone five days when I found in the want ads a litter at Chadron. We drove there and bought a five-week old puppy.

So the puppy, G.R. named Scooter, would have a companion we brought a kitten into the house. Before long they were playing like rambunctious litter mates. Scooter continued to be a friend with all cats.

Scooter was G.R.'s companion for 11 years. His personality and actions were the same as Ted's and his love unconditional.

When his hind legs began to fail, G.R. lifted the heavy dog onto the pickup seat so that he could go with. As time passed, G.R. couldn't bear to accept what was ahead, but the dog's condition worsened.

G.R. said his final goodbye Tuesday before daughter Myndi drove Scooter to the vet. To spare his dad, son John closed the casket and brought him back to the ranch for burial next to Ted.

Family members give their love, but a dog never expects an apology or holds a grudge. I've watched G.R. extend and receive truly unconditional love with his dogs. And he suffers genuine grief at the void.

TED TURNER EXPANDS HIS SANDHILL EMPIRE
- February 2003 -

R.E "Ted" Turner added to his Sandhill "Buffalo Commons" with the purchase February 4, 2003, of the Dan Hill Land and Cattle Company, according to the Sheridan County Clerk. Price paid was $5.358 million for 21,000 acres, the Clerk said, which is about $255 per acre. The Hill property adjoins Turner's 52,000 acre Deer Creek Ranch and extends a short distance into Cherry County. Local ranchers attending the auction say they can't compete with Turner's $255 per acre for prairie land. With the latest purchase, Turner, the largest private landowner in the United States, now owns in excess of 261,780 acres of Sandhill ranch land. Nationwide, he claims more than 1.75 million acres in New Mexico, Montana, South Dakota and Nebraska that he stocks with bison.

Turner first came to the Sandhills in 1995, when be bought the 32,000 acre Spike Box Ranch north of Mullen. At the time, Russell Miller, Turner's general manager, said Turner was drawn to the Sandhills by good grass, good people and good water.

After Jim and Laverna Coble died in an auto accident, Turner purchased their ranch that bordered the Spike Box on the west. Two years ago, following the death of Harry Coble and his wife, Doris Coble, Turner purchased their adjoining 12,000 acre Coble-Newton property. Coble also included several miles of the North Loup River. Those purchases ended a 100 year ranching tradition for the Coble family. Other acquisitions by Turner include the Christensen Blue Creek Ranch in Garden County and the adjoining Decker Ranch. Then he added the McGinley Ranch between Merriman and Gordon that extended into South Dakota and the Deer Creek Ranch in Sheridan County.

Through the early part of the 2000s, Turner added smaller parcels when available, as well as numerous school sections; one in Garden County that Turner paid $496.88 per acre during competitive bidding with a Denver attorney who kept his client anonymous. Turner is the founder of the Cable News Network and the owner of the Atlanta Braves. According to national media, he recently sold more than $5 million in AOL stocks.

Ranch land has been a hot item during the past few years, but mostly in large tracts sold to outside owners. Land prices being paid, at least doubled that of ten years ago appears to put family ranching on the threatened list if not endangered. Nearly 68,000 acres changed hands over the past two months. The last of three transactions recorded the third week of July 2002 brought the total of $17.9 million according to the Cherry County Assessor.

On July 11, R. Keith Christensen bought from Powell Cattle Company a contiguous tract extending over 29.058 acres from the Valentine National Wildlife Refuge west to Nebraska Highway 97. Price paid according to the Assessor, was $297 per acre or $8.6 million.

Powell Cattle Company had its Nebraska beginning in January of 1985 when Jimmy Powell of Ft. McKavitt, Texas bought a 10,400 acre ranch from "Buddy" Beel. The following year he added the adjoining Piercy Ranch and then the Kime Lone Tree Ranch owned at the time by Charley Kramer. Thirty thousand acres, however, was small change for Christensen who in 1993 bought a 100,000 acre Garden County ranch and sold it to Ted Turner in March 2000. A published article claimed Turner paid $192 an acre or $12.4 million.

Barta Land Company LLC of Fremont bought two family ranches west of Highway 97 on May 15, 2002. The County Assessor reported the Ravenscroft Cattle Company covered 19.087 acres and sold to Barta for $260 per acre or $4.9 million. That ranch was run by Jim Ravenscroft (son of Olin) and his sons Rob and Jack.

Jim's nephew, James Ravenscroft (son of Willis), had operated the Three Bar Ranch with his brother John. James moved from the Three Bar to the former Stetter TO Ranch in 1997 and sold it as the 19,575 acre Double A Ranch to Barta for $225 an acre.

Later, James Ravenscroft bought Otto Buechle's horse ranch near Valentine.

AT RANDOM

G.R. and Marianne Beel

Brands & Ownership

U   Brand: Sugar Bowl
Owner: Big Creek Ranch,
       Bernard and Barbara Stichka

V–Λ   Brand: V Bar Open A
Owner: Gordon Valley Ranch
       PH and Beverly Young

C–C   Brand: Reverse C Bar C
Owner: Steve and Kimberly Crowe

VIA   Brand: VIA
Owner: Greg Brown

J–   Brand: J Bar
Owner: Churchill Ranch, L.L.C.

ʊ V–ᴧ C–C VIᴧ J–
'WHEN THE WORK'S ALL DONE'
- October 10, 1978 -

All of us in the ranch business look forward to a time when some credibility will come to the old saying, "When the work's all done next fall..." In this day and age of mechanized efficiency, that saying seems to have become more a fantasy than fact. But when I was a child and wished to go somewhere, my father would put me off with the promise that began "when the work is all done next fall..." And there seemed to be only a short span of time before the work was done.

Moving the stacked hay off the meadows is a fall job that completes the hay harvest. Most ranchers then use the after growth on the meadows for fall grazing before winter feeding begins.

I noticed last year that in places the stacks remained on the meadows. Possibly the after-grass wasn't needed, or maybe the wet fall stopped the rancher from moving the stacks.

Rancher-husband G.R., likes to move his stacks as soon as the hay harvest is completed, if we've had enough rain to settle the stacks. There are several reasons for this: stacks that sit too long on the meadow make weed patches the following year; we need the meadows for fall grazing, and because surface water rises in the fall, the stack moving equipment leaves big ruts on the muddy meadow.

The chance you take with early stack moving, however, is that fall lightning might ignite an entire stack yard.

Years ago, when the stacks were moved by horses, it was essential to move them during dry weather. The stacks were slid across the meadows, and even the moisture of a heavy dew would stop them.

Most of our stacks weigh between four and five tons, and moving them didn't take as many horses as in some other areas. Mrs. Red Neumeyer of Mullen loaned me a picture taken in the late 1930s or early 1940s of hay moving at her brother Floyd Edelman's ranch. The picture was taken near Hyannis and shows 32 horses pulling what must have been an eight or 10-ton stack. Four men each drove a six-horse team, and two men had a team of four.

Red Neumeyer said Edelman "was quite a hand and could work rebellious horses that others had give up on."

I would love to have seen that operation, with only 32 "horsepower" straining in the harness in perfect unison to move a big stack. It is hard to imagine it working, because after World War II we used two surplus Army half-tracks rated at 150 horsepower each. To slide the stacks with the half-tracks, four bridge planks were bolted together for the "log" and attached by cables. The log was positioned behind the stack, and once it broke loose from where it sat, the stack slid along at about 10-12 miles an hour.

In the past few years, stack moving has become a one-man job. A big tractor with a tilt-deck stack mover is now used, and the stacks are picked up and moved rather than sliding them along on the ground.

Modern machinery has made the job much faster. It's strange though, because it seems that we are still always seeking that illusive time "when the work's all done next fall..."

ʊ V-ʌ C-C VIA J-
WIND NEVER HERE WHEN YOU NEED IT
- *January 10, 1980* -

The weather in our part of Nebraska has never been accused of being consistent, rather it is a study in extremes. And we're noted for our wind. Off and on for the past few weeks, however, we've been plagued with lack of wind and realize how dependent we are upon it to water the cattle. When the wind doesn't blow, we put pump-jacks powered by little gasoline engines on the wells to pump the water.

It might be a surprise to city dwellers just how much water a cow drinks in the winter — about 5-10 gallons, or half what they consume during the summer.

Unlike horses, cows won't eat snow. G.R. has always said a cow can survive a long time without feed, but not without water. After a blizzard, his prime concern is opening the ice on the tanks ... then stringing the hay.

Chopping the ice is a cold, bitter job which no one really likes, but it is an important phase of ranching in the winter. And merely chopping a hole isn't sufficient; a large area of open water is needed.

Bitter evidence of this happened one January when we turned the care of the cattle over to a hired hand and were gone for a little over a week. Upon return, the first thing G.R. noticed was how the cows had shrunk in weight.

226

It didn't take long to diagnose the problem. The ice had been chopped each day, but only a "nose hole" and the cattle simply could not drink enough. It would have been fine for one cow, but not when there is the competition of a herd.

Last winter, when January temperatures averaged 4.1 degrees, the ice froze deep, making the job of keeping tanks open, a nasty job. Then the overflow immediately froze into a lake of ice around the tanks making it more difficult for the cattle.

During the winter, officials say it is possible for a cow to survive for about five days without water, but that situation is risky. When water does become available, free choice should not be allowed.

Without water, the animal dehydrates and the sodium or salt content increases in the blood and the brain. When water is reintroduced, the blood takes up the water and sodium concentration levels off, but not in the brain. The sodium imbalance in the brain causes an edema or swelling, and the animal often perishes after drinking.

Of course, there are a lot of influencing factors, such as the condition of the cattle at the time. During hot weather, three days or maybe less without water would be a maximum time.

And speaking again of the wind, it didn't do us much good Sunday when gusts went to 45 miles per hour and dropped the wind chill index to 40 below zero. Besides freezing everyone to the bone, winds of that velocity activate the governors on the mills and shut them all down.

There wasn't much traffic to the windmills, either, because the cattle were huddled together in any available protection from the wind.

It seems we can't make up our minds about the wind. On Saturday, we were wishing it would blow, and on Sunday it did. By Monday, 0 degrees and was calm.

Ʊ V-Λ C-C VIA J-

'WHITE MAN HEAP CRAZY'

- July 3, 1980 -

Every time I drive by an old abandoned farmhouse that is falling into rotted oblivion, I find it a sad and depressing sight. I wonder what became of the family that surely filled the house with laughter at some time.

Most often, the abandoned buildings now have fields of corn growing right up to the empty porches. Occasionally, however, you'll see a deserted farmhouse in a desolate sand swept field.

An Oklahoma paper printed a picture depicting the latter and offered a prize for the best 100-word essay on the disastrous effects of land erosion.

A bright young boy, of possibly Commanche or Kiowa heritage, saw the photo and was not overcome with nostalgia for the former residents. His winning essay had this concise description:

"Picture show white man crazy.
Cut down trees. Make too big tee-pee.
Plow hill. Water wash. Wind blow soil.
Grass gone. Door gone. Squaw gone.
Whole place gone to hell.
No pig. No corn. No pony.
Indian no plow land.
Keep grass. Buffalo eat grass. Indian eat buffalo.
Hide make plenty big tee-pee. Make moccasin.
All time Indian eat.
No work. No hitchhike. No ask relief.
No build dam.
White man heap crazy."

I can't help but try to visualize this land when we moved the Indian onto reservations and "developed" the land in the name of progress.

Maybe we're beginning to realize we have gone too far, but is it too late? We've denuded forests, raped the prairie and polluted the rivers.

We are a progressive, innovative and brilliant people, but did we ignore the limitations of our precious natural resources? It's not a realistic attitude, but I'm afraid I'll have to agree just a teeny bit with that young Indian lad.

Ʊ V–Λ C–C VIA J–

THANKS TO VOLUNTEERS

- September 4, 1980 -

The news is frequently dominated by stories of striking workers who seek higher wages, shorter hours, or better working conditions. A strike has become an accepted practice on the American scene.

With county fair fresh in my mind, I wonder what would happen if all of our volunteers went on strike. There would be no county fairs, no state fairs, no political campaigns and a jillion functions would cease. Volunteers are the nation's unsung heroes ... the backbone of every community.

I like the philosophy of one unassuming volunteer, "It's my way of repaying my community for the privilege of living here."

I concentrated on watching one such volunteer at the Cherry County Fair this year. For the 20 some years that I've attended the fair, farmer-rancher Bernard Miles has been there doing the same job with the same enthusiasm.

Bernard is in charge of the open horse show ... an all day affair.

In my opinion, the special part of the show is that portion developed for the tiny tots, the four and five year old kiddos who show their ponies at halter and then through the performance classes.

Bernard, at the microphone, has the patience of Job. He coaxes those little tykes through the proper procedure and makes their first time in the arena a proud accomplishment.

This year, I watched one little four-year-old girl with long pigtails ride her pony in the barrel race. The pony set a leisurely pace, but tried to go around the wrong side of the barrel. "Pull him up, honey. Take him around the other side," Bernard coaxed and the little girl was able to follow his instructions.

There was never enough speed to make those pigtails fly in the wind, but Bernard made that little girl feel as though she were riding in the Kentucky Derby. "Look at the way that pony runs! Good ride, honey," he said as she crossed the finish line.

One little cowboy, no bigger than a minute, had apparently watched a calf roper get a burst of speed from his mount by switching the horse on both sides with the bridle reins. The little boy tucked his chin and was so intent on flipping the reins from side to side that he failed to let the pony have its head.

The barrel pattern was run in slow motion but Bernard kept praising that little boy... "That cowboy can really whip and ride!"

Those little tykes collect their ribbons and are ready to return in the next age class the following year. Bernard has made their very first participation in competition a winning run.

The bonus for Bernard is that he sees these kiddos return time and again and run like the wind by the time they are eight and nine. Many champions on the youth rodeo circuit made their first appearance in the arena at Bernard's show and returned time and again because of his encouragement.

My own daughter, Myndi, rode her part-Shetland in Bernard's show when she was four years old. This year was her 16th consecutive year and there was considerable difference in her speed, but Bernard remembered her first show.

It is just possible that if she had been discouraged on that first time, she might not have known the fun of further competition.

Too often, we forget to acknowledge the important part that volunteers play in all of our lives. Bernard Miles is only one example of the millions of volunteers who contribute their time and, in turn, improve our lives and their communities.

Today, let's make an effort to say, "Thank you."

ʊ V−ʌ c−c VIA J−

THOSE BLESSED WHITE-FACED CATTLE
- January 1, 1982 -

Stories and legends that surround the winter holiday often extend past Christmas to the first day of the New Year ... the first day of a new beginning. For centuries, people have placed lighted candles in windows from Christmas through New Year's Day. A legend states that the Holy Child wanders the world seeking shelter during that time. Lighted candles guide him to where he is welcome ... just as the star led shepherds to Bethlehem.

As everyone knows, animals are given the power of speech on Christmas Eve so many stories surrounding that first Holy Night have passed down through the animal kingdom.

This year, I took an apple for Tuffy, a trusty old saddle horse with bad teeth and stiff legs. I asked him to tell me of stories passed down by his ancestors. "Why don't you go talk to Maggie on New Year's Eve," he said. "She's very, very old, but her descendants aren't interested in their heritage. They say that she's too old-fashioned for the modern world."

"But why New Year's Eve," I asked.

"Because that's a very special date for hereford cattle," Tuffy explained.

Maggie spends her winters in the barn under special care, because for many years she has delivered the best hereford calf in the herd. I took flaked corn laced with molasses to Maggie on New Year's Eve and finally we talked.

"I'm depressed," she said softly in a quavering tone. "All the young herefords want to talk about is synchronization, AI and embryo transfer. I'm afraid the story told to one of my distant ancestors by St. Francis will die with me." "Please tell me the story," I begged.

Strength returned to her voice and a gleam to her eyes at my interest. "It's a very long story, so I will tell you just the ending, which is the most important."

"Long ago, many large animals preyed upon my ancestors at night. Herdsmen brought them into a circle and built bonfires to frighten predators away."

"Then an angel appeared and told the herdsmen to follow a star, that a savior was to be born. Only a young boy was left to care for the cattle."

"Each day, the lad became more worried. The cattle scattered farther, and it grew harder to find them in the dark, especially the babies. You see, at that time, all cattle were blood-red and they blended into a moonless night.

"He tried hard, but the lad missed a few calves each night so his prayer became continuous: 'Oh, please Lord. Help me find the babies.'"

"New Year's Eve was so dark that it seemed a miracle when he found an animal. 'Thank you Lord,' the lad said each time. Then an angel appeared and said: God decreed that these animals carry the color of Christ's blood to symbolize sacrifice. Now his love and your devotion, too, shall be noted," and the angel touched each animal on its forehead. "You now can find them because their shiny white faces reflect God's love."

"The blood-red herefords white face now shines brightly into the darkest of nights," Maggie said as she drifted off to sleep.

U V–∧ C–C VIA J–

LUNCH-EATING DOBERMAN IS DEEP THINKER

- November 17, 1983 -

A n enjoyable part of living in the country is a relationship with animals. Animal watching, so to speak. When people hear the term, "dumb animals," they think they are exactly that ... dumb. I'm here to tell you that doesn't mean animals don't think. It simply means they can't speak in our language.

Yesterday one of G.R.'s Belgium yearling colts leisurely walked up to the pole fence that divides the lawn from her lot. You know how it is. ... the grass is always greener. V-e-r-y carefully she raised one leg over the fence and then the other.

All of this was done in slow motion ... cool, calm and collected. She tried to raise her hind feet over the fence, but kept hitting the top pole with her hoof until she stopped.

She was a comical sight. ... front legs on one side of the poles and hind legs on the other. When she decided to reverse the action, she couldn't quite get it all put together. Finally, she reared and carefully brought the front half of her body back to the same side of the fence as her hind feet.

I paused to compare the personalities of a draft colt and a quarter horse colt. If the latter had gotten into that situation, it probably would have panicked and torn down the fence.

G.R. said that very soon he is going to teach them to drive. It will be just for the fun of it, because he loves those big, kitten-gentle horses.

When he brought them home from the Three Bar Ranch, I asked him if there would be room enough in his "toy box." (Men and boys, separated only by the price of their toys.)

Next to his horses, he loves his dog. Ted, it seems, is a deep thinker.

A couple of weeks ago, G.R. took his saddle horse and his dog to help our son-in-law, Jim, move cattle. Ted is a Doberman, a dog that is not looked upon as a cattle dog. Most people think of them only as "people eaters."

G.R. said Ted saved him miles of riding while he helped move other cattle out of the way so they wouldn't mix with Jim's herd. When they returned to the pickup, I guess Ted had worked up an appetite. They found out later that somehow he had opened the cooler and eaten half of the lunches.

G.R. said Jim wasn't the least bit understanding. It kinda tickled G.R. because he thinks Ted is so durned smart. "Didn't bother me a bit," he said. "He didn't empty the coffee thermos."

More recently, some deer hunters parked their trailer beside G.R.'s shop where they could plug into the electricity. One day, for some reason, they left all of their big coolers on the ground beside the shop.

G.R. said he was working and didn't pay any attention to a strange noise. Finally, Ted came into the shop with a huge chunk of cheese in his mouth.

"He had fairly well cleaned out the cooler, but he couldn't get the plastic off the cheese. He wanted me to open it for him," G.R. related with a smirk.

I was horrified. "What will those men think?" I asked.

"Oh, they won't care. Ted didn't drink their beer!"

People train their Dobbies as watch dogs. It's been said, "They'll eat you for lunch."

ʊ V–ʌ C–C VIA J–

QUICK TRIP RETURNS LIFE TO FAST LANE
- July 12, 1984 -

Life has returned to the fast lane. The broken ribs are nearly healed and the virus bug left only an occasional cough. The byword of daily summer living seems to be: Full speed ahead and damn the torpedoes. Oppressively hot and humid weather are the torpedoes in my life. On a recent 500-mile story-gathering loop through South Dakota, I found the heat relentless, but the country is green as I've ever seen it. All types of cattle are grass fat and sleek as satin.

Ranchers there told me that the high incidence of hoof rot and pink eye that plague Sandhills cattle this year also are problems on the short-grass prairie. I was told the fly problem is severe and millions of tiny grasshoppers remain in spite of spraying.

A newspaper item about a former Broken Bow resident transplanted to South Dakota caught my eye. Paul Tierney, former world champion all-around cowboy, is still cranking it down in the rodeo arena to currently rank ninth in the national standings. At Belle Fourche on July 4, 1984, he had a time of 3.9 seconds in steer wrestling and 8.5 in calf roping during the second go around. Not too bad!

If you don't believe the fast lane bit, let me tell you about Monday. G.R. and I both had afternoon dental appointments in Lincoln. He thought he was too busy to leave Sunday, so we left early the next morning. When we left the dental office at 5 p.m. he said, "Let's go home!"

I thought if I'd spring for dinner and the motel room, he'd change his mind, but nothing doing. We returned home 22 hours after we had left ... and that is crazy! But it's the hay season you know.

Predictions of severe weather on the car radio and an electrical storm that hemstitched the sky ahead kept us alert. West of Broken Bow a bright moon to our backs created an eerie sight, as it illuminated low, dark storm clouds ahead that looked to me like tornado breeders.

I doubt that I've ever seen more intense lightning. It resembled overdone special effects in a movie. I worried that a herd of cattle bunched along a fence near Dunning might be struck and killed. I remembered some years ago when we found five big cows that had dropped in their tracks on a trail to the windmill that was close to a fence. I think the way G.R. explained it to me, the killing electricity traveled along the fence line from one animal to the other.

More than 2 inches of rain did fall here and 3.5 inches at Buddy's place 6 miles to the east. And a tornado did touch down and cause damage near Johnstown.

Everyone in this area is cursing the rain and wishing it could be re-routed to the Texas drought area. You might say we've all had flood irrigation this year and it has produced a good hay crop. But it also frustrates the head honcho when hay for 25 stacks has been mowed and lies in a couple inches of fresh rainwater.

One rancher told me that he would like to put his idled hay waddie crew to building fence. "Can't keep the posts in the ground," he said. "They float to the top of the post hole as fast as we put them in!"

Give us three days of hay-curing weather and look out for traffic in the fast lane!

ᴜ ᴠ-ᴧ ᴄ-ᴄ ᴠɪᴀ ᴊ-
PHOTOGRAPHER 'GOES FOR THE GOLD'
- *August 9, 1984* -

After watching Olympian feats on television, I decided to exert some extra effort and "go for the gold" myself. You see, for three mornings in a row, I had watched in frustration, as a rouge-red sun edged up into the haze of an eastern sky. That fleeting sight needed to be captured on film, but at the right location.

With that in mind, I awakened at 4 a.m. on Saturday, gathered my cameras and drove to a nearby lake. The morning scene reflected in water should be magnificent. I was excited.

Long before I got to the lake, I turned off the car lights and eased close to shore, not wanting to disturb the waterfowl that had spent the night there. One duck called out in question, not in alarm, and the lake remained quiet.

The next sound I heard was the hum of mosquitoes, but I had remembered to bring repellent. I sat to wait in the cool morning air and savored the song of the bass-voiced bullfrog. Quite often the baritone and tenor voices of ducks joined the chorus.

A bullbat sliced the air in pursuit of mosquitoes. A huge dragonfly flew on gossamer wings to land on the steering wheel and keep me company.

Towering hills cast a dark shadow across the lake, but as the sky slowly lightened I was able to distinguish pelicans gliding effortlessly across the surface ... probably 20 of them. Then a mallard hen swam to a half-submerged log and sat there preening less than 10 feet away. I was unable to determine what caused an occasional splash in the water.

Finally, reflected light from the sky touched the wake left by gliding pelicans and turned it to quicksilver. Long fingers of silver followed the birds as they fed and crisscrossed the lake. A splash sounded when the big fishermen thrust their heads below water to scoop up unsuspecting minnows, and then comically raised their ungainly beaks to swallow.

Other pelicans soared in on fixed wings from a distant lake and landed in quiet slow motion.

Although I was anxious for the dawn I would have liked to suspend time ... to drink in the serenity of the hills and prolong the pre-dawn breakfast ritual.

There was not to be a lingering colorful dawn that morning. The sun vaulted into the sky...a blazing summer sun without an attending court of dancing colors. I was disappointed until I relived the hour spent there in close proximity with the waterfowl of Natures kingdom. Somehow we seldom take enough time to refuel the soul.

I had gone for the gold and it remained out of my grasp. But, I was very content to return home with just the experience of having tried.

ꙡ V−Λ C−C VIΛ J−
SANDHILLS AWESOME FROM AIR
- October 4, 1984 -

Ask me if I want to take an airplane ride over the Sandhills, and you don't have to ask twice. Tim Colvin found that out when he asked me that about 8 o'clock one morning. I was ready to go in five seconds.

The Sandhills never appear the same when viewed from the air. To me the vast expanse of grass-covered sand dunes is an awesome sight. Especially from an airplane, which allows an unlimited view.

I've heard photographers say they can't capture the mood of the Sandhills on film. There are only two times of the day to accomplish that; early morning and late afternoon. That is the time of day when shadows define each individual hill, and the soft light caresses each stem of grass. It's a light that brings total awareness to the inquisitive viewer.

Tim is a very competent pilot which added to an enjoyable ride. The craft seemed to barely skim the hills where grass-fat steers followed the cat walks around a choppy sand hill in search of their morning meal.

Rough hills to the south of the buildings seem in good condition with a vigorous regrowth of native grasses. Those were the hills that burned during a prairie fire last year. Ample moisture during the summer was a godsend to that rangeland.

Four female deer bounced across the meadow into cover along the creek as we flew overhead. Four Canadian geese ignored us and slid into the water. Ducks, however, exploded from the water and flew into the northern sky.

Merritt Reservoir seemed strangely empty on that chilly morning. Not one boat was on the lake and only one frost-covered tent was visible through the pine trees of a camp site.

The first antelope that I've seen all summer were breakfasting on an irrigated alfalfa field. A flock of about 50 Canadian geese were performing the

236

same ritual on a meadow across the hills, only a short distance from a ranch house.

Further on, a buck and several doe were browsing on a grain field stubble.

And of course, all through the hills and valleys, there were cattle; cows with calves, bulls, yearlings and some twos.

Some people call the Sandhills "isolated." Some call it "desolate." Others call it "God-forsaken."

I call the Sandhills awesome and mysterious, and yet friendly. Where else on a short morning trip could you see so many reminders of God's work? Where else would you find such a harmonious co-existence of man and wildlife outside the boundaries of a government refuge? Such an existence requires the open space of a vast territory.

All too soon we had seen every animal and checked every windmill on the entire ranch; a week's job if done by horseback.

Tim and I agreed that the definition of a perfect day would be a day spent in an airplane. But duty demanded that we return to the work-a-day world, which seemed almost sacrilegious.

You see it wasn't even Sunday, but the early morning flight across what Sandhillers call God's country left us with the feeling that we had visited his house.

℧ V−∧ C−C V/∧ J−

PLANTING FLOWERS IN MOM'S MEMORY
- May 9, 1985 -

It was always a mystery to me, as a child, that my mother's hands were pink. Not even her thumbs were green, even though her friends described them as such.

My mother loved any type of growing plants. She especially loved flowers.

Hollyhocks rimmed the yard fence. Iris grew in clumps. Row upon row of annual flowers, were always included within her huge vegetable garden. A variety of flowers bloomed beside the doorstep.

Flowering house plants gathered sun from the windows facing east and south.

237

Mom has been gone for 11 years, but yesterday I planted flowers as a Mother's Day gift. She'll be pleased.

You see, the 60 spindly seedlings were very special and endemic to the Nebraska Sandhills. They are called penstemon haydeni, of which as few as five colonies of about 600 living plants have been officially counted in Hooker, Garden and Cherry counties.

It was in 1979, that I saw my first "blowout bluebell," as the flower often is called. After searching the hills with Dr. Ron Weedon, biologist at Chadron State College, a neighbor woman told me of a colony which she had seen as a child.

Topography is often a formidable defense. The haydeni colony was located on the rim of an active blowout at the crest of a steep sandy hill. A visit to view the flowering plants, the first week of June, is an exhausting trip. Only by walking and climbing can you reach the summit of the hill.

The plant was exciting to biologists. Early attempts to transplant the haydeni on a small scale were made with success. Colonizing, however, seemed to be most successful by using seedlings.

Dr. James Stubbendieck and his colleagues in the Department of Agronomy, University of Nebraska, were successful in developing a method to force germination of gathered seeds.

Dr. Stubbendieck explained that the seeds were found to be coated with a tough, but water soluble inhibitor. Experiments proved that by subjecting the seeds to a water flow the inhibitor was dissolved. Because the coating was extremely hard, Dr. Stubbendieck said, he also cut the seed cover with a knife.

The greenhouse at the university houses dozens of haydeni seedlings that are transplanted into colonies throughout the Sandhills to perpetuate the species. Biologists discourage disturbing the relatively few adult plants that now survive.

When Dr. Stubbendieck offered me the opportunity to establish a new colony from seedlings, I was excited. I knew the exact location —a nearly inaccessible sandy hill to the north of our building site.

The blowout at the crest of the hill is one where resident rancher G.R. played as a child. Deer, coyotes and birds are nearly the only visitors to that lofty spot, inaccessible by vehicle. Humans who venture there leave with sand in their shoes.

The seedlings for a new colony of penstemon haydeni were lovingly planted in that blowout while thoughts of my mother kept me company.

Happy Mother's Day Mom. I knew you'd be pleased.

Ꙩ Ꝟ-Ʌ Ꮯ-Ꮯ ᏉᏆᎪ Ꭻ-
EVEN COYOTES FACE CRISIS
- February 6, 1986 -

Crisis. That word alone seems to be the byword of the day. Agriculture has faced a crisis for so long that we need to coin another word. No one pays any attention to "crisis" anymore.

In fact, there was a reported case of child abuse just the other day, but it didn't make the news. The sheriff hushed it up because he didn't want to record the case on his books. It was that bad!

The sheriff told me that he caught some rancher trying to give his ranch away to his son ... but the sheriff stopped the deal and saved the poor kid from the most brutal kind of child abuse that I've ever heard of.

Things are really tough in this country. You can't even catch a banker anymore unless it's on Sunday. Monday through Friday he's out in the country running the farms and ranches that he's taken over, and on Saturday he hides, so he won't have to take on another one.

Even the coyotes in our country are facing a crisis. For years, the wily predators have enjoyed immunity on the Valentine National Wildlife Refuge where hunting them was prohibited.

When the coyote felt pressure from winter hunting, he merely disappeared into the tall grass and brush of the refuge.

One winter morning, some time ago, our son John counted 50 coyotes on the ice of Pelican Lake. They were drawn to the lake by fish frozen there after the lake had been renovated to kill the carp. John and the coyotes all knew that no one was allowed to shoot them there.

Local ranchers occasionally have called the refuge a "coyote hatchery," especially when the old ones try to feed their young on the meat of baby calves. You know how it is. Leave the refuge, gorge on beef, and then disappear again.

Ole Charlie, however, has outfoxed himself. He developed an appetite for duck eggs, and now he's in a world of trouble.

Fish and Wildlife personnel say that studies have shown that coyotes destroy about 36 percent of all duck nests. That's like figuring a 64 percent calf crop when you have to have at least 90 percent to survive.

Trapping has been allowed on the refuge, but coyotes aren't too dumb about traps. Last year, F&WS personnel eliminated nearly 100 by shooting them from an airplane.

That practice didn't set too well with refuge neighbors. If coyotes were going to be killed, why not let local people shoot them and realize a few dollars from selling the hide? Bootlegging isn't legal and we've all heard about cash flow.

Charlie Coyote had better watch his tracks because the season is now open on his hide. Hunting will be allowed on the Valentine Refuge from now until March 15, governed by a special permit and normal hunting laws, of course. Hunters also will be restricted to shotguns and archery close to the public fishing lakes because there is no open season on fishermen.

ʊ V-ʌ C-C VIA J-
SIGNS OF NEBRASKA HUMOR
- March 27, 1986 -

People from all nationalities settled in the early Sandhills. Perhaps from that diverse heritage, from that melting pot of Germans, Swiss, French etc., came a certain ingenuity and a sense of humor that has become Nebraska's strong point.

I like the sign painted on the side of a truck owned by Ward's Plumbing in Valentine: "In our business a flush beats a full house."

Then there's the one on the back of a photographer's van that reads: "Go ahead. Expect a miracle."

Irene Beaman tells me there's a horse trailer in the Ogallala area with a sign on the endgate that reads: "Slow down. Don't be what you see."

As well as being imaginative, Nebraskans always have been innovative.

Take Lucy McMurtrey for example. She was a bride on an isolated homestead south of the Snake River back in 1915.

Naturally, Lucy often became lonesome, so she took her baby to visit the neighbors in a horse-drawn buggy. She also loaded the churn into the back. By the time she returned home the butter was churned.

Mary Jane Newman lived in a soddie with dirt floors near Pelican Lake. A large population of fleas inhabited the sod walls. To keep them off the table Mary put pans of water under each table leg.

To eliminate the fleas as bed partners she finally scattered a thin layer of straw across the bedroom floor, sprinkled sulfur on the straw and set it afire.

The burning sulfur fumes apparently killed the fleas, but also killed all of her treasured house plants that she carefully had carried in a covered wagon all the way from Minnesota.

The imagination of some was very fertile. Take for example, a silent partner of the Churn Ranch located south of Merriman, back at the turn of the century. He thought they could create additional revenue by selling fur to a felt maker.

The Iowa partner, Herbert Shadbolt, sent out a large number of black cats. He thought they could live and multiply there with little care. When they reached an adequate number he thought their hides could be sold to produce felt for black hats.

Apparently, Kinkaiders contributed extra kittens and the numbers rapidly grew. None of the cats, however, were destroyed unless found guilty of killing baby chicks. Perhaps, cat hats never became popular.

I was raised in South Dakota, so perhaps that's why my imagination is sterile. I can't claim to be a native Nebraskan.

I'd love to be imaginative and innovative, but the best thing that I do anymore is to forget about what I'd like to be. I planned to sign up for a course that improves the memory, but then I forgot.

An innovative friend, however, gave me a little sign to hang over my desk: "I like my new bifocals. My dentures fit just fine. I have my hearing aid turned high, but Lord, I miss my mind."

ʊ V–ʌ C–C VIA J–
NATURE'S VISUALS ABOUND
IN SUMMER SHOW
- July 10, 1986 -

Fields of wildflowers can be found almost anywhere during a Sandhill July ... broad areas, blue with vervain or gold glistening from coneflower petals. Or Queen Ann's lace, black-eyed susans, spiderwart, prickly poppy and many more. Usually, tall spikes of shell-leaf penstomen blanket the prairie for Memorial Day.

Needle and thread grass has matured and shed its barbed seeds, and slender slivers of golden grasses bend freely with the wind. It turns brown by July, because it is one of the cool season grasses that provide the very first grazing in the spring; sometimes in April.

Warm season grasses, such as prairie sandreed, sand dropseed, the bluestems, switchgrass and other native plants, flourish until fall. Cattle convert all those grasses into protein.

And speaking of protein. I'm told that the seed pods on soapweeds are extremely high in protein and found very tasty by cattle. That's why you don't see dry pods in a pasture that is grazed when the pod is soft and edible.

Beef cattle are vegetarians. They convert grass into digestible protein for human consumption in the form of red meat. It would seem to me that the diet of a beef animal should make it one of the most attractive foods available.

I wish for a genie that would see that every human could eat a daily portion of good beef, properly prepared. We'd all have strong bodies.

However, just wishing not always brings what we want.

I'll share a story with that moral:

Once upon a time there was a Chrysler car dealer in a small Florida town. When the first small Japanese imports came onto the market Joe, the dealer, laughed and said they wouldn't last long.

"No red-blooded American would buy imports," he said. But, as time went on, the trickle of foreign cars became a stream, then a river ... and then a torrent. Joe no longer scoffed at the impact of the imports on his business. He grew more depressed because his business was nearly bankrupt. And finally it was.

Joe's wife left him and his children said, "Failure!"

Totally at a loss, Joe decided to travel to London and check out the auto business there. But, Joe was going to walk all the way.

He laid his shoes and coat on the sand of the beach and started walking into the ocean. "Oh how I wish things could have been different," he muttered to himself.

Finally, the ocean water was up to his waist and then to his armpits. A floating bottle kept bumping him until he finally pulled the cork to investigate.

"I'm so grateful you found me," said the genie that emerged. "I've been cooped up for 200 years so I will grant any wish you make."

Joe took considerable time in composing a wish because he was not going to make a foolish wish.

"All I want," he said, "is to be a foreign car dealer in a large city."

His wish was granted. In two seconds Joe found himself as a Chrysler dealer in the heart of Tokyo, Japan.

ひ V-∧ C-C VIA J-
HUMOR KEEPS UP WITH ECONOMY
- August 2, 1986 -

I 've been wondering if perhaps jokes become more caustic, as the farm economy tightens.

For example: Do you know the fastest way to get a political candidate down from a tree? Cut the rope.

Then there's an old story with a new twist. Two lovely ladies were hiking through a small town park one day.

A grasshopper flew through the air and landed in their path.

"Please help me," cried the grasshopper. "A curse has been put upon me by a wicked banker. I'm actually a rancher ... I'm single and I have 1,000 cows on my ranch ... but the only way I can return to normal is by a kiss from a pretty girl. Oh, please kiss me!"

One of the ladies reached down and picked up the grasshopper. She studied it for a moment and then she carefully placed it in her backpack.

"What in the world are you doing?" asked her companion. "Why don't you kiss it and claim yourself a rancher?"

"I thought it over," said the second woman, "and I decided that conditions being what they are, a talking grasshopper was worth a lot more than a big rancher."

I love it! People will never get really down if they can poke fun at themselves.

We've been haying like crazy. For a time it was so hot, 107 degrees on the 29th, that G.R. said the raker had to bunch the hay before it hit the ground behind the mower.

One day, the wind blew so hard the mower cut down grass on a meadow five times because the wind kept blowing his tractor backwards across the field.

Then it rained a couple of inches and stopped the crew. "Not to worry," says ole Grump and Rumble. "It rained so hard it washed the windrows down into the creek behind the beaver dams. To clean up their living quarters, those tidy beavers pushed the hay to shore and stacked it for us."

You might think GRrrr Bear has been out in the sun too long, but strange happenings follow him to the house.

Our birthdays were two days apart in July. We're both Leos (and not compatible according to our horoscope). Myndi, our youngest, invited us in for dinner on Saturday night. I worried about the time element, because when G.R. gets in the hay field he's harder to stop than a runaway team of spooked horses.

He came in on a run allowing about 15 minutes for a shower and a shave. Then I heard him yelling from the back bathroom: "Get me out of here! The door's locked!"

I knew there was no lock on that door so I thought he was kidding. He wasn't, as the threatening tone of his voice soon indicated. The door WAS stuck. The knob turned, but nothing happened.

I passed hammer and screwdriver through an outside window, so he could remove the hinges. Still nothing happened for a time, although I pushed inward on the door.

Use your imagination and you'll visualize his marvelous mood all during the drive to town. "I'm too old for that kind of foolishness," he growled. But grrr turned to genial when other guests were there as a surprise and during a wonderful meal.

When two birthday cakes with the appropriate candles came out, it was our very first experience at viewing an indoor forest fire.

℧   V−Λ   C−C   VIΛ   J−
WELL REPAIR A THANKLESS TASK
- November 13, 1986 -

L ast week, during shirt sleeve weather, G.R. and I tramped across a carpet of green grass. There's just the two of us now. Yesterday we walked across a frozen pond. He walked, I fell through. You might say that's the only time I've carried the most weight around THIS place.

But the pond was shallow having formed when a stock tank sprung a leak and left cows low on water.

Bottomless tanks have a way of breaking out when the thermometer favors the zero mark. Trouble likes company so it usually comes in twos ... and did. Well leathers never like to quit their job unless it's COLD, which they did at the same well.

You may have heard about ranch computers, and I'm quite good at the computer. But I've not seen software yet, that was programmed to bank a tank or releather a well. Sometimes high tech is as worthless as hi diddle diddle.

I first learned of our water problem about 8 a.m., when G.R. came stomping toward the house. His stride told me that all was not well, but I couldn't tell if his breath was turning to steam in the frigid air, or if the blue cloud was smoke coming from out his ears.

When he opened the door, I could tell it was smoke.

"Come help me!" he commanded, "It'll only take a minute."

Knowing from experience the length of his "minutes," I asked for time to find longjohns and mittens. He left again grumbling something that sounded like, "I can't wait all day. Cows are out of water!"

I found a warm jacket, leather gloves, but no overshoes and trudged through 6-inch snow to the shop. We got in the pickup and headed for Duck Lake Flat.

We crawled the barbed wire that circles the base of the windmill tower. Twice, G.R. hung up on a barb, first by his overshoe and then his jeans. He cussed and the mood was set. He was the ole familiar, impatient GRrrr Bear.

The leak from the tank had formed a pond around the well right where we had to stand to pull the pump rod. That's where I broke through the ice and the water that leaked through the holes in my boots had never heard of "warm."

Hand over hand, we both worked to pull the 20-foot pump rod up out from the well, the wet metal rod soaking our gloves. And the cold grew colder.

At the bottom of the rod a threaded gadget had to be taken apart that holds two pieces of cupped leather. Pipe wrenches felt like dry ice, and corroded connections were hard to budge. Then the leathers were too large. That meant bare hand and jackknife.

"This little 3-inch circle of cowhide costs $5 apiece, but they can't even make the *(%'($* thing to fit!" That was GRrrr Bear. I didn't say a word.

That job finished, we chopped into frozen sand and shoveled it around the tank to cover the small leak. GRrr Bear's "minute" became one of the longest I've spent.

Fingers brittle and toes numb I waited for my wages, a thank you. Nothing. Just scowling silence all the way home.

"I'm worth a heck of a lot more than you pay me!" I yelled and slammed the pickup door. Finally ... GRrr Bear grinned.

ʊ V−∧ C−C VI∧ J−
AN ODE TO THE SANDHILLS
- November 19, 1986 -

Thank you, Lord, for the sand beneath our feet. Our gratitude deepens as shadows define the outlines of distant hills during the early evening hours. That's when this land is the most articulate.

First seen, especially when seen from the window of a car speeding down a highway, the Sandhills bring to mind a lot of trite and erroneous descriptions: desolate, bleak, barren, isolated, to name a few.

Remain in the car and those impressions might remain. In that case, the Sandhills have been done a great injustice and a unique experience was missed.

Perhaps the country is best seen at a leisurely pace ... seen over, a horse's ears with frequent stops for exploration ... pauses to meditate and to ponder the land and its inhabitants.

The windswept sand of a creek bank, for example, is not merely an expanse of sand. Thereon lies documentation of life on the prairie. Tracks in the sand tell that deer and an ever cautious coyote drank from the stream ... that sand lizards and mice scurried here and there ... that a badger left his hole for a nocturnal hunt.

On another spot of sand, tiny tracks end abruptly in a flurry of marks, the rodent perhaps snagged by the talons of a swooping hawk or night-hunting owl. Nearby, a snake left behind swinging curves in the sand just because slithering across it felt good to its belly.

Exposed sand of a blowout or cattle trail tell of other stories about the prairie chain of life. More dramatic tales are marked by scattered feathers or bits of fur. Other stories hold less drama and more allure like etchings drawn into the sand with a blade of grass gently bent by the wind ... or of irregular ripples and waves on the leeward side of a blowout.

Stop to observe the story documented in the sand and it will be hard to ignore splashes of color ... color that changes as each wildflower species blooms in its turn.

246

Eyes raised from the flowers will never quite see the horizon, never see that crisp distinct line where the land flattens to abruptly meet the sky.. No matter how high the hill, there always seems to be another hill to obstruct an unlimited view.

From any lofty perch the view might include a broad prairie landscape and a willow-rimmed creek, but never a great, vast land sweeping on forever. Hills rise and fall and rise and fall to shelter their secrets among endless pockets and gullies.

Those same depressions hide about, half of what meets the eye, hide any number of cattle causing cowboys to ride every hill and pocket during round-up. But those same hideouts, cursed during roundup, are praised for the shelter offered there for animals, wild and domestic alike, during the onslaught of a Sandhills blizzard. Bleached bones at the bottom, however, might tell of a critter marooned there during prolonged wind-drifted snow.

The Sandhills can be hostile and have, indeed, claimed the lives of man and beast. At the same time those grass-stabilized dunes can be gentle ... kind to those who understand them and use wisely the prairie grasses that grow up on them.

ʊ V−ʌ C−C VIA J−

PRIVILEGES OF DEER HUNTING
IN NEBRASKA
- November 20, 1986 -

Each fall, deer hunters seek their prey throughout the Sandhills, as well as, the rest of the state. That was not always the case, and perhaps, we've grown to take those game animals for granted.

Did you know, that lack of game laws and over hunting brought deer in Nebraska to the brink of extinction by 1900? The Game and Fish Commission's 1901-02 report estimated only 50 deer in the entire state.

In 1976, I asked the late Bill Stetter about early hunting. Stetter's father, Jacob, a trained butcher, came to Valentine back in 1883 before the town was incorporated.

Bill said his father told him how the soldiers from Fort Niobrara hunted game for market along the Niobrara on their days off. He said they took mule teams with wagons with a high flare box and filled them with deer for the eastern market.

Soldiers were not the only hunters; market hunting was a business for many. An 1887 news item stated that one man shot 500 ducks in eight days and sold them for 20 cents apiece, and that 1,300 ducks had been shot on a lake near Cody. "That type of hunting is an outrage," the editor noted.

Game laws were passed in 1901 and generally ignored. Then the 1907 Legislature prohibited deer hunting. Through migration from the west and re-production, the deer population grew to about 3,000 head by 1940.

The first statewide deer season was in 1961, and present deer population in the state is estimated at about 100,000. According to Carl Menzel, big game specialist for the Nebraska Game and Parks at Bassett, 46,222 deer permits were issued throughout the state in 1985. Some 30,559 deer were taken for a 66 percent success.

In the Sandhills region, which runs from U.S. 83 west to Gordon and South to Arthur, 2,974 permits were issued last year and 1,894 deer were taken. For the past five years, the number of deer checked through the Valentine station has been fairly consistent ranging from 440 in 1982 to 554 in 1984. This year 486 were checked in.

Game management has been a boom not only to hunters, but to the cof-fers of the Game and Parks. I didn't realize, until I put a pencil to it, that the $20 deer licenses plus $7.50 habitat stamps sold in 1985 amounted to $1.27 million.

Throughout the state privately owned land supports most of the deer popu-lation.

Asking permission seems to offend some, and hunters from the eastern part of the state seem to get the most blame. Stories of that are legion, but one landowner north of Valentine said a group with eastern license plates tried to run him off his own land. "Brazen," he said. "Told me I was trespassing."

Then, there is the mistaken identity problem. Don Colburn told me that it's a matter of record in the sheriff's office that an 800-pound steer on his place was found dead in his canyon pasture, shot twice ... once in the flank and once behind the front leg.

Deer hunting is now a privilege gained through careful game manage-ment. But it seems only common courtesy to ask permission to hunt on private land. That, too, is a privilege.

ʊ V-ʌ c-c VＩA J-
'THANK GOD FOR GREATER NEBRASKA'
- June 4, 1987 -

About this time in the week you might hear people mutter TGIF ... Thank God it's Friday. It's almost Friday, but this is my TGFGN column ... Thank God For Greater Nebraska ... and I might add ... its people.

Ours is a rural part of the state where people seem to genuinely care about their neighbors. Let me cite examples.

Visualize women dressed in pretty frocks attending a shower for two young women who had lost all of their possessions in a recent fire. Some of those same guests soon left the party to enter a nearby building filling with smoke to help carry out merchandise in the face of another fire. The building belonged to the shower honoree's family.

It's certain that those party dresses became soiled or at least absorbed the offensive smell of smoke. That was the least of the women's concern.

There were dozens of other people who rushed to help and worked on into the night, perhaps not because they were close friends, but because there was a need.

That happened Monday in Valentine, small town, mid-America. Would the same thing happen in New York, big city, East Coast? I wonder.

Then there were the volunteer firemen, businessmen who perhaps must lock their stores to go fight another's fire ... sometimes on through the night. They don't get paid, unless perhaps with a thank you. A thank you may be small pay, but it's important to the recipient. Let us not forget.

A kindness or a thoughtful act need not be dramatic to deserve appreciation. My thanks go to Mrs. Jack Smith of North Platte, who sent me information about the courthouse at Nelson. I was curious to find out when that magnificent old building was erected.

Smith referred to a book published on Nuckolls County. Information there, she said, noted the first frame courthouse was built in 1873 where the present library now stands. (That's 10 years before Cherry County was even organized.)

The present courthouse apparently was built in 1890, the cornerstone laid on June 20 of that year. An entire block for the site, valued between $8,000 and

$10,000, was donated by the city of Nelson. Taxpayers paid 60 cents on every $1,000 assessed for the bond issue.

Cherry County's own Nelda Keller is nearly the same age as the courthouse. She lives with her daughter, Eldora Muirhead, and celebrated her 98th birthday on Monday.

She taught her first school in 1905, in a log building along the Niobrara River when she was 16. Valentine High School offered only 11 grades at the time including a normal training course.

Nelda Keller is 98, one of our last true pioneers. She is an example of the people who preferred life on the prairie and who helped make Greater Nebraska a good place to live.

Thank God for Greater Nebraska and the people who live there.

ʊ V–ʌ C–C VIA J–
ELECTRICITY EXAMINED, FEARED
- July 16, 1987 -

Electricity frequently charges the air during the Iran-Contra hearings. We are not daytime TV soap watchers, but our television set has been on all through the day for more than a week. An attempt to understand what —we feel— is our duty.

We'll leave analyzing to the experts, but it would appear that a considerable amount of national laundry is being washed in public. Secrecy and lies have separate definitions.

Deceit is an unfortunate tool, no matter what the motive. We admire heroes. We would like to feel they would be above reproach because youngsters emulate their heroes. But as we listened to testimony, it substantiated a little ditty learned at our mother's knee: "Oh what a web we weave when we practice to deceive."

A different type of electricity recently has been closer to home. We feel more qualified in analyzing its effects. You've read about storm damage in the Sandhills area recently, but we would like to elaborate about the mysterious effects of lightning.

One week ago, we were at the edge of Valentine and observed the angriest sky to the south, we've ever seen. White twisting wind clouds in the shape of a mega-sized cigar hugged the ground at the base of a sky turned black. Lightning stabbed and jabbed with dreadful power. Thunder was deafening.

Cattle were killed during that electrical storm. Only those insured are investigated, so an exact number will never be known. We know of two bulls and perhaps a dozen cows. One calf apparently was nursing when it and its mother were struck and killed.

Ron McCoy had been combining rye south of town. Hail began to fall, some larger than golf balls and lightning turned vicious. His daughter was driving another big tractor, but they abandoned the equipment hurriedly.

The next day, a rear tractor tire was flat, a big 18-438 that costs about $500. In a short time it was found that all four tractor tires were ruined. Replacement cost, without fluid, runs about $1,300.

Ironically, the business band radio in that particular tractor was not damaged. One in the combine parked 75 feet away was knocked out.

Denny Doolittle of Colburn's Tire Shop said he'd never seen anything quite like it. Wherever each tire made contact with the ground, there were about 500 holes the size of match heads, he said.

He said fluid in the tire probably acted as a better conductor for electricity, but he wondered what would happen to a person had they been in the machine at the time.

Another question arises. Now that steel belts are a part of passenger car tires, would lightning be more of a threat to passengers?

That same night lightning struck two power poles in the heart of town. Reports from only one sales and service business listed 30 service calls after the storm within a 20-mile radius; one-third of them satellite dishes and the rest antennas and TV sets.

Bruce Phipps said that during a separate storm lightning struck a tree beside his house. It left a hole two feet in diameter and 10 inches deep, then entered the house to blast the door off the fuse box and scatter fuses across the room.

Nature's electricity often leaves a trail of irreversible damage. Let's hope that the sparks flying from the Iran-Contra hearings do not do the same to our nation.

LEAP YEAR DAY FULL OF CALVING HUMOR
- February 25, 1988 -

L eap Year gives us an extra day to cope with. Whether that's good or bad depends upon what you're doing. Most Sandhills ranchers have extended the calving season, so it's possible a little excitement may enliven a routine job on the 29th.

A neighbor, we'll call Pete, stopped the other day and got to reminiscing about one calving season that he spent in South Dakota. The men were howling with laughter because they could relate to the story. But in passing it along you'll miss the best part, that of Pete's facial and physical expressions.

Pete said one particular night was especially dark as he walked through the springers with a flashlight.

"The calving lot was long and narrow, but not too big," he explained.

"My light picked up a first-calf heifer having trouble. Only one foot out. She was stretched out and didn't see me, so I thought I'd just ease up behind her, get both of the calf's feet in the chain and pull it. You hate to rile cows by getting them in the barn if you don't have to."

For those unfamiliar with the bovine maternity ward, let me explain the calving chain. It's lightweight, about three feet long with round links on each end large enough to pull back through and make a loop. The loops are slipped over the calf's front feet for pulling leverage.

When you're alone, you have to make up for the lack of a third hand. Pete said everything went as planned ... for a couple of seconds.

"I needed to work fast before the heifer realized I was there," Pete explained. "I formed a loop at both ends of the chain and slipped one over the exposed leg. I needed both hands to get hold of the second leg, so I slipped the other loop around my wrist to keep it from dangling. Once I got a hold of the second leg, I could slide the chain right off my wrist and over the hoof. Ten seconds would do it."

But with only one loop secured, the heifer jumped to her feet.

"She took off on a dead run a kickin' and a bawlin'," Pete said, "and a pulling me by my wrist. Around that lot we went, her a bawlin' and me taking steps 20-feet long. I swear that lot seemed big enough to cover a full section."

252

Pete, somehow, was able to stay on his feet, and finally the heifer sprinted into close quarters beside a tank and a windmill. She stopped and Pete went on by with enough force that he was able to pull the heifer off her feet.

The cowboy grinned and asked, "Have you ever heard of bulldogging a critter from the rear?"

Pete was able to remove the loop from his wrist before the heifer took off again, losing the chain somewhere in the lot.

"I sat there for quite a spell before I could breathe normal again. Later, I drove the heifer in the barn, and with very little effort pulled her calf."

Pete laughed in remembering.

"At the time it sure wasn't funny," he said and the men nodded in understanding.

℧ V-Λ C-C VIΛ J-

NOT EASY FOR HUMANS TO OUTSTMART CATTLE

- October 13, 1988 -

Reader response adds a postscript to the story about Jim Van Winkle loading a wild bull into a trailer parked in the middle of a big pasture. The principle was easy does it ... patiently circle the bull in close until stepping into the trailer becomes his own idea.

A possible theory may be that if you "worry" a not-so-tame animal long enough it seeks a place to hide. But there may be danger in passing along a brand new method.

Wayne Jenkins, down in Callaway country, said my credibility was in doubt as some of the locals gathered for coffee at what he called the "Liar's Club." Apparently, some who read the story doubted that I had ever lived on a ranch or helped work cattle.

Jenkins said he came to my defense. He had visited this ranch when G.R.'s father, L.C., was alive and he remembered that I was raised on one in South Dakota.

The place where I was raised was much smaller and so was the herd. Few numbers made it easy to tame them. Consequently, our methods of handling cattle often were quite different from those we now use in our Sandhill pastures scattered over 16 sections.

My earliest memory of a bull, however, was that of a horned hereford that grew wild and mean. Dad wanted to be rid of him and was able to corral him only by bringing cows in with him. Getting him through the plank gate to the loading dock was another story. Dad stood in the narrow alley and when the bull charged him it was my job to latch the gate.

Never have I been so scared ... certain that Dad would be gored.

Some ranchers tell me that as a last resort, a shotgun blast to the rump is a convincing bull persuader. Some use birdshot and others use shells loaded with salt.

Although I've always lived on a ranch, none of my family claim to be "buckaroos" - cowboys who wear leather hats, "chink" chaps and dislike riding slower than a gallop. But I've helped drive cattle enough to know that you alter the method to fit the animal.

Just last week, G.R. encountered a high-headed, wild-eyed black cow. Her typical behavior was either to attack or high-tail through the nearest fence. So G.R. backed the trailer with the open end just through the metal gate and slowly hazed the cow into the big plank corral.

"She ran around and around, but I just sat quietly on my horse. After so long, she jumped into the trailer. No big deal. Had I whooped, hollered and crowded her, she'd have wrecked the place."

Peter Seberger writes from Cozad, that he and a brother shared a holstein bull back during the 50s. "They could be mean," he wrote, but the bull was hauled back and forth so often to breed both herds that when they'd park the trailer the bull jumped right in. "Knew where he was going," Peter wrote.

He had less success with a skittish, first-calf heifer that he wanted to milk. After repeated tries to get her in the barn, he lost his patience and whistled for the dog. A few laps around the corral with a dog at her heels and the heifer went right to the stanchion.

Perhaps, handling animals is all a matter of getting their attention ... usually with a 2 x 4 for a mule, I'm told. Like people, God didn't make any two animals exactly alike. Some are quiet and gentle while others are mean and obnoxious.

Success just might depend on the human species outsmarting those of the animal world.

U V-∧ C-C VIA J-
AMERICA'S LAST, MYSTERIOUS FRONTIER
- July 18, 1989 -

It would seem to me that throughout the inhabited United States, Nebraska's Sandhills area still remains somewhat of a last frontier. Novels have been written and movies have been filmed in states from Montana to Texas and from New York to California. To my knowledge only a short scene from the movie, "Sea of Grass," was actually filmed in the Sandhills.

Even novelists, with the exception of Mari Sandoz and Nellie Snyder Yost, skirted the interior as did the early explorers.

Mystery enshrouded the early Sandhills, a land described in 1795 by Scotsman James MacKay, the first white man to skirt its eastern edge, as "a great desert of drifting sand without trees, soil, rocks or animals of any kind."

Lt. G.K. Warren was similarly impressed during excursions in 1855 and 1857 and described the Sandhills as "unfit for man or beast."

Warren, however, reported a large party of the Ponca tribe, and some 380 lodges of the Dakota Sioux or "Burnt Thighs" along the Niobrara River. Archaeological evidence, however scant, shows that prehistoric man had, indeed, settled along the river valleys within the Sandhills.

It wasn't until 1879 that cowboys entered the heartland. Cattle being held for the government beef issue drifted south across the Niobrara during a March '79 blizzard and cowboys were sent to find them. To their surprise they found hundreds of strays that had over wintered within the hills that were in comparable, or better flesh, than those that had drifted.

From that time, cattlemen and settlers alike, moved deeper into the hills. But the Sandhills remained virtually unnoticed by the rest of the nation. Sooner or later, however, even an isolated area gains recognition.

The first "real" story that I saw appear was a color spread in National Geographic that called the Sandhills "the land of lingering shadows and long sunsets."

Since then, there have been Sandhills stories accompanied by colored photos in the Smithsonian, GEO, Better Homes and Gardens, Farm & Ranch Living, Country Woman and Sports Afield, to name a few. GEO featured the 54,000-acre Niobrara Valley Preserve where six major ecological systems meet and mix as part of the two million acres owned or managed nationwide by the Nature Conservancy.

A lot of history has been compressed into the past 100 years, but has remained virtually untouched until some of it was recorded in "A Sandhill Century," a two-volume set printed to commemorate Cherry County's centennial.

It's just possible that a novel and movie are going to be based in the Sandhills. Early in December, I fielded a call from Katie Asch, research specialist for Columbia Pictures. She said it was possible that a writer was going to base a story in the Sandhills for a movie. She ordered a set of our books, and I referred her to North Platte Historian, Nellie Yost.

ᘮ V-ᴧ c-c VIᴧ J-
TAKING TIME TO SMELL NATIVE FLOWERS
- September 21, 1989 -

It would seem that I'd better retract my words of "end of the season for grasses" that I wrote last week. Even though heavy frost turned our world to white and temperatures were in the mid-20s, it now appears that frost did not kill the native grasses.

Perhaps, because rain had fallen and soaked the ground before the cold front moved through, plants were more resistant to the killing effects of frost. My garden went flat on the first night, but flowers close to the house are still in bloom.

We were afraid that the leaves would turn black on the trees, as they have in years before, and cling with a death grip all during the winter. But I see that woodbine along the fence line is turning crimson and here and there golden leaves are brightening the cottonwoods.

I climbed in the wagon with G.R. the other day and took a leisurely trip up to the cows where he scattered blocks and fixed a little fence.

We travel in the "fast lane" so much of the time, that forced into a slow pace by lumbering, grass-fat Belgian horses is a pleasant experience. And the spring wagon is equipped with rubber tires and padded seats, so riding in one is not unlike the luxury of a rocking chair.

There is a certain music to the jingle of tug chains and creaking harness leather as the horses move along, keeping the beat with their hoofs pounding the ground. And sometimes G.R. added the lyrics of "Move up Babe! Whoa back Bill!"

For the most part, flowers of fall seem of much sturdier species than those of springtime. Resinous stems hold boldly erect the blossoms of black-eyed Susan and black Sampson. Heath aster appear like clouds of miniature daisies along moist areas, as well as, several varieties of sunflower.

We stopped the team at a small dam along the Gordon Creek so that G.R. could feed the fish he has seen in the overflow pool; bass, pike, bullheads and, of course, the dratted carp that stirs and muddies the water. His hope is that the fish will begin to surface and strike at the grain and slices of bread that he feeds them.

While he sat on the exposed end of the culvert feeding his fish, I crawled the barbed wire fence and walked the creek. Bug-eyed frogs watched me approach and then slipped off into deeper water. And a turtle took one glimpse and then dived.

Down along the creek, sheltered by steep sandy banks were yellow bursts of color. I'm not certain if the clumps of flowers were that of the tickseed sunflower or that of beggar-ticks, but they were lovely. And then bright spots of lavender caught my eye and I waded the shallow creek to investigate the other bank.

At close range, I recognized them at once as lobelias, but I had previously seen them only along the Niobrara. The delicate flower has two lips, split in the middle with white into the throat. Then closer to the ground I found the tiny cup-shaped slender gerardia. A new discovery, and my book on native flowers says the blossoms last but one day.

Our little excursion into the "wilderness" was most refreshing to the soul and put new meaning into a favorite, but mostly unheeded phrase, "Take time to smell the roses."

ʊ V−ʌ c−c VIA J−

GOOSE GUMPTION
- March 1, 1990 -

Eleven Canada geese flew over last evening at tree-top level. The song that they sing surely must be the most compelling of any wildfowl in nature's world. This, perhaps, is a resident flock because we see them on the feedground behind our calves, eating any spilled corn or grain. Last summer, we counted numerous families of gosling's being raised on the smaller lakes nearby and to the west.

It's said that the Canada goose mates for life ... in sickness and health until death does them part. Who could not admire that built-in instinct for devotion.

It seems incredible that this large heavy-bodied bird is even able to fly. On takeoff from water, we've watched them run along the water until the five-foot wingspan is able to take over and the birds finally become airborne.

Even more incredible, however, is the ability of a flock of geese to land on a small pond at the same time. What type of built-in radar keeps them from crashing into each other? With the air filled with extended wings, how do they avoid a traffic jam that would damage flight feathers and cause them to fall?

The human race could learn a lot from geese according to an article contained in the newsletter of the Society of Range Management, New Mexico Section.

By flying in a "V" formation, the entire flock adds 71 percent flying range than if a single bird flew alone, according to the article. As each bird flaps its wings, it creates an uplift for the bird following.

Can we take a lesson? People who share a common direction and sense of community can get where they are going quicker and easier, because they are traveling on the thrust and "uplift" of one another.

Should a goose fall from formation, it suddenly feels the drag and resistance of trying to fly alone and quickly moves back into formation to enjoy the lifting power of the bird immediately in front.

If humans had as much sense as the goose, we would stay in formation with those who lead in the direction we want to go, accept their help and give ours to others.

When the lead goose gets tired ... the one at the point of the "V" ... it rotates back into the formation and another goose flies into the point position.

It pays for humans, too, to take turns during the hard tasks and to share the burden of leadership. As with geese, humans are interdependent on each other.

The goose in the lead strives to keep up its speed because the rest of the formation continuously honks encouragement from behind.

We who follow our leaders need to make certain that our honking from behind is encouraging...not biting away at those backs that go before us.

When the goose grows sick, or becomes wounded in flight, two geese drop out of formation to follow it down to help and to protect it, the article says.

258

They stay with it until it is able to fly again or dies. Then they catch up with their original flock or join another formation.

If we can claim the same level of intelligence as the wild Canada goose, surely we too, can stand by each other through more difficult times as well as when the flight is easy.

SURPRISED BY NEW FLOWER SPECIES
- *August 9, 1990* -

I n recent years I've thought that if I should ever be reincarnated, I'd like to return to the Sandhills ... but as a trained botanist. I do love plants. And I have a burning curiosity to learn all of their traits and to watch them flourish. Native plants that grow on the prairie are my favorites, but I also seem unable to discard an ailing house plant until it sighs its last. I administer TLC until the very end.

I went through a mourning period last winter, after the thermometer dropped to a minus 30 degrees. To conserve heat, I had lowered the thermostat and closed the door to a separate living room heated by electricity.

The door should have been left ajar. During that fateful night, the apparently overloaded heaters, threw a breaker and all of my beautiful plants froze to death. Lost were two giant ferns, a three-foot cactus and two other plants that reached the ceiling.

So, it was with great expectation, that I visited the spring prairie. Wild flowers were magnificent and ever changing species continue to display their colors. The prairie seems a peace loving environment.

I can't tell you how exciting it was recently, to find a flower species along a Highway 2 road ditch that I'd not seen before. It was brilliant with purple tulip-like flowers. Later, when I checked my reference book, I found them to be prairie gentian; a showy wildflower with lasting ability when cut. That's unusual.

One flower and stem was cut to take home for identification. It was hot in the car and with no container of water the flower wilted. The next morning, however, leaves were erect and the blossom reopened. Now I covet a sample of the hardy plant to add to a plot I've planted with native flowers.

I also have a garden of veggies, but I'll have to alter my strategy. I use no fertilizer. But soil brought from the corral seems overly fertile. Plants that I had spaced far apart now entwine like a jungle. Tomato plants in their wire support are my height so I cut the tops. The weighted plants still fell to the ground and pulled the wire supports with them.

I caught G.R. one morning when fog delayed going to the hayfield. He brought in heavy wire panels and we propped the jungle-like plants up and off from the ground. Perhaps there is a chance the fruit will ripen now that it is exposed to sunlight.

Everything in my garden seems overly vigorous ... especially the dratted moles or gophers that invade peaceful territory daily to dine. Gourmet gophers, perhaps. I've found beets, onions and potatoes with sides gnawed out. Some were completely devoured. Nothing escapes the invaders. Not even cucumbers. One potato plant was cut off just below ground level.

Mine has been a chemical-free garden. I use no insecticides. But enough is enough already. I'm declaring war on the invaders that sneak in below ground. I've tried diplomacy ... discourage them by plugging their runs. I'd appreciate any war strategy that anyone can give me. Surely, there is something that will defeat the aggressors that want to control my highly productive, but peaceful territory.

Diplomacy is out. Obviously it won't be effective. Ground combat is inevitable. Come to think of it those words have a familiar ring.

U V−Λ C−C VIA J−

DESERT SANDHILLS HOLD FLORAL BEAUTY
- June 27, 1991 -

S urprising, isn't it, what a few hot days will do to excess water in the Sandhills. Sun and wind are drying the meadows recently flooded. But much of the lowland grasses subjected to flood waters look dried and brown.

Little grass frogs on the meadow are so thick they resemble speckled green carpet. Bull frogs are more numerous than normal and there always seem to be sand turtles crossing the highway. Only the alert driver avoids crushing them.

Flood water recently washed out three of our crossings at the Gordon Creek, but the water also brought a lot of fish. As the men rebuilt the fences along the water gaps, they said they saw a lot of bass as well as the not-so-desirable carp in the waters.

Howard, our right-hand-man, said he's found several duck nests that predators had violated. The eggs remained, but with holes in the end. Apparently a raccoon or skunk emptied the eggs for breakfast.

I no longer explore the prairie, as much as I'd like. I need to avoid midday hikes, so I'm not overcome by heat. Walking the prairie during early morning hours, however, is comparable to entering a native flower greenhouse. Flowers are everywhere.

On Tuesday, I found a clump of wild begamot for the first time. The lavender flowers somewhat resemble Rocky Mountain beeplant, but the leaves smelled a bit like oregano.

My reference book said the flower was of the beebalm or mint family and the leaves were dried and used in a tea to relieve abdominal pain by the Teton Dakota and for sore throat by the Lakota.

Another beebalm grows just west of our house. The white flowers stack one above the other to look as though they were pierced by a stiffly erect stem.

Color my backyard prairie yellow with goat's beard, coneflower, puccoon, prickly pear and coreopsis or green-thread wearing golden tresses. Or dust my prairie white with prairie larkspur, slender beardstongue, prickly poppy, soapweed, yarrow and Queen Anne's lace. Or color it blue with verbena, blue lettuce, chicory, lobelias and even an occasional dayflower.

The tiny scarlet gaura is possibly the most delicate blossom on the prairie. Eight slender stamens with reddish-brown antlers protrude from the petals and spikey tails somewhat resemble a flying insect. When first open, the white blossom changes to pink and then scarlet during one day's time.

G.R. brought me a small bouquet from the Snake River pasture, and among the smaller species was a bird's egg vetch plant with six pods that really do resemble bird eggs.

Of all of Nebraska's grasslands, the Sandhills area remains mostly in pasture so it has fared the best. The natural undisturbed beauty is, indeed, a bonus for the prairie dweller.

RARE FLOWER CAPTURED FOR A MOMENT

- July 18, 1991 -

Capture the moment. How often have I wished ... when it was too late ... that I had done just that? We're all in such a hurry. I've begun to resent that. We should take more time to smell the flowers.

And while we're speaking of flowers, I have to report on the magnificent display this year of bush morning glories.

Near the refuge headquarters, the hillsides are literally abloom with the pink trumpet blossoms. Never have I seen so many bush morning glory in bloom.

Nature has provided well for the plant. Several inches below the surface, the root becomes a huge, spindle-shaped water storage tank up to two feet in diameter that might extend five feet into the sand.

There are several of us prairie dwellers who thrill at our native flowers each season. And we share information on a possible new discovery ... sort of a "prairie petals" network.

Nothing less than a new find, would have stirred me out of the house on Saturday when the thermometer was pushing 100 degrees. But when Floss Garner called to give me the location of two prairie fringed orchis, I grabbed my cameras and salt pills. No matter that I had to drive 35 miles.

In case you don't know, the orchis is in the orchid family and reported as one of our state's rarest flowers. I had never seen one.

Floss told me she saw the orchis in a road ditch. As I traveled, I feared that some tourist might have picked it, not knowing that it was rare.

I walked and walked the road ditch. Deer flies and sweat bees left itching welts across my body. Sweat dripped salt into my eyes. I grew dizzy from the heat.

I was on the brink of admitting defeat, when I found the flower and all thoughts of discomfort disappeared. Believe me. It was worth the trip.

Description eludes me. The blossom is elegant, magnificent, breath taking. And the scent is sweet. The texture resembles that of an orchid. The petals remind me of some costumed dancer with chiffon flowing outward in graceful motion.

262

I took photos from every angle in color, in black and white and on a video camera. I had, indeed, taken time to smell the flowers ... thanks to an alert from Floss.

So it was, that I passed along the information to Gayle Hanna, who lives about the same distance in the opposite direction.

Later, when I answered the phone, she said "Thank you," several times. She, too, said the sight was worth the trip.

I become very excited about the visuals that the good Lord provides for our enjoyment. And I'm going to pursue more avidly the philosophy I learned from the orchis:

Capture the moment.

ʊ V–ʌ C–C VIA J–
BEST TRADE EVER MADE
- September 5, 1991 -

About six years ago, G.R. returned to the ranch from town driving a 25-foot motor home. I nearly fainted and asked if his lapse into insanity was temporary or permanent. Now to argue my case, here's a man who will seldom leave home for a Saturday night in town, and he comes home prepared to travel! If we ever did leave on a trip we drove 12-13 hours a day and on the third day it was head full-speed for home.

I think I've spent overnight in the thing about three times. Then two years ago, we took Myndi and two grand-kiddos (and Doberman Ted, of course) with us to Lander, WY, to visit son Lorin.

In my concept of a vacation, that trip ranked about minus three on a scale of 1 to 10. Too-oo-oo much togetherness, too hot, too many miles and too many hungry people. A self-contained camper is no place to vacation for a woman grown weary of cooking.

Last winter, son John did take the motor home about 14 miles west, where we had moved our cows to feed them hay that we purchased from a neighbor.

The temperature dropped to a record low, John couldn't get the heating stove to work and about froze to death. I think he spent only three nights there even when the weather warmed.

The third weekend of August, G.R. decided we should vacation in the motor home. "For how long?" I asked. When he said a couple days, I refused to pack any food.

About 15 miles down the road I asked why the heater was on. By then it was 90 degrees both inside and outside. Then G.R. remembered that he and John had removed a heater valve at cow camp. Now there was no way to stop hot water from circulating.

I sat with feet in the aisle and turned the air conditioner to "freeze." But the heater was the more powerful.

Highlight of that hot trip was approaching Devil's Tower and being told there was no admission fee in honor of its 75th anniversary. Back in 1906, President Teddy Roosevelt made it our first national monument.

Back at Deadwood, G.R. was grumpy as he tried to maneuver up the canyon to a cramped KOA campground. After he paid an $18 fee and had the campground breaker blow from our one air conditioner, he was decidedly crabby.

Just out of Rapid City at 10 a.m. on Monday, he said he wanted to check a dealership. His old pickup passed 160,000 miles and he's been looking.

Without a second thought I said, "Trade this thing in on it." And I'll be darned if he didn't.

It was 103 degrees in Rapid City and only slightly cooler in the motor home. I spent until 5 p.m. loading belongings into big trash bags...the only thing available.

The new pickup was ... I mean loaded! We'd also picked up airplane skis at Sturgis.

Only G.R. would leave on a rare vacation in a motor home and return three days later in a pickup ... but thank God, a cool one. Packed in as tightly as we were, Doberman Ted and I, were grateful for those last cool hours.

ʊ V−ʌ C−c VIA J−
BOOTS RETURN HOME
- April 2, 1992 -

G.R. says it is increasingly hard to find a good pair of work boots — boots that don't stretch out two sizes during the first month. He tells the truth. Once the boots are worn enough to be comfortable, he needs to wear two pairs of heavy socks. I think it's ridiculous. There is enough leather running around this ranch to boot an entire army. But G.R. says that cows are a lot more comfortable wearing that leather than he would be.

Cow hide is too thick, he says. Once the leather is split to wearable thickness, the strength is lost. Thus the stretch. The English and French are noted for fine tanned leather, but we can't seem to compete.

Boots are a bit like hats. They follow a pecking order. When new boots join the "foot family," then the older pair is worn for work. And the pair with holes in the soles are saved for "just in case."

For years, G.R. sent his foot measurements to M.L. Leddy and bought his boots by mail. They were wonderful, and the tops lasted through several new bottoms. The company attached new bottoms on the old tops time and again, and the "half-new" pair was cheaper.

That was back when French calf was affordable.

Recently, G.R. was in town and stopped at the Paradise Boot Shop. He thought he might order a pair made.

He noticed a pair of old boots in the shop and told Mike Dyke that they looked just like French calf boots that he used to wear.

"In fact," G.R. said, "those are my boots! I recognize them from the wing tips right up to stitching on the white tops."

"Sure they are," Mike said with a smug grin. "I tell you what. If you can get them on, I'll fix them up for you."

G.R. said he'd be back as soon as he went for his dental appointment. But there was another reason for delay. He knew that he had on two pair of heavy socks and the Leddys would never fit.

After leaving the dentist, he bought a pair of light socks and returned to Paradise. He pulled the boots on and Mike said something like, "Well, I'll be darned. I didn't think they could be yours because I bought these from a young man at a yard sale in North Platte."

That young man, G.R. told him, had to be Theo Schuff, the son of Sally Schuff, who is now editor of the Colorado Farmer in Denver. It must be close to 10 years ago that Theo worked in our hay field, and G.R. couldn't stand to see anyone without a pair of boots. He gave Theo a pair of Leddys that were a bit tight.

At the time, G.R. was about 40 pounds heavier and probably suffered from fat feet. I told him the condition probably moved about five feet higher.

All of my life, I've heard tales about lost dogs that return home after years of absence. I honestly never dreamed I'd hear of cowboy boots that have the same homing instinct.

ꙅ ᐯ–ᐱ ᑕ–ᑕ ᐯIᐱ J–
VALUING ROOTS –
IN TREES, LAND AND FAMILY
- October 22, 1992 -

Dried, brown leaves rustled underfoot as I walk across the lawn. But overhead the weeping birch is aglow with leaves that glisten in the sun like spun gold-like treasured memories.

The birch towers above the house. Slender tendrils bend groundward under a cascade of notched, golden leaves. The white bark and bright leaves of fall have caused the tree to be a favored backdrop for family photos through the years.

Tuesday evening, daughter Myndi initiated a photo session with five little grandkiddos beneath the birch tree. That really pleased me because, for me, it had become tradition.

When I planted the tree, more years ago than I wish to remember, G.R.'s father, L.C., predicted that it would never live.

Perhaps, I gave the weeping birch more care which kept it alive. But I suspect L.C. was just challenging my sense of responsibility. He held a special affinity with growing things.

L.C. was especially fond of the soapweed. So I feel he approved of the one I sketched that was carved onto his tombstone. And his daughter, Maxine, planted a soapweed at each end of the stone. Both now produce magnificent spring blossoms.

Perhaps, living so close to the land as ranchers do, we bond more easily with plant life that is nurtured by the land, and with the animals that depend upon the prairie plants.

I'm in a pensive mood this morning. More than likely, I'm feeling grateful that we were given the opportunity to live our life on the prairie.

Ours is not a leisurely life. At times, it can mean stressful long hours and exhaustion. Perhaps, we could make more money elsewhere, but we treasure this way of life. To live elsewhere surely would wither our souls.

We do not own this land. Rather the land owns us and we bend to its will. That philosophy is accepted family tradition.

Last night, five little grandkiddos, the oldest 7 and the youngest 2, played beneath the birch tree. We delighted in their laughter as they ran noisily through the leaves.

266

I silently wished that L.C. could join us. He would have loved watching his energetic little great-grandkiddos.

Oh, that L.C. could return to drive through the weaned calves, sleek, tame and contented. We would drive him through the hills so that he could relish the dozen shades of greens and mauves and rusts that now paint the prairie landscape.

I'd hope that he'd approve of what he saw. Our heritage was to appreciate the prairie, its fragile environment and its animals.

In my heart the towering birch tree is symbolic of the opportunity L.C. provided. He taught us to anchor our roots deep into the sand so that we might grow as tall as our hopes and ambition allowed.

℧ V−Λ C−C VIA J−

TELLING CATTLE STORY, SINGING TO CHOIR
- October 12, 1997 -

Three weeks ago, I did a little research and was going to share a bit of what has changed in the cattle business. But you may have noticed that I've been absent on what we'll call an unscheduled vacation. We'll get to that later.

As I considered what I should write, I thought to myself, "Here I am talking about the cattle business on the ag page of a newspaper published in the heart of a rural state. I might as well be singing to the choir." You all know how that works. The choir knows the words and music much better than you. So does anyone listen?

Perhaps the thing that keeps me singing to the choir is that every once in a while readers send letters. They say they clip and send my columns to friends or relatives — that sometimes what I write helps others better understand life in the rural lane.

Three weeks ago, we had just delivered our yearling steers. In a way, it was history repeating itself because they were sold at the ranch. In other words, the price was agreed on between buyer and seller and the cattle weighed at the ranch where the buyer took delivery. The alternative was marketing through a livestock auction.

For some years, buyers seem to favor purchasing through the auction market. In a way, it's easier to let someone else set the market for the day. And if

267

there are not sufficient buyers in attendance that day, the sale becomes a truly buyer's market and a producer's wreck.

Years ago, it seemed that the bulk of our cattle sales were at the ranch. As I studied G.R.'s dad's old day book, it is noted that in 1949 we drove his steers from the ranch to the yards and scales at Ballard Marsh on U.S. Highway 83. An Iowa farmer/feeder bought the steers that averaged about 1,100 pounds. I believe there were a dozen semi-trucks there to haul the cattle. Now we're talking big, 3-year-old, grass-fat steers. They weighed 1,100 pounds, but this year we sold yearling steers that weighed 935 pounds. Put a pencil to the figures and you'll find that back then, 3-year-old steers weighed only 165 pounds more than our present yearlings.

But there got to be about 30 seconds a year when you could sell a steer at three or even at two. Through genetics, many cattlemen are making the same number of acres produce more pounds of beef in less time. And it is called survival.

On a personal note, I'm back after seven days in the hospital and 10 days of being pampered at the home of daughter Myndi and her family.

It was a respiratory thing that caught me totally by surprise. Something about no air moving through my lungs. But that's behind me and I'm here for the long haul. And God willing, I'll keep singing to the choir.

ʊ V−ʌ C−C VIʌ J−
A JOURNEY TO CURTIS
- February 1, 1998 -

A recent 3 1/2-hour trip on good roads to Curtis brought back so many memories for G.R. On the return trip to the ranch, he told me stories that I'd not heard before. It was a lesson in just how very much times have changed.

Back in the fall of 1940 when G.R. entered high school, his parents selected the Nebraska School of Agriculture at Curtis. Many other parents throughout the Sandhills also chose the school that operated from 1913 - 1968.

Having just emerged from a decade of drought and the Great Depression, it was a time of very few roads, very little money and long before the invention of four-wheel drive.

268

That era was also before a time when many mothers moved to town with the youngsters in school while leaving her husband at the ranch.

On that initial trip to Curtis, G.R. remembers that his parents drove a 1939 Ford. They left about 4 a.m. and didn't arrive in Curtis until about 5 p.m., he said.

The Great Plains Highway was a distinct misnomer. It was merely a deep sand, sometimes graded trail that wound north-south through the hills. Local ranchers usually were responsible for any maintenance.

From the ranch, the trail zig-zagged across steep hills, past Lone Tree Lake, through Brownlee and south to Seneca; then south from Seneca across the old bridge on the Dismal to Tryon.

"I think it was about 10 miles north of North Platte that we hit a stretch of oil road," G.R. said. From there on the road was gravel into Curtis.

"Quite often," G.R. said, "parents from Wood Lake to Hyannis would meet along the way and travel as a caravan, because someone was sure to get stuck. To get over the steep hills at Seneca and the Dismal, we usually had to get out and help push someone's car."

Sometimes they traveled to Brownlee, came to a stretch of gravel about 13 miles north of Thedford, drove to Anselmo, south to Arnold and then good gravel to Gothenburg and south to Moorefield and Curtis. Highway 83 between Valentine and Thedford did not become reality until after World War II and to North Platte in the 50s.

But there were railroads. Several times, G.R. said, he boarded the train at Valentine with long layovers at Chadron, Alliance and Sterling, CO, before getting to Curtis.

He said he was terribly homesick, but because of the distance, was able to go home only at Thanksgiving and Christmas.

The dormitories weren't built until the 1942-43 school year. Students stayed in the homes of Curtis residents. G.R. was unhappy where he stayed as a freshman, so Dick and Cecile Green and their daughter, Margaret Nell, opened their home to him. G.R. said they were so good to him and he spent many hours in Dick's barber shop building model airplanes.

G.R. retains a definite loyalty to the school and to the Greens. Our trip to Curtis was so he could serve as pall bearer for Cecile Green who died at 98 years. He said he felt honored to do so.

U V-Λ C-C VIΛ J-

NIGHT HORSE IS SPECIAL ANIMAL

- March 29, 1998 -

L ast week, in this space we discussed how some people pass retirement age still full of vitality, albeit what detractors may describe as somewhat creaking. Advancing age does not mean productivity ends. Now let's discuss that quality in a member of the equine species. His given name is Freddie Rabbit. We call him Fred.

G.R. bought him as a 5 year old gelding from Doug Mulligan, who knew G.R. wanted a good cow horse.

Fred is tall, about 15.5 hands with a long back and long strides that makes for easy riding. And he was a tough horse with a mind of his own.

G.R. and Fred had quite a few fights to determine who was boss. But cattlemen, like a spirited horse, that as G.R. describes it, "Doesn't have to be peddled."

Once a man finds a horse that really fits him, he is reluctant to ride any other. Sometimes, especially during calving, G.R. rode Fred day after day. A horse with less heart probably would have quit him.

If nothing else, Fred was all heart and all business. There was never need for spurs, just soft pressure from a boot heel or a snap of the reins and Fred shifted gears.

The big horse wasn't much for fooling around. One time, on a trail ride through McCann Canyon north from the Niobrara River, apparently Fred grew unhappy about what he probably thought was dinking around. Stepping over fallen logs and around rocks was not to his liking.

For a time, there was quite a conflict of wills, but Fred finally gave in and was docile the rest of the day. But it's funny. We could tell by the look in his eyes that he wasn't a happy camper.

Fred was at his best while corralling a reluctant sow. Once, he was certain which animal was the target, all the rider had to do was keep his seat and a loose hand on the reins.

Fred now is 25 and retired. His joints are painful from age and arthritis. We don't sell our faithful old horses. When his time comes he will be buried on a hillside overlooking the meadow beside Tuffy and Kilbars.

Each calving season, Fred is grained and kept close to the barn for an emergency; usually nighttime. A night horse is a special animal, sure footed, well trained and cooperative.

They must have night vision and be sure footed on slick ground or frozen cow chips. They don't shy at every shadow. They can out-think a cow, and most of all, give their heart to the job at hand.

Recently, our night man faced an emergency. His horse was at the far barn, so he saddled Fred to corral the cow.

The next morning he said to G.R., "I've never ridden a horse like that. He turned so hard he almost lost me."

G.R. said he can relate to the horse. "Fred is old and his legs hurt. Once he knows which cow you want you can turn off your flashlight and hang on."

∪ V−∧ C−C VI∧ J−

MAKING DO WITH BARBED WIRE
- August 2, 1998 -

O ften I wonder, who will be "Mr. Fix-it" when G.R. is no longer around. There doesn't seem many things that he can't fix without going to town for new parts. He runs a tractor on a double-mow outfit, but when something else goes wrong, it's G.R. to the rescue. His job is full time with "go-fer" thrown in.

Many years ago our neighbor, Billy Piercy, told G.R. that he could have any old windmill heads that he found in the Piercy blowout.

G.R. gathered them up and rebuilt them, one by one. He still rebuilds old windmill heads... for us and occasionally for a neighbor.

"I guess I got that from L.C.," he told me recently. His dad was inventive in making do with items at hands. Often, G.R. said, it was with baling wire.

After a day of mowing on Duck Lake meadow, G.R. said he reminisced as he mowed. He shared those memories with me that evening and I thought, "My, how times have changed." Early on, L.C. hired several single men and sent one down on Duck Lake to feed hay with four horses. The man left his team and came back to the ranch for a hame strap. He said one had broken.

For those not familiar with harness, the hame strap is a short leather strap that holds the wooden hames tight together at the bottom of the collar. The rest of the harness is attached to the hames.

I guess L.C. didn't take kindly to the man's lack of judgment. He asked why he left his job when he was standing beside a barbed wire fence. A short piece of barbed wire would have made do.

G.R. said that L.C. paid the man up that night. Perhaps that lack of judgment was just the proverbial "straw."

L.C. liked to tell his kids about the time he was driving his 1917 Buick down the sandy roads when a front wheel bearing burned out near Don Hanna Sr.'s ranch, west of Brownlee.

L.C. borrowed a saw from Don, and with permission, sawed a slice from the top of a hardwood post and drilled a hole. With plenty of grease, he inserted the make-do bearing and was able to drive to Thedford where he purchased a new one.

G.R. explained that wheel bearings were shaped differently at the time. I think he said they were cone-shaped.

Those memories brought others back to mind.

G.R. told of when Loren Boyer, now of Seneca, carried the mail from Kennedy west during the 1930s. Loren's vehicle had a cracked block and money was scarce. So, after every trip, he drained all of the oil and replaced it just before he left on his mail route.

I remember the late Bud Aufdengarten telling of traveling to Ogallala or perhaps Grant. Along the way his fan belt broke, and you don't move when that happens. Bud used a little innovative thinking, borrowed his wife's panty hose and tied them into a loop. The sturdy nylon did the job until he was able to buy the real thing.

There are many times when G.R. must buy new parts. Other times he goes to his shop, and, quite often, is able to build the part that he needs to save hundreds of dollars.

ʊ V−Λ C−C VIΛ J−

BLIZZARD CHANGED NEWLYWED TO PIONEER
- January 3, 1999 -

A fter barely "getting by" for a time with very little, I renew my appreciation of those every day material items found throughout the house. We get so used to them that we take them for granted.

A short list would include electricity, telephone, deep freeze, well stocked pantry, reading material, running water, bathroom and thermostat-controlled heat. A car in the garage. I enjoyed none of the above one January through May.

On this 50th anniversary of the infamous Blizzard of 1949, I vividly remember the onslaught. I especially remember the living conditions during the months following the blizzard.

We couldn't blame the weatherman for a "cloudy with light snow" forecast. The storm system that hit here on January 2nd was far too complex.

On that Sunday this area was enjoying shirt-sleeve weather. But boiling up from the south was one storm; another came from the northwest. Those storms met in mortal combat over eastern Wyoming, western Nebraska and South Dakota revolving counterclockwise.

Then the resulting storm system doubled back on itself. Wind velocities drove the snow at 60 to 70 miles per hour. A huge area was brought to a standstill, trains were snowed under and travelers were marooned for days.

Snow depths varied up to 42 inches in the west, but packed by the wind, the drifts were like concrete. Here drifts reached from the ground to the eaves.

At the time, REA had not reached our ranch. Electricity was provided by a 32-volt Kohler engine and stored in batteries. A small amount of meat was stored in the freezer compartment of a Skelgas refrigerator. The rest was in a rented locker in town. But ranchers usually keep a couple weeks supply of groceries on hand.

The Sunday blinding storm caught me and G.R. in town and we were unable to make it to the ranch. We spent until Thursday at the By the Way Ranch. Jack Harvey landed with a ski-equipped three-place Piper to take us home.

Overnight we loaded meager supplies from ranch shelves on a drag sled to make a day-long trek some 15 miles to an isolated cow-camp. We were there more than two months to care for the cows and 2-year-old steers.

We always had wind. Day after day it created ground blizzards and zero visibility. I worried each time G.R. left in search of cattle. Should I need to go for help, there was only a saddle horse for transportation.

I don't remember what we ate. G.R. says we had canned salmon and potatoes.

We were blessed with a Coleman lantern, but nothing to read. Thank heavens we covered our supplies on the sled with a tarp. Later, we used it as a bedspread so we could shake off the snow that blew in through cracks in the wainscoting.

Army dozers moved in to clear paths and drifts from around stacks, but wind usually blew everything shut and it crusted even harder.

Newcomers might scoff at tales of Nebraska's hard winters. It can happen. It turned this naive newlywed into a seasoned pioneer.

℧ V–Λ C–C VΙΛ J–

BRANDING: A SPRING TRADITION
- May 19, 1999 -

William

We scheduled a branding for Friday. Thunderstorms, possibly severe, were accurately forecast for Thursday night and Friday. We branded anyway. Branding part of our calves during a downpour caused me to reflect on how times have changed. Long ago, we would cancel and pick another day.

The calendar fills rapidly with neighborhood brandings and makes it touchy to reschedule. Everyone is anxious to turn out to pasture once calves are branded.

In recent years, we've gone to a tilt-table to work the calves, which causes much less stress on both animal and crew. Calves are pushed down an alley to a head-catch, and then turned sideways on the tilt-table. Men brand and vaccinate at waist level, which relieves back strain.

The reason we could brand while it rained, is that son John set up the tilt table and alley inside the big calving barn. Doors at both ends are left open. Cows and calves are brought into the north corral, cows sorted off and calves brought inside the barn to paneled stalls. Wet hides dry quickly there.

Large fans hung from the rafters to blow the branding smoke away. Once the calf is branded, it leaves through the open south door to join its mother.

A plus for the cook is that it takes only about five men to do the job. But since calves are handled one at a time, only about 200 are done at a time. Several days are needed.

If G.R.'s dad, L.C., was watching from the Lord's corral, I imagine he shook his head in disbelief. Especially on Thursday, when the crew from another branding came by to help us corral about 300 cows and calves. The roundup went smoothly with two men on horseback, and of all things, four on ATVs, or what we call four-wheelers.

For the traditional branding, about a dozen men on horseback complete the roundup. Then about three ropers heel the corralled calves and drag them to three sets of wrestlers. It takes two wrestlers to flip each kicking calf to the ground and hold it. Depending upon the situation, bruising often is expected on calves and men alike.

Several men handle the hot irons and branding takes on an assembly line atmosphere.

I'll never forget the first branding dinner I prepared, way back when, during my second spring on this ranch.

I was told there would be about 20 men. So I added a couple and guesstimated the amount of food. Because of my tiny kitchen, the men would eat on the lawn. My meager collection of china and silverware, at the time, had to be supplemented with paper plates and plastic.

That year, we branded with portable corrals set up in a distant pasture. I didn't see any of the crew until they drove in to eat.

I'd been nervous before, but when I saw that 20 men brought 25 kids because school was out, I about had a heart attack. There was no way I could stretch the food to feed 45.

The kids were great. They waited and we made do with wieners and buns from the deep freeze and ice cream instead of pie. Later, I heard that not one youngster got to go to the very next branding.

LEST WE FORGET

Brands & Ownership

Brand: Bar Eleven Bar
Owner: Elver and Georgia Lord
          Bobby and Donna Lord

Brand: 4 Open 6
Owner: Gene Carver

Brand: Duck Bar
Owner: L.C. Beel and Son

Brand: T O
Owner: Stetter Cattle Company
          William J. and Bob Stetter

Brand: 7 Diamond
Owner: Joe Hammond

-||- 4, b ⊢O 7⧫

FRANK CARVER

- January 10, 1978 -

There's an empty saddle in this ranch country tonight, and the man who rode it will be sorely missed. Frank Carver was 82; his funeral was Friday.

Just a month ago, during my last conversation with Frank, he made a statement that I think typifies his life. He was a quiet, unassuming man, and in that same tone he said, "I'm a lucky man, as I've known a lot of wonderful people. I've never sold a horse to anyone who hasn't remained my friend."

That statement was so true...but it didn't just happen by accident. Frank Carver was one of our last "old timers" who survived hard times, drought and depression. He made it by hard work, ability and old-fashion integrity. He was slight of build but a giant in the eyes of the young and old who appreciate honesty and good horses.

Frank Carver added Quarter horse breeding to his cattle operation near Crookston in the early 40s, before the Nebraska Quarter Horse Association was even formed. He started with a good broodmare band of Morgan and Indian ponies and a Texas Quarter horse stallion he named "Judge Carver."

He said he always bred for conformation and speed...and wouldn't settle for anything less than best in his horses. His horses built a record of champions, register of merit and race track wins much too long to list here. He said his aim was to raise good "using" horses.

For the past few years, I've made it a practice to watch for his 4J brand. I've seen it on horses ridden by 4-H youngsters, in the Quarter horse show ring, on the race track and in the arena at rodeos from Little Britches up to professional shows. Many ranchers in this country claim their Carver horses are their best using horses and show a lot of "cow sense."

Frank Carver was proud of his horses, and folks who bought them were proud to own them. He also had a special rapport with youngsters.

About five years ago, our teenage daughter Myndi wanted a 4J horse more than anything in the world. Frank helped her pick a buckskin Kilgore-bred colt. Myndi was responsible for breaking the colt, and Frank would stop to check on her progress as he made his annual tour to check on his horses.

Myndi was extremely proud of that horse and a bit touchy about any criticism of it. Frank loved to tease, and he chuckled when he told me about one horse show when Myndi was waiting to take "Mr. Kilbars" into the arena and didn't see Frank. Just loud enough for her to hear, he said, "I wonder where that poor girl got that ugly horse."

"There was fight in her eyes until she saw it was me," he laughed.

Frank was always at the county horse show to watch, as he said, "his kids and horses." For the 1977 show, close friends Randy Peterson, Harry Stokely and Bernard Miles planned a tribute to the man — a tribute that most of us felt was long overdue but hadn't done it.

The show was proclaimed "Frank Carver Day," and a hand-tooled leather plaque was given to Frank and his wife, Greeta, on behalf of the Cherry County folks who rode and loved his horses. Men, women and small children led or rode 4J horses into the arena to surround the couple during the presentation.

We are all grateful now that we didn't wait too long to say "thank you." We are also grateful for the events during the last weeks of Frank's life, they seem so fitting.

Frank was a family man, and his life centered around his family and horses. I asked him one time to name his favorite horse, and he said, "Would you ask me to name my favorite child?"

His son Gene and family live at the ranch. Recently, Frank and Greeta took a trip to visit the other two children and their families. They visited Frank Jr. and their first great-grandchild in California, and then daughter Maurine in Mesa, AZ.

While in Arizona, they watched Jerry Bennett's horses on a race track at Tuscon. Jerry had trained horses for Frank and was a long-time friend. He greatly respected Frank, noting that, "Frank has put a lot of cowboys horseback," which in the vernacular of the horse circuit means the best of horses.

After the races, Frank said he was terribly tired. The end was quiet and quick.

Frank Carver's last days were spent with his wife, his family and horses... everything he held most dear.

We will miss him, his friendship, his wit...and his horses. His saddle is empty, but his legacy lives on. His horses are exactly what he said they were: good using horses.

MEMORIES OF MOTHER'S MAGIC HANDS
- May 16, 1978 -

For me, Mother's Day was filled with memories of my mother, a farm wife. Searching back into the hidden corners of childhood memories, it seems I remember my mother's hands before the image of her face materialized. Maybe it was because her hands were at the eye level of a little tow-headed girl.

Hers were strong, capable hands...hands that never found a job that was impossible.

I remember those hands gently holding my baby brother for my close inspection when I was four. I had waited with such anticipation for his birth. He was so tiny, I said he looked like a Mickey Mouse. He was forever after burdened with the nickname, "Mick."

Mom's hands never seemed to be idle. Standing with my chin resting on the table, I watched those hands sharpening a knife to cut into pieces a beef that Dad had butchered...then tightening the lids of the quart jars as she canned it.

There were memories of watching her knead bread dough, rolling and flattening, rolling and flattening...and her hands lifting the sweet-smelling loaves from the oven of the wood-burning stove. Mick and I favored the yellow, sweet zwieback rolls. She seldom used a recipe and described her cooking as "by gob and by gosh," a pinch of this and a dab of that. Her hands had a magic touch as they added just a few dried corn cobs at a time to keep the oven at that perfect temperature for crisp, golden crusts.

I was always watching her hands...guiding cloth through the sewing machine, cutting homemade noodles, capping the root beer, slicing her homemade soap, milking the cows and rendering lard. I watched them scattering grain to her beloved chickens, then holding her apron into a "basket" while she gathered eggs or rhubarb.

I can almost feel her cool hand on my fevered brow as it burned with scarlet fever, chicken pox, measles and pneumonia.

Her hands also mixed glasses of "cure-all" hot lemonade laced with whiskey and sugar — a hated concoction which I poured into the hot water bottle and then watched tremulously as those hands took the cooled vessel to refill it, wondering if she'd discover my secret.

Her hand was seldom felt on our backsides. She and Dad were firm in their discipline, and each was in complete support of the other.

In her garden, my mother's hands treated the plants and soil almost reverently. She loved her garden; it was her sanctuary. The produce filled the cellar and was shared with neighbors. She'd sit in the white wooden rocking chair by the kitchen window and, hour after hour, shell peas, snap beans or string cranberries and popcorn for the Christmas tree.

Proud hands held binoculars during the 2,550 hours she logged for the Civilian Ground Observer Corps during World War II. Her oldest son had joined that world war, as her bridegroom had the first one.

Those hands darkened with liver-colored spots, then swelled, twisted and became painfully crippled. Our home was desolate from the lack of her efficient hands while she was away for months of therapy.

Her will was stronger than the crippling arthritis, however, and her hands returned to their duties. They now were slower hands, twisted and stiff, which made each job painful. But she found a way...a new way to hold a knife, a needle or pen, and to minister to my ailing father.

Those hands laboriously wrote a multitude of letters, unhooked a jillion fish and tuned the radio to late, late programs after Dad died.

When I said my last goodbye two months and four years ago, Mom's hands seemed to be softer, straighter...and younger. The Lord had touched her and her face, like her hands, had regained a certain youth.

I had to feel there was an urgent need waiting at the Lord's house for my mother's capable hands...the hands of a farm wife.

-||- 4, ㅂ ┣O 7/◇

FORMER REFUGE MANAGER
LEAVES HIS MARK
- September 18, 1980 -

We stood on one of the highest hills in the area overlooking lakes and marshes which complement this tall grass prairie. It was as though we were looking into tomorrow. The spot was symbolic.

282

I was one of a large crowd who gathered near Dewey Lake for dedication of a marker in memory of a man who had left his mark on our Sandhills by having the courage to look ahead.

Some 530 acres of native grassland on the Valentine Wildlife Refuge has been designated as the George Wiseman Natural Area. The memorial is unique to the state of Nebraska.

When George was refuge manager during the 1950s, he won the confidence of area ranchers. They, in turn, used range management practices on their own land which George carried out on refuge pastures.

His flexible policies created harmony between community and big government. He also saw and convinced the U.S. Fish and Wildlife Service of a need to restrict the influence of man from certain areas. That natural area would serve as a contrast to grazed areas of the Sandhills and allow study of plant genetics and disease on an undisturbed prairie.

To the west of the marker is a living memorial to George. He had some 15,000 cedar and pine trees planted on the treeless prairie. The shelterbelt not only provides wildlife habitat, but acts as a snowfence for a winter road.

George was a 4-H leader and he and his family were very much a part of the community. The Sandhills, I believe, left a mark on the Wiseman family because they have maintained contact, although their lives have taken them to other locations.

His wife, Hope, their four children and nine of the 12 grandchildren returned for Saturday's ceremonies. It had been more than 20 years since the family had been transferred out of state so there was a lot of "catching up" to do during the dinner and social evening following the dedication.

Lynne Wilson is the oldest daughter and the only one to remain in Nebraska. She and her husband, Will, farm near Maywood. Lynne was remembered by a good many young people as their first babysitter.

Larry and his wife, Sue, are veterinarians in Colorado Springs. Vicki is married to David Kirby, a veterinarian at Big Harbor, WA.

Bruce chose to follow in the footsteps of his father and is refuge manager of 600,000 acres in Oregon. That refuge is much different because it is a big game refuge with mountain sheep, moose and elk.

Bruce is now a quiet professional man but he was the brunt of a lot of teasing. We all remember him as a mischievous little boy with unlimited energy. What he couldn't think of doing in mischief wasn't worth mention.

They are a nice family and reflect George's strong quiet influence. George left warm memories from his tenure in the Sandhills as I'm sure he did elsewhere during his 30 years of service to the Fish and Wildlife Service.

But I think the hills must have left a mark on the family as well. They chose a spot in our Sandhills as an appropriate spot for a marker, which in effect says, "George Wiseman was here."

-||- 4, b FO 7/◇

FRIEND MISSED IN SANDHILLS
- December 18, 1980 -

There is a void in our community and our holiday season. My heart aches for a family that loses a loved one during the Christmas season. William J. Stetter, better known as "Bill" lived all of his life in Cherry County.

One reason his death December 12, 1980 at 80 years seemed such a shock, was his eternal youthfulness. Bill looked and acted like a man many years younger. His full head of hair was only streaked by gray and his walk was brisk.

My big regret is that I waited too long. I had often felt I should take more time to spend with Bill and his lovely wife, Ann.

You see, Bill had a deep interest in the early history of this area and he had taken photos for a long, long time. He kept a host of information and pictures in meticulous scrapbooks and I always meant to go through them with him.

Bill had a versatile background and I could always rely upon him as a source of information about early history. As a young man, he was a fur trader and then a rancher. While the youngsters were in school, the family moved to Valentine and operated a western store.

He has recorded some of the early history and told of his father, who arrived in Valentine in 1882, a year before the village was incorporated. He soon answered a community need and opened Valentine's first meat market.

Other stories were told him by his uncle, George Schwalm...of the market hunters who came to the Sandhills to shoot huge quantities of game for the Chicago market...and the soldiers at Fort Niobrara bringing in wagon loads of deer to sell.

In 1899, Bill's father acquired a portion of the TO Ranch, some 30 miles south of Cody and in later years, full interest. In 1926, it was sold to George Brandeis of Omaha, who frequently hunted there.

284

The TO brand didn't go with the ranch and the story goes that Brandeis used three K's on the left side...at a time when the Ku Klux Klan was prominent in the news.

It seems that Brandeis took a lot of kidding about being a German Jew who employed an Irish Catholic foreman and a Negro chauffeur yet branded with three K's. The brand was soon changed to the Three Bar and remains on that ranch now owned by the Ravenscrofts.

The elder Stetter then purchased the Nels Rowley ranch nearer to Valentine. Bill and Ann were married and moved there in the early 30s.

Still standing on their ranch is the original log house built by Rowley in 1883, one of only two, which still remain in the Sandhills.

Bill's stories were fascinating and often filled with humor. My favorite goes something like this: Jim Mogle ran a filling station at Cody and one day a couple stopped for gas who were driving a grand car with New York license plates. The man asked Jim if it were true that having to live in such a desolate and God forsaken country didn't cause a few residents to "go off their rocker."

Mogle assured them it was true so he was asked what was done with those people. Mogle's reply was, "We send most of them back to New York to teach school."

I live with regret that I failed to tape record his stories...to spend more time taking notes from his scrapbooks. Bill Stetter was a friend to all who knew him. He was one of the last survivors of an era when a man's word was better than a written contract.

DEAN PEARMAN
- February 26, 1981 -

I'd like to tell you a story about people of the Sandhills. This one is a bittersweet story that makes me sad, but at the same time, so very proud to live in the Sandhills of Nebraska. The story begins with Dean Pearman, 30, who was born and raised in the Seneca-Mullen area — a man handy with horses in a quiet manner which is his personality.

He married Clarine Hamilton from the neighboring Thedford community. The young couple shares the joy of daughter Casey's (now seven) dark beauty that mirrored each of their own. They also dealt with sorrow of the loss of their little son.

Two years ago, Dean's sudden illness was diagnosed as an inoperable brain tumor ... the dreaded cancer. He received the maximum treatment of radiation allowable, and by last spring, he had a clean bill of health. Sabrena was born in July.

Last fall, Dean was disabled with symptoms similar to a stroke. Doctors said although the tumor had been greatly diminished, apparently "fingers" had extended and eluded X-rays. They couldn't treat for something they weren't sure of.

"Dean was in such good physical condition that he looks great although he's bedfast in the Mullen hospital and can't talk," Clarine said, "and he isn't in pain. We're locked into limbo though. We can't turn back time, and we can't make plans for the future."

Friends the young couple had made over a wide area refused to remain idle. They decided fund-raising benefits would be one way to help. Two were held simultaneously a week ago Sunday. The other was Saturday night.

Don Younkin of Seneca, population less than 200, promoted an auction sale. Town and country people donated desirable items, women prepared and sold lunch and food for a bake sale, and some 300 attended.

Jim Patterson and John Sutton volunteered their auctioneering expertise and bidding was spirited. A rooster was sold and resold until it brought $100. Younkin donated a day's labor and that sold for $110. There was something for everyone, a load of wood, a stallion fee, furniture ... to name a few. Total of the sale: $8,700.

"It was a huge success beyond my wildest expectations," Younkin said. "It made me proud to live in this community."

Gordon Kostman, president of the Arthur Roping Club, and Doug Garner organized a team roping on the same day. The club donated its time and talent which included Margaret Hawkin's barn and announcer Gene Olson, and the roping steers were donated by Bruce Huffman, Chet Kramer, Allen Swanson and Mary Walz. The Pack-Backers club sold a benefit lunch.

The license plates on vehicles were from three states and seven Nebraska counties. Three sets of roping reins, donated by Dave Hebbert of Hyannis, sold and resold for $702. Total raised for the Pearman family was $1,907.

All the while, the competitive spirit of 114 teams was bright. Top time in the open class went to Jim Alworth and Butch White with 5.98 seconds and in the mixed class. Lori Clark and Troy Trenary clocked 7.2.

286

Saturday night, Dave and Cathy Sullivan promoted a "fun night" in Mullen. At the club, there was a cake raffle, bingo, kissing booth and you name it ... the evening ended with a benefit dance at the Lariat where the Sundance County Line band donated most of their fee. The dance proceeds of $1,100 boosted the grand total to nearly $12,000.

You must remember these are small towns — Arthur and Seneca have less than 200 people and Mullen about 700. It didn't make any difference if those people lived a mile from the Pearmans or 100 miles. They gathered together in "fun" events to help a young family whose husband and father was stricken during the prime of life; their future now based upon hope and prayer ... and Sandhills people share that, too.

Clarine said she is so deeply grateful and overwhelmed by people's compassion. "Only in the Sandhills ... could this happen."

A TRIBUTE TO A BRAVE FRIEND
- October 8, 1981 -

Dark heavy clouds hung low over the Sandhills Sunday night and spilled nearly two inches of rain onto the dry sand. For me, the weather was symbolic. The raindrops were tears of mourning shed for a fellow Sandhiller, Norman Muirhead, whom everyone called "Red," died as the rain fell Sunday night.

It will never be said that Red lost his battle with life, rather that he won an eight-year battle over death. His courage and a determined will to live remains an inspiration to all of us who knew him.

Red migrated to the Sandhills from Kansas during the 30s when drought-devastated the country. His first job was at the Carl Weise Ranch on the Loup River near Thedford. Wages during the depression were meager.

I imagine it was there that he met Eldora Keller, a ranch girl of a pioneer family near Purdum. They were a quiet, God loving and hard working couple who raised three sons with strong family ties.

They spent the 40s working for Harry Minor on the Minor-Adams Ranch near Hyannis and the Jurgeson farther to the north. Minor's son, Dick, said he remembers Red putting up all the hay with horses and a crew of Mexicans.

"He was all business," Dick said. In 1951, Red moved his family to G.C. Young Ranch near Valentine. For the next 23 years they tended the ranch and cattle as though it belonged to them. Eldora and the boys, Neal, Wayne and Marvin, worked by his side.

Red was a gentle man and the cattle responded in like manner. His neighbors called Red a "helluva cowman."

He was loading a couple of bulls in a horse trailer in 1973 when the animals accidentally pushed him against a fence and injured his chest. That injury took him to the doctor and it was then that he found that he had cancer of the pancreas. He was 59 years old and given only three months to live.

Doctors said they couldn't touch the pancreas so bypass surgery was done, but Red would be a diabetic.

His health rapidly deteriorated and one day Eldora left to take him to his doctors in Kearney. By the time she reached Broken Bow he was so ill she entered him in the hospital there. Red lapsed into a coma. After two weeks with Eldora constantly caring for him she was told she could move him to Valentine.

"Harry and Dick Minor came to see him," Eldora remembers, "and although Red didn't respond they talked about old times on the ranch. During the middle of the night Red spoke to me for the first time in weeks and said he had dreamed about the Minors."

She told him they had been to see him and their voices had apparently pierced his subconscious. She said he seemed to rally and said "People really do care, don't they?"

Red took up the battle to live. That summer their son Marvin, Greg Perrett and Eldora were putting up the hay. "Red was terribly weak and on crutches, but one day he came with me to the hayfield to watch. He waved me over and told me to check a flat tire on my rig. While I was looking at the tire he pulled himself onto the tractor and left me standing. That took a lot of guts, but he was determined to be useful."

His health forced him to leave the ranch in 1975 but he never gave up. Between sessions with the doctors and the hospital his activities included stacking hay with a hay buster and working at the Thedford Sale Barn to mention a few.

Doctors called him a "miracle case" and said that only a strong will and a determination to live had extended his life from the anticipated three months to eight years. There was no other explanation.

288

He was able to see his three sons graduate from college, determined that they have the education he didn't. He also knew the love of five grandchildren; three of them born after 1973.

Red was a quiet man but he retained his subtle low-key sense of humor. He frequently had a joke to tell but never talked about himself or his illness...just the plans for what he would do tomorrow.

Red Muirhead was the most courageous man I have ever known. Our entire family knew him and loved him. He enriched our lives with his love of life and we too, will miss him.

DISTAFF PIONEERS REMEMBERED
- March 10, 1983 -

History tends to minimize credit due the brave women for their contributions of settling the West. They worked beside their men under almost primitive conditions. Days started at dawn and ended in darkness; there was little rest or recreation. All accolades offered the men settlers should be shared with the courageous ladies who were partners and helpmates every step of the way.

That was written by Helen Belsky Weyerman when she wrote about her parents who settled in my county during 1906. I thought it worthy of sharing with you during the week dedicated to women's contribution to history.

Cherry County is in its centennial year. This week might be the appropriate time to honor some of our pioneer women — the weld which bound the family together — the strength of spirit which overcame incredible obstacles ...

Dr. Mary Baker came to the western portion of the county in 1886 by covered wagon when she was 40. When a young man with a gunshot wound was brought to her, she saved his life by amputation on her kitchen table. Her patients included young women in the throes of complicated childbirth and a burned child who was trying to fill a mother's place to her orphaned brothers and sisters.

At the same time, she taught school and organized a church far from the nearest village.

Josephine Story was left with six small children in 1907 when her husband left for adventure in Canada. She ran a small cafe in Kilgore to support her family, sold fresh baked bread, kept boarders and was the community midwife until she was in her late 70s.

In the Brownlee community, Mrs. Ed Lee taught her first year of school in 1892 and her last year in 1942. In the Mullen area, Maggie Prindle Marshall lived in a one-room granary with her three children during one summer until their sod house was finished. Three days after moving into the house, a son was born.

Dora Simonson was pregnant with her 11th child when the family settled along the Boardman Creek about 50 miles southwest of Valentine in 1910. They lived in the wagon and tents and carried water from the creek. A daughter was born in September after the sod house was finished.

Essie Davis of Hyannis was widowed when her son was 4 months old. She built the OLO Ranch to its present size. In 1927, in the Purdum area, Emma Keller was left with four children, 137 cows, 100 horses and mortgaged land when Harry died. Quietly, by hard work, she paid off the land there as well as land in Canada which her husband had purchased.

Living conditions during those times, however, were primitive. Near Thedford, Minnie Wiese battled bedbugs and fleas with coal oil, lye and boiling water. On Pelican Lake, Mary Newman scattered straw sprinkled with sulphur and burned it. She got rid of the fleas and her treasured house plants she had brought from Minnesota.

Philipine Carpenter planted moss rose on her sod roof. Elizabeth Nicholas braided rugs which rotted on the earthen floor. Bertha Stilwell raised 15 children in the Simeon community.

Hattie Goodfellow was a college graduate when she moved with her husband to an isolated ranch south of Cody after the turn of the century. She burned cow chips without complaint until she found the men had traveled to the Snake River to cut wood for a branding fire. Then she rebelled. Lizzie Kime Wolfenden of the Kennedy community attended only three terms of school (two of them only three months long) but taught school when some students were older than she. She didn't leave the ranch until she was past 80 although she had been widowed for 15 years.

Lucy McMurtrey lived near the heart of the big county. When lonesome, she went visiting in her team and buggy and took along a container of cream. When she returned, the butter had been "churned" while bouncing over rough trails.

At one time, Ada Adamson didn't leave their ranch south of Cody for three years. Edna Wallingford Sears in the Kennedy community didn't see another woman for a span of eight months. A son was born with only her husband in attendance.

Although these women might not be recognized in any history book, they were the vital pulse of each home and each community.

I have only one question. How much history would have been written without such women?

PERRY FRANKS / TIM NUTTER
- September 1, 1983 -

Before we submit an update of an earlier story, let's review the first. Perry Franks, who now puts the polish on cow cutting horses, was at the ranch at the time. He had left the calf roping arena in 1958 after spending 12 very successful years roping at big rodeos such as Denver, Cheyenne and Chicago. It was during a time when matched roping was popular, and he once averaged 12.2 seconds on 12 head.

Perry remembered winning 'big money' — $3,700 in 1947 at Chicago. "We all had nine calves to rope during 22 performances," he said. "I was the only man to rope all nine on the first loop."

Six years ago I wrote a story and I was positive it was only the first chapter. Now it's time for an update. We were going to brand our spring calves and G.R. thought it would be fun to instigate another matched roping ... Perry and our little neighbor, 9-year-old Timothy Nutter. We called him Timmy then.

Some said Timmy was born with a rope in his hand. While other youngsters were roping, he could be seen practicing his loop. Later on he had a roping pony just his size. He was, and is, a quiet young man who smiles more than he talks. At rodeos when his father was dogging a steer, the lad might be found along the sidelines roping a saw horse.

Timmy was the only one who didn't know he was going to be matched calf for calf with Perry. "Don't put too much pressure on a little kid," G.R. said. The branding crew was anxious in anticipation of the event and guarded the secret well.

The branding crew gathered and Perry shook his head when he examined Timmy's soft limp rope that he said belonged to his sister. "Couldn't find mine," he said.

Perry was off double-checking the flex of his nylon rope, but Timmy was waiting by the corral while the branding irons heated. He rode into the herd time and again, twirled his loop on a hind leg, and dragged the calf to the branders. The crew gleefully kept silent tally: 5-0 in favor of the young cowboy.

When Perry realized he had to play catch-up, his loop often was jinxed and missed its mark. To make matters worse, one of Timmy's loops snared two calves and his lead increased.

Perry good-naturedly conceded the contest and the men urged Timmy to quit, not to overdo. He kept right on roping, but did say he hoped he didn't catch two at a time again. It was hard for his pony to pull two.

During the branding dinner the men found that Timmy had blisters across the palm of his roping hand, but he refused to complain.

Perry took a lot of good-natured teasing about being "wiped out" by a boy of 9.

"That kid is something else and we haven't heard the last of him," Perry said.

That was six years ago when Timmy Nutter was 9. Now Tim Nutter is 15 and he won the calf roping championship at the National Little Britches Rodeo last week. It was his first year of competition in the senior division. His average time on three head was 12.3 seconds ... close to the 12.2 that Perry set in 1947.

Tim appears cool and calm in competition. Perhaps, in part, because of the philosophy rather than pressure offered by his father, Doug Nutter, who was National High School Rodeo president in 1966.

"I tell him to forget the other ropers and their scores when he goes to rope," Doug said. "I tell him just to rope against himself, just to do the best he can."

Tim also ropes on two other circuits, High School Rodeo and the Nebraska State Rodeo Association. He and Jeff White team-rope together and hope to make the top 10 and qualify for the NSRA finals in October.

That's an update to the story. I'll repeat the same ending I used six years ago.

"There will be more chapters to this tale but you'll have to follow Tim Nutter and his calf roping to learn the rest of the story."

-||- Ꮞ Ꮯ ⊢O 7◇

TRACING A SANDHILLS FAMILY
- July 19, 1984 -

The well-kept lawn that surrounds Don and Claire Hanna's ranch house lends a feeling of freedom and space. Actually, the white rail enclosed lawn serves two houses with abundant space in between.

"It takes me seven hours to mow it," said Don E. Hanna II, who has lived on that spot for the past 69 years — since he was 3 years old.

Looking beyond that yard, a vast hay meadow is dotted with stacks of sun-cured hay, winter feed for cattle during the inevitable Nebraska winter. In fact, hay meadows and rangeland for this particular Hanna family stretch to the west for 22 continuous miles. The Hannas are five-generation Cherry County ranchers.

The patriarch of the clan, "Milt" Hanna, and his brother, Jim, brought cattle from Iowa to the Bar 7 Ranch on the Middle Loup River in 1883. After working on the ranch for two years, the brothers filed claims near Dunning.

In 1896, Milt and Della moved their family of six children to a house north of Seneca, which burned because of a faulty chimney. The family spent the summer in a sod chicken house and a tent borrowed from George Higgins of the Box T Ranch.

By 1908, Milt and a partner bought the Pass Ranch 10 miles west of Brownlee. The Pass was the eastern portion of the old Standard Land and Cattle Co.'s 101 Ranch that also included Big Creek and the Carver. Four of Milt's sons, Don E., Jim, George and Seth, bought the Pass in 1915.

Don E. and Nona's three sons, Don Jr., Francis and Bob, were born in a sod house 3 miles northeast on what is now the Pound ranch.

The land transactions of Milt's sons were numerous during the following years. George sold his share to Don E., Jim sold to Seth and bought land in Canada, and Don E. and Seth bought the original Faddis and Steadman Triple L in 1948; Don trading his share for Seth's share of the Pass.

At the same time, Don E. found time for community service —county commissioner from 1930-38, Nebraska Legislature 1941-49 and was a member of the Nebraska Highway Advisory committee when he died in 1954.

Don Jr. and Claire Frink were married in 1934, by Chet Paxton, then Thomas County Judge. Like his father, Don Jr. served in the state Legislature.

Don and Claire not only celebrated their golden wedding anniversary last Sunday, but 50 years of living on the Pass Ranch.

Friends, neighbors and relatives gathered on the spacious lawn for the party. Hosts were the three Hanna children; Don III "Sonny" and Susie Hanna, Jimmy and Lynda Hanna and Bernard and Barb Stichka, and the three children of each couple.

Apparently ranch life has kept Don II and Claire youthful; Don is straight and slim and Claire is as petite as her daughter and two daughters-in-law and her gracious smile never wavers.

Don and Claire have perpetuated the Hanna tradition of land expansion. In 1978, the family bought the Big Creek Ranch, also part of the former 101 and later owned by Brass and Meyers. Each of their three children now operate their ranches as separate entities: Sonny and Suzie at the Pass; Jimmy and Lynda on the east portion of Big Creek and Bernard and Barb, who own the old Brass and Meyers Sugarbowl brand, at the original Big Creek headquarters to the west. Live water is provided by 15 miles of the Loup River and about nine miles of Big Creek.

Don said he and Claire no longer own any cattle but they still own land, which they lease to their children. But ... they wouldn't think of living anywhere other than the ranch.

SPECIAL WOMEN FRIENDS REMEMBERED
- April 4, 1985 -

While searching for something special about April, in addition to Easter Sunday, I remembered that several women, important to my life, were born during April; I believe the diamond is April's birthstone. There's an inner quality that compares to that popular gem in each of the women I'll introduce.

G.R.'s mother, Sadie, was born April 1, 1890. Her importance is for obvious reasons. She was also the "Jewish mother" of the Beel clan; ministering with delicious food and genuine concern to all who stopped by her house.

Her entire life revolved around her husband, children and grandchildren. I think she was loved by all who knew her. That's a coveted memorial.

Sally Schuff, associate editor of the Nebraska Farmer, has contributed tremendously to my professional needs. I admire and respect her writing ability, but Sally also has a huge capacity for fun. We've had some great times while riding horseback or sharing the joy of photography. Her birthday is the seventh.

Janet Magnuson is the type of friend who is always there whether circumstances be good or bad, happy or sad. She recognizes your weaknesses and likes you anyway. We've walked the beaches, fished through the ice and sold rodeo books together. Most of all, we laugh together. Her birthday is the 11th.

Alice Cumbow will be 91 on the 15th, a day her CPA son Bill won't easily forget. Alice is the most noted artist in her native Cherry County. Yet she is a very humble unassuming dear of a woman. She is self-taught, and the type of talented person who says "we," not I.

Nadine Beel's birthday is the 25th. She alone probably saved my skin when I was introduced to ranch life by the job of cooking for a 12-man haycrew. She taught me how to cook, continually furnished me with recipes and soothed my fears. She wiped my brow during childbirth and helped me in so many other ways too numerous to list. Can you have any idea of my gratitude?

Last, but far from least of my April birthdays, is our daughter, Myki, born the last day. It was close enough to Easter 1954 that a colored Easter egg was placed in the bassinet when she was brought to my room.

Myki was the first of our two daughters who introduced a delightful femininity to our home previously dominated by two sons. More than just a thoughtful daughter, I call her friend.

Myki VanWinkle delivered a little grandson last year on Good Friday. There will be another addition expected late in September. I've ordered a little toe-headed girl, and being a dutiful daughter. ...

All of these women were born in April under the signs of Aries and Taurus. They have added greatly to my enjoyment and appreciation of life as well as to the quality of life for others. I am proud of them as women, and I hope I may always call them "friend."

Lest I forget on their special days, Happy Birthday and God Bless to each and every one of them!

-||- 4̖ ᔌ ꟾO 7⟡

RED NEUMEYER
- June 6, 1985 -

P erhaps the good Lord has been depressed lately and felt the need for someone to maintain high spirits throughout his kingdom. Why else would he have called Red Neumeyer home?

No one could stay in a black mood for very long around Red Neumeyer. He wasn't happy if he wasn't telling a joke, pulling a trick on some unsuspecting soul or initiating some shenanigan.

It was 10 years ago when we first met the tall and lanky cowboy. He must have been 53, but he was pulling down the cinch on a saddle bronc at the very first Old-timers Cowboy's Rodeo at Hyannis.

Red made a pretty ride. Then after the eight-second whistle it was legal to touch his hat, so Red fanned his bronc wildly with his Stetson.

"That's the way we used to ride broncs and it doesn't seem natural if you don't fan your hat," he said later with a laugh.

It was easy for Red to laugh. He could relieve a serious and stressful situation with his sense of humor. Red Neumeyer has been described over and over as "one in a million," and he dearly loved the sport of rodeo.

Sunday, the Hyannis High School Rodeo Club held their annual high school rodeo. Marty Retchless had his horse positioned in the box ready to rope his calf. But he had to wait because it was time. At exactly 2 p.m., a saddle bronc carrying an empty saddle bucked out of the chute in tribute to a member of the rodeo fraternity. That cowboy memorial service for Red Neumeyer was scheduled at the very same time as Red's funeral began in Mullen. The touching ceremony never fails to leave a lump in the throat. Red and his wife operated Red's Cafe in Mullen where Red held court with a jovial sense of humor. He was considered sort of a local "character."

Gordon Most ranches and sells TV satellite discs as a sideline. Red said, no he didn't want one.

The next time Gordon went to Mullen he saw that Red had constructed his own TV disc on his front lawn across the street from the cafe. Red had used a children's plastic saucer sled, a couple of chrome table legs and a bathroom plunger to build his disc. He had a lot of fun doing it.

Some strangers might have been surprised while driving into town from the west when they saw a figure sitting in an outhouse on Red's lot. When they looked a second time they saw the occupant was only a stuffed dummy wearing a cowboy hat and Levis.

A sign on the outhouse read, "Campaign office" and a political poster for Mullenite, Jack Kemp, was tacked below the sign.

Of anyone lacked a sense of humor, Red was a good teacher.

A sign affixed to barbed wire that enclosed Red's parked vehicles read, "Sanford and Sons."

It's easy to visualize Red chuckling to himself as he added those personal touches to his property along Highway 2.

Don't think he always spent his time playing pranks. When he wasn't cooking or dozing the state gravel pile west of town to lofty heights he was attending some branding or building fence on some ranch. He seemed to be in perpetual motion.

No matter where he might be you could count on hearing his hearty laugh; a laugh that was infectious because it spread through any group he might be with.

Red's memory will live on and on as his friends laugh while telling and retelling his stories. Red Neumeyer would like that.

DEAL BARNES
- June 5, 1986 -

As Hudson had done in the beginning, the new owner expanded ranch boundaries that added to Barnes' responsibilities.

As Barnes' 80th birthday approached, painful joints didn't keep him from his horse. He'd say, "I've got work to do! Cattle to move!"

His loyalty to the owner was returned in full. When Barnes' failing health kept him from the saddle, the ranch house was to be their home for as long as they wanted.

The good Lord was kind. When failing memory often brings agony, Barnes remained happy. He would talk a bit with visitors and then say, "I've got work to do. Cattle to move!"

Barnes' grandson, who worked with him for years, is now manager. And the Bow & Arrow cattle brand, the third registered in Cherry County, begins 119 continuous years as the owner's signature on the same ranch.

When Hudson died, he had lived on his original claim 75 years, longer than anyone in the county. Barnes' 40-plus years as manager of the same ranch may well be some kind of record.

There is an empty saddle at the Bow & Arrow Ranch. Friends and family gathered Tuesday to say goodbye to Deal Barnes.

Words written by his grand-daughter might have been Barnes' own: "I have lived a good life; a cowboy's dream come true. Thank you, Lord, for I'm now ready to ride into eternity; me, my horse and you."

You may not have known him, slight-built with an ever-present Texas-size cigar as his trademark. In later years, the cigar was there. He just didn't light it.

Barnes holds a permanent place in the history of the Bow & Arrow, a ranch in the Simeon community where Sam Hudson filed his homestead back in 1883. Sam's trademark was a Texas-sized handlebar mustache.

Hudson had no children. After his wife died in 1947, a kindly woman became Sam's caregiver in the home he built in 1889. A rancher and good friend, Harold Harms, managed the ranch affairs.

In 1954, Harms brought Barnes and his wife, Ruth, to the ranch as resident manager. Long ago, Barnes told me his first job was to rebuild miles and miles of neglected fences.

When Hudson died in 1958 at 97, Harms' young son became heir to the ranch and the brand. Barnes, known for his fierce loyalty, stayed on.

Barnes wasn't always a cowboy. A Rapid City, SD, high school Golden Gloves boxing champion, he also was a winning pro in the lightweight division. After a stint in the Navy, he trained horses for then South Dakota governor, Tom Berry. He also was a jockey for quarter horse racing.

While at the Bow & Arrow Ranch, Barnes helped train Valentine boxers and was an active Mason and Shriner.

The 1970's were a financial wreck for the cattle industry. The Bow & Arrow was put up for sale. Barnes chuckled when he told me an Alabama man said he was interested in buying only if he remained manager. The ranch sold, Barnes stayed on and Ruth ran the books.

OUR MARVELOUS PIONEERS
- June 5, 1986 -

Our pioneers are marvelous people. The only thing Etta Simons wanted for her 91st birthday last year was a party. So her daughters, Harriett Cozad and Marg Richards, invited guests to a birthday luncheon at the Celebrity in Valentine.

You ought to know that Etta remains youthful as she lives alone during her 10th decade in Cherry County.

In fact, the 10 ladies who were invited to the party all live alone and care for themselves. All were at least 90 with Virginia Galligher and Mary Reagle 95 and 94, respectively. Arline Hodges, Fern Lovejoy and Anna Woods all were 93. Those who were the same age as the honoree were Alive Cumbow, Hazel Wilson, Rose Simons and Minnie Tetherow.

The group had such a good time the party was repeated again Saturday for Etta's 92nd birthday. Three additional ladies have reached the 90 mark, so they were added to the guest list: Fannie Estes, Esther Haynes and Olive VanMetre.

Not all were able to come because of previous commitments. They are a busy group of ladies; hardy, ambitious pioneer women.

The marvelous traits of those ladies are their independence and their joy for living. If there be wrinkles on their brows, I didn't notice, because wrinkles certainly have not creased their hearts.

Their collective attitude reminds me of my own mother's words of wisdom long ago: "Life is a picture. Paint it well."

Speaking of birthdays, Nelda Keller celebrated her 97th on Sunday.

Nelda Hoefs was four years old when her family moved to Cherry County near Wood Lake. Then prior to her marriage to John Keller in 1914, she filed a Kinkaid near Good Creek. The couple moved to Canada for a couple of years, but Nelda returned the required time to prove up on her claim.

Nelda was a true pioneer. Her first term as school teacher in 1909 was in a log school near McCann Canyon for 34 students in eight grades. Her salary was $40 a month and she paid $10 for room and board.

Later, she lived in a homestead shack. While in Canada, she cooked for their threshing crew on a topsy stove, but the second year hail claimed their crop and they returned to the Sandhills. Health had failed for John's parents, so

Nelda sold her claim for a good price of $1.56 an acre and the couple returned to the home ranch.

Nelda was Cascade postmaster for 27 years before the couple moved to Valentine in 1947 and became involved with the historical society. Nelda lived alone for the next decade after John died in 1971. Through those years she crocheted about 25 afghans which she gave as gifts or donated to support community fund raising causes.

Nelda's hip failed and she has not walked for a year. She now lives with a daughter, Eldora Muirhead, who quit her job at the hospital to care for her mother. Sharing the home with an elderly parent is a tradition of pioneer families.

By example, Nelda Keller instilled in her family a willingness to share. And so it seems fitting that the Keller name will live on in the Keller Park State Recreation Area that will be dedicated Saturday near Ainsworth.

Nelda and John Keller's son, Neal and his wife Pauline, recently donated 197 acres of picturesque land in Bone Creek Valley as the newest addition, to the Nebraska state parks system. The couple said they wanted to share the spot with all Nebraskans.

Our pioneers are marvelous people.

MEMORIES THAT ARE SURE TO LIVE ON
- July 31, 1986 -

We never know what card will be dealt next from the deck that is called life. If we all could but remember to savor each moment, appreciate each blessing and really LIVE each hour we would allow no time for worry about the "what if's" that are the future.

It's quite possible that if young Joe Ensminger from Valentine could have known the future, he wouldn't have worried about his performance in cow cutting at the recent national rodeo. But had he known he would be champion of that event, half the fun of competing would have been lost.

He was dealt the Queen of Hearts, the kind lady with a smile.

Jody Hollopeter of Colome, SD, was dealt a different card during that rodeo. Her father, Jack, died several days after it started.

300

But Jody went on. He would have wanted it that way, but I'm sure the loss was an added strain to the usual stress of competition. Jody claimed a national second in goat tying, and I'll bet she offered her efforts up in her dad's memory.

Memories do live on and on and on.

The memory of Elizabeth "Bess" Heelan remains strong in our town. She died recently; a proud slim 86 years.

I doubt that I've ever been to town and not seen Bess Heelan walking somewhere in the town. She always walked and often graciously turned down an offered ride.

I had an impromptu lunch with her in the spring after we both attended a hearing at the courthouse. Bess was an intelligent woman who was vitally interested in all that went on ... and very knowledgeable about civic affairs. Some people did not always appreciate that because she had the courage of her own convictions and she wasn't afraid to voice her opinion.

Bess was an Egan from Whitman. Her husband, Will Heelan, became Cherry County Attorney in 1921 and practiced law here until he died in 1954. Bess had been secretary for Judge Osgood in Hyannis, and later practiced in Valentine as a registered abstractor until just four years ago.

She had four very bright sons, and I've heard people say that Bess Heelan could have passed the bar exam if she had ever wanted to.

Mrs. Heelan was always well groomed; her hair in a neat coil atop her head and I can't remember her without her earrings and white gloves.

More importantly she was always concerned about people, and she ministered to them in hundreds of ways. But she also was a very private person and few outsiders knew of her generosities. She preferred it that way.

She would have been very pleased to know that the honorary pallbearers named for her funeral were 11 women who were very pleased to be so honored.

I was not aware that women ever were named as honorary pallbearers, but I thought it was a marvelous idea. Somehow I find it appropriate with Bess Heelan's wishes.

She lived her life well and she will live on in our memories.

-||- 니 ᄂ ╞O 7

BAD GUYS USE IMAGINATION
- October 20, 1987 -

T he death last week of former State Sentor, Otho Kime, is a reminder that stories of those who experienced another, sometimes more colorful era, are gone forever unless they are recorded.

Otho's father, Frank, joined the railroad survey crew at Thacher in 1882, a year before Valentine emerged as a tent town. Five years later, Frank homesteaded on Lone Tree Lake about five miles southwest of this ranch. Otho was the fourth of nine children, all who became marksmen. Young Otho was noted for shooting coyotes with a pistol from the back of a galloping horse.

He was very tall and thin with deep-set eyes and craggy eyebrows, the image of a frontier lawman. He was Cherry County Sheriff from 1935-1948, except for a two-year leave of absence to serve with the Army Counter Intelligence during World War II.

A couple of years ago I studied the scrapbook he kept during those years and he elaborated on some of the more colorful experiences.

Prohibition had ended by 1935 when Otho took office as sheriff January 3, but liquor problems hadn't. At midnight on the 10th, Brown County Sheriff Reed called to tell him a habitual criminal had hijacked a truckload of liquor, shot up the place and was headed west.

After a chase, he and his deputies were able to stop the armed man five miles west of town. Otho explained that Rat Peters bought liquor from a Long Pine dealer saying he would open a store at Rushville. Then he refused to pay the dealer, beat him with a flashlight, and accidentally shot his driver in the arm with a .45 pistol.

Rat Peters wasn't stopped for long.

"After haying that fall, Erba 'Hub' McMurtrey turned his horses out to pasture, but 12 horses and three mules were missing after Peters passed through headed east."

"Hub checked into a hotel in Ainsworth and contacted Sheriff Reed. Later Hub overheard Peters say he was going to load out at 3 a.m. Reed held Peters, but two of his hired hands disappeared with the horses at Ainsworth."

Otho and his deputy arrested a man named Blacky at Wood Lake who had ridden with Peters and who confessed they had used the Doc Middleton method of stealing horses.

302

Blacky said that in preparation, Peters hardened his two best horses by graining them for a month. Then Peters and Blacky rode 50 miles southwest from Hay Springs to camp on Dry Valley north of the Wolfenden Ranch. At sundown, they ran the stolen horses down Dry Valley past Swansons, the Kennedy post office and on to Wood Lake avoiding the ranch building sites.

"Peters branded the horses on the jaw through a wet blanket, which blistered the hide but didn't burn the hair, a method used by Texas cattle rustlers," Blacky told Otho.

Half of the horses had gone to Indiana by rail from Wood Lake and half trucked to Ainsworth. Later the man hired to truck them remembered the mules, describing them as "terrible animals."

Peters was sentenced to five years.

"He didn't change," Otho said. "Later he was sentenced in Sheridan County for stealing hogs."

Otho laughed, remembering a 1937 Crookston incident. "Two Wyoming safe-crackers hit four safes in one night," he said. "When we caught them one said they had rolled the safe from Babcock's filling station down the hill to the railroad yards on the cement walk. He said it was the 'deadest town' ... said he rode the safe downhill while yelling, 'Whoopee, I'm a cowboy!'"

Of the early lawless, Otho said, "They weren't short on imagination."

-||- 4, ♭ ⊢O ⁷◇

GOD HAS TAKEN A LIVING ANGEL FROM US
- April 18, 1991 -

Some of us believe that angels really do spend time on Earth. Those whom we consider as such seem to have a special personality. They are good, but without being "goody-goody." They are concerned without being intrusive. They are compassionate and giving without expecting anything in return. And those traits are humanized by a sense of humor.

Just knowing such a person has a way of making us feel good about ourselves and the rest of the world. And we might even grow to feel that they will be with us forever.

But God, if he does indeed send an angel among us, decides upon the time when he calls them home. When that call is met with calm and peaceful acceptance, it would seem the message to us who remain behind is, "do not mourn."

We will, indeed, miss Ann Stetter. Sorely miss her presence. But I think the unspoken message she left for us was "celebrate life each day."

Several hundred filled the church, the choir loft, and the cry room to say their final goodbyes to Ann. A huge crowd doesn't always turn out for someone who has lived 88 years. Quite often most of their friends have gone before them.

There were so many, both young and old, who knew and loved Ann Stetter. During the funeral service Father Jim called her an angel. And he told us of her faith and calm acceptance as she prepared to depart this life on April 10, 1991.

From her hospital bed in Omaha with her three grown children at her side, Ann calmly asked for a piece of paper. With their help she wrote her obituary, selected her pall bearers and even chose her final dress. That compassion for others was so like her. She wanted to spare her loved ones of those sad details. Six of her favorite one-time students, now grown men, proudly carried her casket.

Father Jim also told us of a time when friends came to visit Ann in her home when she wasn't feeling well. Later in the afternoon the friends said they must go, but Ann invited them for dinner. "But Ann, you're not feeling well," they said. I'm positive that her eyes twinkled as she said, "But I won't be doing the cooking."

It's easy to visualize that exchange, and the way Ann laughed while she said it. She had a marvelous sense of humor and usually had a cute little story to tell. Hers was a marvelous talent for nurturing friendships. Ann also had the courage of her convictions, and she spoke out when she felt the need. But hers was a manner that didn't seem to ruffle any feathers.

Last fall, Ann told me that as a young woman in the 1920s, she rode the train alone from Iowa. "I was a little scared, but jobs were hard to get and I was accepted to teach high school mathematics in Valentine."

During her 60-some years in the Sandhills, Ann Stetter touched so many lives with a loving hand. During the 24 years she and Bill Stetter spent at the ranch, after they moved to town in 1968, her energy seemed endless. She was there for friends in times of sorrow and times of happiness. Her heart and her home were always open to family and to friends. It was truly a privilege to have known Ann Stetter.

HISTORIC HANNAS
- January 2, 1992 -

I have an award I call "GRAND Parents" that I want to publicly award to a ranch couple. There will be no trophy or certificate, just this space to acknowledge what I consider to be an ultimate gift that this couple gave at Christmas time.

The honorees I've selected are longtime ranchers Don Hanna Jr. and his wife Claire. They are originally of the Brownlee area and more recently, Mullen residents. Don Hanna III is now head honcho at the home ranch.

Through the years Don and Claire enlarged the ranch, raised two sons and a daughter, and if my count is accurate, now have 17 grandchildren and six great-grandchildren.

Don, the eldest son of former state Sen. Don E. Hanna, is a marvelous source of local history and a great story teller with a meticulous memory. I've yet to see Claire, a petite wisp of a woman, without a broad smile or a kind word. She is one classy lady.

As a third-generation ranch couple they have lived through historic times. Married during the Great Depression and drought, they watched the demise of horses and the overshot stacker in the hayfield and the advent of mechanized machinery. They knew firsthand the hardship during the infamous Blizzard of 1949 and the highs and lows of the cattle cycle.

They remember the day when they watched neighboring cowboys in the Brownlee Roping Club action. Don Hanna Sr. observed: "I had to ride into Valentine those 50 miles on horseback to serve on jury duty. That was quite a trip, but my kids think nothing of driving in for a movie."

Don's father was no stranger to horses. He won a silver mounted saddle at Grand Island in 1908 as state saddle bronco champ and rode that saddle for the next 25 years.

Long before he became state senator, Don Hanna Sr. rode the rough stock for outfits such as JF Minor, the UBI and the 101. In 1944 when the Thomas Dewey campaign train stopped over in Valentine, Hanna entertained Dick Lee, political editor of the New York Times, with a wild tale about "Old Blue." Caught in a blizzard, Old Blue fell and broke his leg, Hanna said. To save himself, Hanna said he gutted the horse and crawled into the rib cavity out of the storm. Before long the carcass was frozen shut with Hanna inside.

Two wolves began to tear at the carcass, so Hanna reached out and grabbed each by the tail. By yanking and steering he was able to head them towards home. His wife ran out, shot the wolves and rescued Hanna with an ax. Lee thought the story was hilarious, printed it back east and it was reprinted many times over the years.

Don and Claire gathered this story and others that include three brothers and a sister along with marvelous old photos, and compiled a book, "The Family of Milt & Della Hanna, 1858 - 1996." A nephew, George Hanna Jr., contributed a complete genealogy chart of the Hanna family. This book was Don and Claire's Christmas gift to their children and grandchildren.

The book begins when Milt, Don Jr.'s grandfather, came to the Sandhills in 1883. He was delivering cattle for Hanna's great grandfather, John Parker Hanna, who bought and sold cattle in Iowa.

This book would seem to me to be the ultimate gift. Family history all in one source for future generations. Perhaps other grandparents will begin their book for their family next Christmas. I can't think of a more treasured gift from GRAND Parents.

SPRING'S RETURN BRINGS MEMORIES OF L.C.
- May 13, 1993 -

A sweet fragrance of wild plum blossoms enter the house through open windows. Now I believe that spring has truly arrived. Memories of L.C. return, especially at plum blossom time. He planted the clump in our back yard that now is in full bloom. He favored blossoms of the Sandhills, especially those of the wild plum, chokecherry and soapweed.

L.C. Beel was my second father. Somehow I never thought of him as a father-in-law. It was my privilege to have him as a mentor for 22 years.

He was a tall, quiet man ... born of a time when a man's word was better than any written contract. After completing the sixth grade he had left home to work and help support the large family.

He was not a demonstrative man. In fact, I never heard him say, "I love you," to anyone. But he was a gentle man and dealt with family members in a loving manner.

Each of our four kiddos adored him. Grandpa was among the first words that they spoke. And as soon as they were old enough, he stopped by the house to take them with him as he checked cattle and pastures in his pickup.

L.C. rode the railroad from Iowa to the Sandhills shortly after the turn of the century. He was delivering bulls to the John Bachelor ranch on the Boardman Creek. That's about 14 miles west of our present location.

On that initial trip he decided that a Sandhills ranch was the end of his rainbow. He returned and worked as a ranch hand and purchased Ben Bachelor's original homestead. With a lot of hard work and frugal management, he eventually built his own ranch of considerable size.

Early entries in L.C.'s old daybook note his attention to detail. Every penny spent was recorded: "My expense to town, 75 cents."

In fact, everything is recorded in that old book. Each animal that he acquired or sold. And each animal that died, the cause and the monetary loss.

He was 34 when he married Sadie, his best friend's sister, in 1913 at the Episcopal manse in Valentine. Never known to waste a trip, he then joined the Masonic Lodge while his bride and a friend attended the picture show.

He had built a homestead shack for his bride-to-be who filed a 640-acre Kinkaid adjoining L.C.'s land as did her mother. After they married, the couple lived there five years. Their first big surprise was twin daughters.

After L.C. built the family home, he moved his wife's claim shack to the building complex as a ranch cook house. It still stands, now seldom used other than as a summer bunkhouse.

Those early ranchers were tenacious, common-sense environmentalists long before it became a buzz-word. "Take good care of the land and it will care for you." That was his doctrine.

His belief became our heritage. I wish that he could visit one more time. His approval would mean a great deal.

LENARD KIME DIED WITH HIS BOOTS ON
- April 27, 1995 -

When you hear a cowboy say, "Let me die with my boots on," he is not being fatalistic. He simply means he wants to live his entire life doing what he has always done.

When a man's life is spent caring for animals and caring for the land on which he and his animals mingle with the wild ones, he has a deep sense that he is in the presence of the Lord.

And why wouldn't he? He feels that his prairie environment is the creation of a higher power. When a man looks upon the land and knows that he is its steward, he is likely to say, "I don't own this land. The land owns me."

There are those who say you don't worship a higher being if you don't worship in church. And some prairie dwellers say they can worship from a tall hill 60 or 70 miles from the closest steeple.

Such a person was Lenard Kime. Each Sunday he would return from a trip through the hills and cattle and say to his wife, Joan, "I've just been to church."

Lenard lived life to its fullest. He loved to tease, play cards, tell jokes and more than a few tall tales. He liked to visit, so it's been said that he never met a stranger.

Lenard was also a serious cattleman. He learned the meaning of a family ranch from his father, Jake. Then he and his brother, Buzz, continued the tradition to include Lenard and Joan's son, Duane, and his family.

He was modest about his role in community affairs such as longtime director for the Bank of Mullen.

On April 5, Lenard died with his boots on. He died with spurs attached to his boots because only minutes before, he was riding his horse. He died just outside his home unexpectedly and without warning.

His loved ones knew devastating shock and sorrow at their loss. And there were tears of mourning in private. But the Kimes are strong people.

The mood at the wake and at the funeral was to celebrate the life of a man who loved life. Emphasis was on the good times shared, on Lenard's sense of humor that made people laugh.

Mourners who joined the family found themselves laughing at the stories retold. He had a special relationship with dogs and one called Lady was a constant companion.

Among Lenard's favorite sayings was, "If your dog bites you, why get a second opinion?"

Retaining a sense of humor softens adversity. And the Kimes know adversity all too well.

Joan Kime says she will face the future by taking one day at a time. She is a strong woman because that is how she has lived for several years.

Some of you may remember that I wrote about Joan, who was victim of a horrible accident. A loaded semi-truck upset on the car in which she was riding five years ago.

For some time her very life was threatened. Some injuries were permanent. Partial recovery has been painfully slow. But Lenard was there for her.

The couple played cribbage during the evening hours and they laughed together. Now he is gone; her companion of nearly 45 years.

But it was Joan's wish that his life be reviewed at his funeral with joy, not sorrow. So the minister repeated stories that brought chuckles, not tears.

Lenard Kime celebrated life. So it seemed fitting to his loved ones to continue that mood at its end.

It would seem logical that the world would be a happier place if we could all claim the epitaph, "He made people laugh."

LOOKING BACK AT OLD FRIENDS
- December 1997 -

I've read that it may be normal to feel a certain melancholy at this time of year. One of the reasons cited is change. It would be a waste of energy to dwell on the past. But it is OK to remember those who made a difference and to pay homage.

A recent incident drew my thoughts to the late Frank Carver of Crookston. For several decades it was common to see any number of top performing horses carry Carver's brand.

Frank took great pride in raising performance horses. His animals were comfortable on the track, in the timed event arena and as a ranch using horse. The animals also were handsome and ranked well in the halter class.

Frank Carver was considered a congenial one-stop source for anyone wanting a horse for whatever reason. During youth or adult rodeos, there usually was a horse carrying his 4-J brand and performing well in every event. Most owners claimed those same horses were tops at working cattle with born-in cow sense.

We were fortunate to own three of those Carver horses. Bo was one of the last colts sired by Mr. Kilgore before the stallion was killed by lightning.

Bo was a brother to Bill Hammond's Clay, a bulldogging horse that carried him to his third consecutive state title in that event.

I looked upon Bo as the most beautiful horse on this ranch. A buckskin with a dorsal strip, he was used mostly for ranch work, but also for youth rodeo, for trail rides and even once as a pack horse.

That was then. This is now and he must not be subjected to another winter. G.R. fed him a last meal of grain before the vet arrived. Bo was retired, 30 years old and very thin. A grave had been dug in preparation. The injections were merciful and the old horse passed over without so much as a quiver.

There now are three horses buried in their own special spot. Bo joins Kilbars, another of Mr. Kilgore's get and Tuffy sired by Tough Bars. All three carried the 4-J brand.

Daughter Myndi bought Kilbars as a colt in 1974. With G.R.'s help she trained him to drive on a sulky as well as ride him in 4-H events. Years later her little daughter, Megan, began running the barrels on him during the youth horse show of the county fair when she was about 4-years-old.

Kilbars died of a heart attack, but he was brought to the ranch and buried on a hill overlooking the west meadow.

Tuffy was G.R.'s working cow horse. "Get that horse on a cow and he can turn on a dime and leave you change," G.R. would say.

His registered name was 'Tough Bars Prince and he exhibited a bit of a royal attitude. He'd prance while carrying a rodeo queen. But after winning the champion gelding trophy he yawned for the photo.

We actually caught a photo of Tuffy grasping the caker rope in his teeth, and giving it a firm jerk to dump cake onto the ground for his equine buddies.

We retired Tuffy and he had the run of the ranch. One night he lay down in a patch of clover on the summer meadow and never moved again. His horseshoes welded onto a metal plate marks his grave.

ROY ERICKSON: "HORSE WHISPERER"
- April 26, 1998 -

They called him the "Horse Whisperer", the man who could gentle problem horses. A book was written, and Robert Redford filmed the movie in Montana. When I read the book, I wished it had been written about Roy Erickson, 1889-1973. There could be much more drama but most difficult to capture on film.

Roy was a friend of my Dad and visited often. But rather than to rely on stories told then, I'll refer to eye witness accounts recorded in Olin Waddill's book, "Saddle Strings."

Roy's ability with horses was legend in the Sandhills. He was born about 10 miles west of this place, and raised horses and cattle along with his father, "Bill America" Erickson.

"Horse Psychic" may have been a more appropriate title for Roy. He said most important was to gain a horse's confidence and he'd spend long hours just sitting in a corral. He said he would catch a horse when its mind was right, according to Waddill's book.

Roy traveled the country breaking problem horses. Walter Adamson watched as Roy broke eight head for John Bachelor.

He'd single one out using a fishing pole to steer and guide them. He'd walk along beside them touching with the pole until the horse began to follow him. Then he took them to the barn to halter. He'd often use a willow switch, not hitting the animal, rather hitting the ground and talking gently to the horse.

George Stetter sold a big Appaloosa to a cowboy who hit the horse over the head when he couldn't saddle him. After that the horse would bite and strike. Roy used his method with the Appie and when it responded he gave it oats from his pocket. When Stetter returned Roy sat on a nail keg and called the horse to him.

At the Dumb Bell Ranch, several bronc riders were unable to ride one horse. Jim Haney said if Roy could break him, there would be a job.

When the men came in from the hayfield, Roy's son, 10-year old Charles, was bringing in the milk cows on the horse.

Such stories are legion and probably hard to believe. Many told of how it took Roy anywhere from 15 minutes to an hour to gentle a horse. Often to prove his success, he'd sit under the bronc and strike a match for his cigarette on a hind hoof.

My favorite story is told by his daughter. Roy gathered a corral full of wild mustangs to break and sell to the U.S. Cavalry. A "doubting Thomas" bet Roy that he couldn't take four of them and drive them down Valentine's Main Street by late afternoon. She said Roy collected his bet when he drove the horses shortly after noon ... and all without bridles.

These stories are but a sample of the unique way that Roy dealt with problem horses.

He was never injured while working with horses. But in the 1940s he was sitting cross-legged on a gentle horse when it fell and crushed his ankle. Blood poisoning set in and that leg was amputated. Later, he lost the other.

Roy spent 30 years in a wheel chair, but he was not idle. He painted marvelous western scenes, hand-crafted leather and sculptured his beloved horses from wood. His handwriting looped and swirled into intricate designs.

His talents were many. In her book, "Call of the Range," Nellie Snyder Yost wrote about good horseman, "... but top of them all was probably Roy Erickson of Cherry County, who became a legend in his own time."

TOMBSTONES MARK THEIR PLACE
- May 24, 1998 -

Lest we forget, tombstones mark their place. Throughout the year, I visit cemeteries during traveling through the Sandhills. A few isolated burial plots carry inscriptions dated only into the late 1890s. Weeds may hide the stones, but I like to think the spirits of those resting there know that I visited.

To the best of my knowledge there are two markers within Cherry County that have the most unusual history. Both permanent markers were placed by rancher friends many years after the deaths of those who lie beneath them.

A white marble marker stands alone in a small fenced plot on the south shores of the Niobrara River south of Kilgore. The inscription reads: "In memory of James Williamson, killed by Indians May 6, 1879, aged 28 years."

Williamson, from the McCann Ranch riding a green-broke colt, and another cowboy were sent out to gather horses from winter range before the big spring roundup. Near the Snake Falls, Williamson's horse refused to cross the river and he was killed when attacked by a band of Indians, said to be Cheyennes. Felix James escaped.

Williamson's body was brought back and buried. Billy the Bear, employed by Sharp's Ranch, fashioned a casket from cedar and burned the letters with a hot iron.

While fighting a 1914 prairie fire, forest ranger Gordie Lord, covered the marker with sand to save it. Much later, rancher C.J. Anderson replaced the marker with a marble duplicate. The original marker eventually was preserved at Fort Robinson.

An impressive granite marker with an engraved picture of a cowboy stands at Mt. Hope Cemetery in Valentine. One might wonder what kind of a man would inspire his friends to erect such a monument to his memory 22 years after his death in 1906 at age 45.

The inscription reads: "He was hospitable, generous, kind and true. A cowboy, ranchman and humorist too."

"Death makes us all alike as we lie beneath the sod. But in life there was only one 'Arkansas Bob.'" Robert Gillespie hated cotton farming and wanted to be a cowboy.

By chance, he met Sam Hudson who was recruiting drovers to trail herds north.

At 19, Bob was on his way to becoming a seasoned trail hand. Both Gillespie and Hudson eventually chose to stay in the Sandhills; Hudson homesteading on the Niobrara and Gillespie a foreman on C.J. Anderson's Diamond Bar Ranch. Later he and his brothers established the TO ranch on Boardman Creek which currently is the location of the Ravenscroft's Three Bar.

Arkansas Bob had a reputation of being "fair and square" as well as quick-witted and a story teller. One time a doctor asked him how he got bucked off and broke his collar bone.

"Can't understand it," Bob said. "I was well-balanced, had a quart of good whiskey in each pocket."

When an easterner questioned Bob how he delivered cattle into Chicago from the east because of the lake. Bob was quick. "You'd thought lake if you'd been with us. We swam those cattle for 14 days."

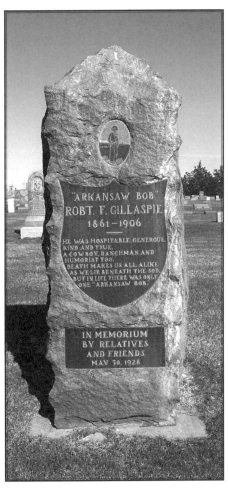

When he first visited Bartlett Richards' new U-shaped house in Ellsworth, Bob viewed the bathrooms with disbelief.

"Never saw so many dipping vats in one house before," he said.

Those who knew Arkansas Bob said, "He was as full of stories as a Swede is of fish." Early in the century, Arkansas Bob was found unconscious with his horse standing over him. He was returning from Cody with the ranch payroll. Apparently, he was robbed and left for dead. Partially paralyzed and going blind, his wish was to die at his ranch.

By 1928, rancher Dan Adamson was instrumental in getting the monument erected to the memory of an unforgettable personality whose stories linger on.

A tombstone marks his place.

RUTH HANNA
- October 18, 1998 -

She was a tiny woman, but with an indomitable spirit and a big heart. One of her personal traits that I greatly admired was having the courage of her convictions.

The funeral for Ruth Fianna Joint was on Wednesday. Covering the coffin was one of her magnificent quilts that she lovingly stitched for her family members.

Row after row of stitches were perfectly spaced by hand. Flowers appliquéd around the center were a work of art.

Meticulous was another of Ruth's traits.

Born far from town on the Hanna's Pony Lake Ranch without benefit of doctor or midwife, Ruth was an example of hardy independence. Widowed since 1958, Ruth lived alone and remained active to the age of 90. She needed no help when she bought a new car last summer.

Some may say that her personality was a bit feisty. But I called it honest. If she felt something was wrong she didn't fall into the "don't make waves" mentality. She wasn't afraid to speak up and her word was good as gold.

Her brand of honesty, in my opinion, represents a dwindling number of pioneers of whom it's been said time and again that one's word was better than a written contract.

Ruth was a longtime supporter of our Cherry County Historical Society Museum and many pre-generations of the David Hanna family. Theirs is a rich history, but not without personal tragedy.

David Hanna, Ruth's grandfather, came to the Sandhills in 1884. Music filled the sod house while David played the violin, his wife, Janet, the organ and their son, Neil, a guitar and harmonica. That organ is but one of many items now in the museum.

David was elected sheriff in 1890 and later to the State Legislature. When his only son, Neil, married in 1905, he and his bride moved to the ranch. David moved his wife and three daughters to Wood Lake and purchased half interest in the bank.

Florence used her father's violin and became a skilled violinist. She collapsed and died while rehearsing with the Chadron College orchestra. Mary married a Wood Lake banker, was widowed after 19 years and left with two children. Charlotte married Dr. Orville Ralston, Nebraska's only "Ace" of World War I. After Pearl Harbor, he was commissioned a major and was an Air Force flight instructor when he was killed on a training mission.

Ruth was the first of two daughters and two sons born to Neil and Nannie Hanna. She and her sister, Louise, remember playing in their grandmother's attic with treasured toys from the childhood of three aunts. Those miniature dolls and doll furniture were also donated to the museum. Ruth covered pillows with her needlepoint and sewed other items as fund-raisers at the museum. She and her support will be sorely missed.

When the government established the Valentine National Wildlife Refuge in 1935, the Pony Lake Ranch fell within its boundaries. Neil bought a ranch in the Goose Creek Valley operated now by Ruth's brother, Dick, and Dick's son, Jeff.

Ruth was buried in the well-manicured Wood Lake Cemetery beside so many of the Hanna family members who represent the values of early Sandhill settlers.

-||-　ᴸᴶ　ᴮ̲　ᕼO　⁷⟡

RANCH PARTNERS 50 YEARS
- February 12, 2003 -

Fifty-year anniversaries are becoming more common as people are living healthier and living longer. Frequently we read in the paper that children and grandchildren are hosting a 50th celebration for loved ones. We recently learned of a 50th anniversary that passed with little fanfare. It wasn't that the partners were hostile, rather quite the opposite.

Gordon McLeod is our closest neighbor five miles to the west. He is one of the few longtime neighbors who have not been absorbed by absentee owners. A local historian, he said his Scottish ancestors adjusted well to the Canadian wilderness before moving to Nebraska in 1886.

When asked, Gordon talked fondly about his partner of 50 years, a Piper Super Cub also known as a PA-18. The two actually are into their 52nd year. He said he hasn't flown for about a week during the colder weather.

"I owned two airplanes before this one," he said. "I obtained my license in 1946 and bought a Piper J-3. Then in 1950 I bought Chris Abbott's Piper PA-11."

"In 1952 Bob Cole northwest of Whitman wanted a larger plane so I bought his PA-18 with only 120 hours (on the logbook) for $3,000."

"I now have about 5,000 hours on the plane and it still could sell for about $35,000. But that is because a dollar is worth about nine cents today compared to about 90 cents when I bought it."

The last acquisition with wing flaps allows more control for pasture flying and landing. McLeod said he flew to keep the hay crew in repairs when they hayed south of Wood Lake. Checking cattle and windmills is a year-round chore.

He built an open-sided T-hangar on the meadow near the building site. He said the structure was sufficient to protect the fabric from the sun and that snow blows on through. In spring, however, when water often covers the meadow he is unable to take off or land.

"Age is not a factor if the craft is maintained properly," he said. "Most pilots get in trouble when they take a chance on bad weather. If you lose the horizon you're going to be in trouble," he said.

He did make a forced landing once when he ran out of gas. He landed on the prairie south of Valentine, walked to Highway 83 and caught a ride.

McLeod said when he logged 3,500 hours he hired Bud Sheer at the Ainsworth Airport to install a new engine. In 1980, Scheer replaced the fabric.

"Scheer was the best," McLeod said. "Give him a Piper J-3 and he could out-fly the Red Baron."

Apparently, McLeod is no slouch as a pilot. At 81-years he has been flying the same airplane for more than 50 years. Both must hale from sturdy stock because neither appear to show their age.

Ranch headquarters for Gordon, his son Gary and their wives is where B.E.B Kennedy filed. McLeod's father, Gilmore, settled near Brownlee and bought land in 1884 to the north including Kennedy's homestead. At that location Gilmore's mother, Sarah McLeod, was named postmaster of the fourth class Kennedy post office in 1911.

GEORGE YOUNKIN
- February 22, 2003 -

For men raised on the prairie during the early 1900s, a horse most likely was their best friend. A favorite saddle horse willingly carried the cowboy through rain and snow and never betrayed a confidence.

Much of the early cowboy's work was done with harnessed draft horses while harvesting or feeding hay. The most admired horse on the team never balked at the job, rather leaned into the collar to keep the tugs taut.

Perhaps the willing horse loved the job and most likely the man holding the leather lines shared the same work ethic.

Two weeks ago George Younkin saddled his horse to drive to the corral, his steers assigned to auction that day in Valentine. Then he drove a pickup pulling one of two trailers from his ranch north of Mullen.

George Younkin was 93 years old and able to continue doing most jobs a rancher needs to do. But he never made it home that night. The pickup and empty horse trailer went off a steep curve on icy roads. It is believed that death was instant.

A Hispanic orphan, who came to the Sandhills, 19 years old on the Orphan Train, he had no thought of retirement. He is among the few whose health allows them to stay on the job ... to keep a taut tug. He didn't wear glasses and had never lost a tooth.

In was in admiration for the man that G.R. said a bit wistfully, "George died in the harness."

We asked several men 20 to 40 years his junior to describe him. Most gave the same response: He was just a "good, good" man. He always knew you, never forgot a face, and was always the same. He was an honest person with values of the Old West.

The elderly Younkins didn't adopt George, rather looked upon him as ranch help, George said in a 1997 story. He left school after the eighth grade to work full time and bought cull cows to start his herd.

He said he liked working with a lot of cowboys at the big outfits like the Carver. "I was always accepted," he told his eight children.

The young cowboy who rode bareback rodeo horses on occasion married Rana Dalton, the daughter of a ranch cook. He said the first small place they bought wasn't much, but "she never once complained."

Through frugal management and family help the ranch expanded to a dozen sections. Rana died 15 years ago. The family expanded to great grand-children.

He loved a good rodeo. For more years than the family remembers he went early to claim the same seat near the bucking chutes at the Buffalo Bill Rodeo. Daughter Judy Most and her husband, Gordon, took him to Las Vegas to the pro finals at least 13 years and grandchildren the last few years.

George Younkin was humble and unassuming. His family selected a cedar casket with rope handles that displayed his Lazy Diamond Bar X brand. A favorite hat rested on his chest. Grandsons were pallbearers.

So who can explain why Mullen's Lariat Hall, capacity about 700, was close to capacity with people decades younger who came to bid farewell. At 93 years most of his friends were gone long before him.

George Younkin was not a wealthy man with political connections. In the words of one at the funeral, "He was just a good, good man who touched a lot of people."

Special Thanks...

The column, "Sand In My Shoes" (SIMS) was written over a period of 26 years and published in the *North Platte Telegraph*. Through those years readers would often ask, "When are you going to do a book?" As time went on they seemed to get more serious. "Someday," I would say, "but I'm just too busy right now." No one should claim to be too busy because it's really called procrastination. My intentions to do a book, my <u>good intentions</u>, left all the tear pages in the boot boxes.

I apologize because when I found the time to work on the saved papers, my health turned immediately fragile; Chronic Obstructive Pulmonary Disease (COPD), diabetes, and osteoporosis.

I required too much oxygen to work on musty papers, so Gerald (I call him G.R.) took command. He would say, "I don't know a darn thing about computers, but I'll find someone who can." It turned out that G.R. and I hit gold at the same moment. I was talking to Devin, not knowing that G.R. had found Bob Stetter. Before I knew anything about it the day was over and Bob had ordered printers and scanners and copiers. Most of all he found Dee Jaye to operate this complicated program that transferred yellowed newspaper print through copiers and scanners and other quirky things to end up as a book, we hope. All this gear was set up in a spare room at Cherry Hills and those that could, worked there sometimes long hours into the night. I was never able to help there.

My thanks to George, Devin, Dave, Bob, G.R. and especially Dee Jaye Fowler, who all put in a lot of hours.